The New Negroes
and Their Music

*Jon Michael Spencer is the
Tyler and Alice Haynes Professor
of American Studies and
Professor of Music at the
University of Richmond, Virginia.*

Also by the Author

Re-Searching Black Music (1996)
Self-Made and Blues-Rich (1996)
Sing a New Song (1995)
The Rhythms of Black Folk (1995)
Blues and Evil (1993)
Black Hymnody (1992)
Theological Music (1991)
Protest and Praise (1990)
Sacred Symphony (1987)
As the Black School Sings (1987)

The New Negroes and Their Music

*The Success of the
Harlem Renaissance*

Jon Michael Spencer

The University of Tennessee Press / Knoxville

The paper in this book meets the minimum requirements of the
American National Standard for Permanence of Paper for Printed
Library Materials. ⊗ The binding materials have been chosen
for strength and durability.

✪

Printed on recycled paper.

Library of Congress Cataloging-in-Publication Data

Spencer, Jon Michael.
  The new Negroes and their music : the success of the Harlem
Renaissance / Jon Michael Spencer.—1st ed.
    p. cm.
  Includes index.
  ISBN 0-87049-967-X (pbk. : alk. paper)
1. Afro-Americans—New York (State)—New York—Music—History and criticism.
2. Music—New York (State)—New York—20th century—History and criticism.
3. Harlem (New York, N.Y.)—Intellectual life—20th century.
4. Harlem Renaissance. I. Title.
ML3556.S77 1997
780'.89'9607307471—dc20   96-25273
                                    CIP
                                    MN

Contents

Illustrations

Acknowledgments

The several staff at the Moorland-Spingarn Research Center at Howard University to whom I owe a word of thanks are Helen Rutt, Esme Bhan, and Donna Wells. I am grateful to archivist Fritz Malval and his staff (Donzella Willford, Cynthia Poston, and Deborah Greene) at the Hampton University Archives for their gracious assistance in facilitating my research. To director Michael Dabrishus and former staff worker Norma Ortiz-Karp at the Special Collections Division at the University of Arkansas at Fayetteville, I likewise owe special thanks. And to the staff at the Beinecke Rare Book and Manuscript Library at Yale University, I am indebted. Additionally, I would not have been able to do research at several of these institutions were it not for the financial assistance from the Arkansas Humanities Council.

I am grateful to Judith Ann Still, the daughter of William Grant Still, for helpful information and photographs; to my former colleague, Kenneth Jenkin, a historian, who inspired me with healthy debate on the Harlem Renaissance; to my wife, Michele Bowen-Spencer, a burgeoning historian who was very helpful with her comments on my manuscript as it was in preparation; and to Dominique Rene de Lerma and Cynthia Fleming for their careful readings and remarks. Finally, and not least in importance, I say thank you to the staff of the University of Tennessee Press who saw this project through to fruition—Meredith Morris-Babb (and her assistant Kimberly Scarbrough) and Stan Ivester.

Prologue

The life of the protagonist in James Weldon Johnson's book titled *The Au-tobiography of an Ex-Colored Man*[1] commenced in rural Georgia a few years after the Civil War. The protagonist's father, whom the protagonist did not recall as a child and would meet but once as a young boy, was a white man. His mother, who raised him single-handedly, was a colored woman who could pass for white nearly as well as her son. As a youth the boy was taken by his mother to a town in Connecticut, where he was raised "a perfect little aristocrat," privileged to be taking piano and organ lessons, singing in the boys choir, and studying music theory. One day, while in grammar school, the "little aristocrat" stumbled upon the realization that he was "colored." Though initially daunted by this discovery, it was upon hearing his colored friend, Shiny, rendering an inspiring oration at gradua-tion (Wendell Phillips's "Toussaint L'Ouverture") that a redemptive seed of racial "vindication" was planted in his heart. At that moment the boy felt proud to be colored, and he began to dream about becoming a great col-ored man who would bring honor to the Negro race.

It was this transformation in his life that led the boy, when he became a young man, to choose a black college, Atlanta University, as the place to prepare for the pursuit of his dream. On his way south, however, the money he had secured for his schooling was stolen. With his mother having re-cently passed away, he followed the advice of a Pullman porter and went to Jacksonville, Florida, where he found work as a cigar-maker. Although he continued to be the cultured young man his mother had raised, he also learned from his co-workers at the cigar factory how to be careless with his money. As a result, he continuously and then indefinitely postponed going to Atlanta University.

Eventually the skill the young man had acquired for making cigars took him back north to New York City, where, in Harlem, he first heard ragtime, which was just then becoming the rage. The "barbaric harmonies" and "intricate rhythms" with their wild syncopations intrigued him so much that he set out to learn to play the music, indeed to master it, eventually becoming the best ragtime pianist in Harlem. Because of his training as a classical pianist, he also became the first musician to perform ragtime renditions of the European classics, his most popular ragged classic being Mendelssohn's "Wedding March."

As a ragtime "professor," the colored man played regularly at a Harlem nightclub and earned a decent living. But it was when a millionaire white man began to patronize him that his life took a turn for the better, for the millionaire paid him generously to provide the musical entertainment for his private parties and personal enjoyment. The young pianist viewed this as a turn for the better, even though he had to agree not to fill any similar engagements for others without the millionaire's instructions but rather would be occasionally "loaned" to some of the millionaire's friends. The colored man played long hours for his benefactor's dinners and parties and was often awakened in the middle of the night to play for his benefactor's personal enjoyment. "He seemed to be some grim, mute, but relentless tyrant," recalled the colored man, "possessing over me a supernatural power which he used to drive me on mercilessly to exhaustion."

Eventually this arrangement took the colored man to Europe for the first time. And after an extended stay with his benefactor in Paris, London, and Berlin, the colored man became "a polished man of the world." This leisurely life abroad was not to be long lived, however, for the colored man decided to return home in order to live for a while among the least polished of society—the colored folk of the rural South. This decision came in Berlin when the colored man was carrying on his usual task of entertaining his benefactor's party guests. In a flurry of excitement over ragtime, one of the party guests insisted on sitting down at the piano. Taking up the theme of the tune he had heard, the German pianist played it through in straight chords and then developed it in every known classical form. "I sat amazed," the colored man recalled. "I had been turning classic music into rag-time, a comparatively easy task; and this man had taken rag-time and made it classic. The thought came across me like a flash—It can be done, why can't I do it? From that moment my mind was made up. I clearly saw the way of carrying out the ambition I had formed when a boy."

All these years the colored man had been wasting his time and abusing his talent, he felt. Now he could become the great race man he had dreamed of since his grammar school graduation. He would become a great composer and voice the joys, sorrows, hopes, and ambitions of the Negro in classical musical form. He announced to his benefactor his intentions and said he would be leaving Europe. His patron asked why he would want to throw away his life living amidst the poverty and ignorance of a people involved in a hopeless struggle to be free, and he insisted that the colored man would be placing a terrible handicap upon himself by working as a Negro composer who would never receive the hearing for his work that it might deserve. He said further that he doubted that even a highly recognized white composer could bring to fruition the notion that an American music should be built upon the use of Negro musical themes.

The colored man sympathized with his benefactor's argument, for he knew that his own people generally preferred to sing the standard Protestant hymns in church rather than the spirituals. He thought it was natural that they would feel this way since they were still very close to the conditions under which the "slave songs" were created, but he also believed the day would come when the spirituals would become the Negro's most treasured heritage. Despite his benefactor's discouragement, then, the colored man returned home, all the way home to the place of his birth. Through rural Georgia he traveled, collecting melodies and future compositional themes from the various forms of Negro folk music he heard. He went about his work feeling certain that the root of the race problem in America lay in the racial attitudes of whites, attitudes that could be changed by people like him. These racial attitudes could be changed, he believed, not by strictly imitating white culture, which he said whites would take in a "comic-opera sense," but by depicting the life, ambitions, struggles, and passions of the Negro race within the "higher" classical musical forms.

The rural South and its colored people were as intriguing to the colored man as Europe was. The South was also horrifying, however, for it was there that he witnessed a Negro burned alive by a mob of whites. This experience, which caused him to have immense shame for being part of such a despised race, was as dreadful as when in grammar school he discovered he was colored. He decided at that moment of the violent act that he would return north to New York City, take a new name, and pass for white. In New York he entered the real estate business, married a white woman, and raised two children. But after his wife died, the ex-colored man frequently pondered the fateful decision he had made to pass for white. Haunted by his neglect to live up to his grammar school dream of contributing to the vindication of the Negro and impressed by those who did live out this dream, the ex-colored man said at his narrative's close: "My love for my children makes me glad that I am what I am and keeps me from desiring to be otherwise; and yet, when I sometimes open a little box in which I still keep my fast yellowing manuscripts, the only tangible remnants of a vanished dream, a dead ambition, a sacrificed talent, I cannot repress the thought that, after all, I have chosen the lesser part, that I have sold my birthright for a mess of pottage."

So ends the story of a man who chose the lesser part. But for every colored person who chose to pass for white, there was another Negro—a New Negro—who chose to take his or her birthright and vindicate it with a self-conscious racialism (a conscious acceptance of the concept of race and of being racially black). Thus, we need not wonder what great symphonies, operas, oratorios, ballets, and other concert works and performances might have burgeoned from the melodies and themes on those yellowing manuscripts in the little box of the ex-colored man. To know we need only listen to the famous work of those composers and performers who did capture the life, ambitions, struggles, and passions of the Negro race within the "higher" classical musical forms—that famous work that was part and parcel of the historical epoch called the "Harlem" or "Negro Renaissance."

Introduction

It was Mary Kemp Davis, formerly a professor of African American literature at the University of North Carolina at Chapel Hill, who suggested that
for this book I make use of James Weldon Johnson's thematic treatment of
black music in *The Autobiography of an Ex-Colored Man* (1912). After re-
reading Johnson's book, which I had not read since my teens, I felt as
though a great symphonic theme had been recommended to me, for I
found that the major motifs important to an understanding of the Negro
Renaissance were present in this work. This was possible because Johnson
had written a story that he said was based on essential truth. He said, "although it cannot be stated that the story of the hero is the true life of any
individual; yet, it is made up in every important fact and detail from the
real life experiences of several persons I have known, and from incidents
which have come under my own observation and within my personal experience; so, in every essential particular, the biography is truth and not fiction."[1] It is in this respect that Carl Van Vechten, in his introduction to the
1927 reprint of the book, suggested that it be read as a "composite autobiography of the Negro race."[2]

The title of Johnson's book suggests the dominant theme of "passing" (a
fair "colored" person passing for white), and even in this aspect the book is
truth "in every essential particular." Johnson explained that one of the main
reasons for writing the book was to reveal the unsuspected fact that racism
against Negroes in such large cities as New York was exerting a pressure
that constantly forced a large number of fair-complexioned colored people
to pass for white.[3] But Johnson is not simply interested in the intrigue of
passing, as Charles S. Johnson pointed out in his introduction to the 1948
reprint of *The Autobiography*. Charles Johnson explained that the problem

of "passing" was not the principal issue that the author wanted his reader-ship to be concerned about, but rather the social situation in the country which made passing an option for survival and happiness.[4]

Indeed, Johnson's *Autobiography* had drawn from the real-life tenor of the times, as evidenced, for instance, in a letter written in 1911 by Carl R. Diton, a black American studying music abroad in Munich during the 1910–11 academic year. Diton was writing to another young black American who was studying at the University of Berlin, having just completed three years at Hertford College (Oxford University) as the first black Rhodes scholar. Diton told that young Rhodes scholar—Alain LeRoy Locke—that it had been his desire for six years to make "serious" and "famous work" in music composition his life's aim. Due in part to his tendency "to lean toward our race," wrote Diton, he thought the Negro vein would be the proper idiom for his work. "And later on it occurred to me that that medium would not only be the best for me because it is easier for me to think in that more so than in any other," he explained, "but because it would give to the art of music a new kind of expression hitherto far from being thoroughly explored." Diton went on, "I may not succeed in doing all I want to do, but my aim is certainly worthy of being striven for. And the only thing that will cut me completely off from it will be the absolute necessity of . . . bread-earning. But I hope that my life will be, pure and simple, that of the scholar in music."[5] Drawing his letter to a close, in response to an earlier letter from Locke which evidently spoke prophetically of a future in black culture that would come to be referred to as a renaissance, Diton said:

> Let me say, in conclusion, that your letter gave me a peculiar kind of pleasure for even as slightly acquainted as I am with the work of two of our most important men in America, Du Bois and Washington, it seemed to tell me that you—(and may I add my humble self?)—and I, together with those at home who are con-temporaneously looking to great things, are, in time, to point out a new era in the development of intellect among negroes. And I ar-dently hope that the day is not far distant when we may swoop down upon the sentiment of the whites in America so they won't know their heads from the[ir] heels—a veritable retribution for innumerable injustices, past and present.[6]

About a year later, in mid-1912, *The Autobiography of an Ex-Colored Man* was published, Johnson's first book, which he had begun about six years earlier in New York. With regard to the book being based on essential truth, there are several themes in the book that are also found in Diton's 1911 letter to Locke, one being a theme that would burgeon into the central philosophy and practice behind the debut of the New Negro (the Renaissance man and woman). One of the themes in Johnson's book which burgeoned into the central philosophy and practice of the Negro Renaissance was what Diton identified as racial "retribution" and which Locke later called the "vindication of the Negro." This "retribution" or "vindication" would occur by Renaissance artists making "serious" and "famous work" the aims of their professional careers. Johnson himself was such an artist and his *Autobiography of an Ex-Colored Man* was such a "famous work."

Following *The Autobiography of an Ex-Colored Man,* Johnson went on to write or edit a number of books that came to be considered important to the corpus of Negro Renaissance literature. Most notable with regard to music are *The Book of American Negro Spirituals* (1925), *The Second Book of Negro Spirituals* (1926), and *God's Trombones* (1927). But in his other books, particularly *The Book of American Negro Poetry* (1922) and *Black Manhattan* (1930), music continued to be an important part of the discussion. Thus, had Johnson not been tragically killed in an automobile accident in 1938, at the prime of his life, he might have been compelled, as Alain Locke was, to write a monograph on the music of the Negro Renaissance. As it turns out, however, Locke's *The Negro and His Music* (1936) remained for well over a half-century (up to the point of the present book) the only monograph on the music of the Negro Renaissance.

As Locke was returning to the United States from his tour of southern Europe, the Middle East, northern Africa, and Russia at the close of the summer of 1934, he wrote his benefactor, Charlotte Osgood Mason, about his plans to write a series of pamphlets. One would be on black music, which he vowed would "put things simply and squarely." "I'll have to do as you once said," wrote Locke to Mason, "'burn the Harvard and Oxford wrappers up.'"[7] Locke did put things simply and squarely in *The Negro and His Music,* the little book that came out two years later. That Locke put things "simply and squarely" is in fact one of the book's strong points. However, that the book, according to the periodization I will present for the Renaissance, was published approximately two and one-half decades before the Renaissance even ended, makes it (certainly through no fault of its author) an incomplete assessment of the music of the Renaissance.

Nonetheless, Locke's book must have reaffirmed for composers Will Marion Cook, William Grant Still, William Dawson, and Ulysses Kay, performer Roland Hayes, scholars James Weldon Johnson and Benjamin

Brawley, and benefactor Charlotte Mason (all of whom Locke sent complimentary copies) that music was a central part of the philosophy and practice of the Renaissance. Hayes, after reading the book cover to cover, told Locke it was a "significant treatise," the best-organized and most comprehensive text on Negro music and musicians he had ever read.[8] Kemper Harreld informed Locke that he was using the book in his music classes at Spelman College.[9] Still wrote Locke to say that up to that point he had considered Maud Cuney-Hare's *Negro Musicians and Their Music* (1936) to be the most authoritative book on the subject of Negro music but that he found Locke's scholarly approach to be "a little more satisfying."[10]

Cuney-Hare's book, also published in 1936, was the first comprehensive text on black music by a twentieth-century black scholar, its predecessor being James Trotter's *Music and Some Highly Musical People* (1878). In her book, Cuney-Hare gives a general history of black music beginning at its African roots and including musicians of African descent in Europe. But compared to Locke's book, she provides unsatisfactory coverage of 1895 to the early 1930s, the period in which Locke considered the Negro Renaissance to have burgeoned. While Cuney-Hare discussed Roland Hayes, Paul Robeson, Marian Anderson, and Jules Bledsoe, and gave a reasonable amount of attention to R. Nathaniel Dett and William Grant Still, she mentioned William Dawson only in passing and completely ignored his most important work, *The Negro Folk Symphony*. Dawson's symphony should have been covered in Cuney-Hare's chapter titled "Folk Themes in Larger Forms of Composition." That chapter, as I believe James Weldon Johnson's *Autobiography* foretold, also would have been the ideal one for a general discussion of the Renaissance philosophy and practice. However, Cuney-Hare made absolutely no mention of the Renaissance and altogether avoided the term "New Negro." This is probably why Locke's book, though less historically comprehensive and half the length of Cuney-Hare's, was more "satisfying" for a New Negro such as Still.

Samuel Floyd's edited book, *Music in the Harlem Renaissance* (1990), though not a monograph, is helpful in trying to understand the musical component of the Renaissance. It focuses on those forms of music—black music in classical forms—that were in fact viewed by the artists and intellectuals of the epoch as part of the Renaissance movement. It would have been most fitting for Floyd to begin his edited book with an essay on James Weldon Johnson, an essay that addressed his thematization of music in his many books, beginning with *The Autobiography*. In the absence of this, however, it is appropriate that the first article following Floyd's introductory overview of the Renaissance and its music is a piece titled "Vindication as a Thematic Principle in the Writings of Alain Locke on the Music of Black Americans." While I disagree with the author, Paul Burgett, that the idea of vindicating Negro music suggests "a psychological undercurrent of cultural inferiority about Negro music," a disagreement I will expound on in chapter 1, I do agree with his conclusion: "The theme of vindication, whatever criticism it might sustain, was supported by its own special and not uncomplicated logic and was an appropriate response to conditions of the time."[11] To Carl Diton, as his 1911 letter to Locke revealed, the conditions of the times—the "innumerable injustices" that whites long heaped upon blacks—logically called for vindication or "retribution" to "swoop down upon the sentiment of the whites in America so they won't know their heads from their heels."[12]

After Burgett's essay, the two most important pieces in Floyd's edited book are those that cover R. Nathaniel Dett and William Grant Still, both of whom, as I will show respectively in chapters 2 and 3, sought to vindicate the Negro through their "serious" and "famous work" in music. Georgia Ryder, in her essay on Dett, identifies what she finds to be no mere coincidence with regard to the composer's possible relationship to the Renaissance. She points out that Dett's major compositions based on the spirituals—the motet titled *The Chariot Jubilee* (1919) and the oratorio titled *The Ordering of Moses* (1932)—span the period during which the Renaissance is generally understood to have thrived. She also points out that Dett's published writings during that period demonstrate his intellectual kinship to many of the better-known Renaissance artists and advocates.[13]

Rae Linda Brown, in her essay devoted in part to the music of Still,[14] is able to reveal much more about this composer's kinship with the Renaissance artists and advocates between 1919 and 1931 because it was a much more explicit kinship. In 1919, Still joined the Pace and Handy Publishing Company, which had moved to Harlem from Memphis in 1917, and two years later, in 1921, joined Eubie Blake's orchestra for the successful debut of the musical *Shuffle Along*. Although *Shuffle Along* was not, in Still's own estimation, an example of Renaissance art in that it was based on popular music and texts rather than on classical or "serious" ones, Still was nonetheless interacting with Harlem musicians such as Hall Johnson, who himself eventually encased the peculiar black musical idioms in classical forms. After touring with Blake's orchestra, Still returned to Harlem in 1923 and became the recording director and conductor for the two-year-old Black Swan Recording Company founded by Harry H. Pace, the company's president and general manager. In 1930, Still was still living in Harlem when he completed his most famous Renaissance composition, *Afro-American Symphony.*

In addition to what Rae Linda Brown has told us about Still's rather explicit relationship to the Renaissance that was burgeoning in Harlem, there are some additional connections. Not only was Renaissance promoter Alain Locke a personal friend of Still, such that when *The Negro and His Music* was released he sent Still a complimentary copy,[15] but Locke also facilitated a collaboration between Still and Renaissance littérateur Richard Bruce, which resulted in the ballet titled *Sahdji.* Still also collaborated with Langston Hughes, one of the most famous writers of the Renaissance. With Hughes as the librettist of Still's opera, *Troubled Island,* the year 1949 saw the premier of the first opera by a black composer to be performed by a major opera company. A year later, at the close of that decade (yet still within the Renaissance era according to the periodization I will present), Still wrote a group of songs under the title *Songs of Separation,* which were based on poems by five black writers, including Renaissance poets Langston Hughes, Countee Cullen, and Arna Bontemps. Additionally, some of these literati, and others, gained fame by publishing their works in the pages of the National Urban League's *Opportunity* and the NAACP's *The Crisis,* the same magazines in which Still published several articles on music beginning in the late 1930s.

Although Floyd's *Black Music in the Harlem Renaissance,* with its essays on Dett and Still and Locke's philosophy of "vindication," does not permit a singular perspective on the music of the Renaissance movement because it is an edited book, his introduction nonetheless gives a hint of what such a singular perspective might comprise. Floyd writes insightfully:

> The Harlem Renaissance has been treated primarily as a literary movement, with occasional asides, contributed as musical spice, about the jazz age and the performances of concert artists. But music's role was much more basic and important to the movement. In fact, the stance of the black leadership and scattered brief comments about music during the period suggest the primacy of music to the Renaissance philosophy and practice. . . .
>
> Generally . . . the Harlem Renaissance used and was supported and accompanied by music. The music of the black theater shows, the dance music of the cabarets, the blues and ragtime of the speakeasies and the rent parties, the spirituals and the art

songs of the recital and concert halls all created an ambience for Renaissance activity and contemplation.[16]

Floyd also says that despite its obvious importance to the Renaissance, black music was taken for granted because it had always been a pathmaker and a central part of black culture.[17] In this regard, Floyd wonders whether the 1919 founding of the National Association of Negro Musicians, an organization whose intentions seemed to anticipate the burgeoning of the literature of the Renaissance, was perhaps the entity after which Renaissance intellectuals Charles S. Johnson and Alain Locke modeled the era's literary movement.[18] Essentially Floyd is repeating what Martin Blum wrote in an article of 1974 fittingly titled "Black Music: Pathmaker of the Harlem Renaissance," in which Blum says black music not only contributed to and benefited from the Renaissance but in fact spearheaded it by example.[19]

Renaissance artists working in areas other than music did in fact seem to look to music as an example of the progress that needed to occur in their own artistic fields. For instance, in an article on black drama published in *The Crisis* in 1919, Renaissance playwright Willis Richardson asked: "Is it true that there is coming into existence in America a Negro Drama which at some future day may equal in excellence the American Negro music?"[20] James Weldon Johnson, in his preface to *The Second Book of Negro Spirituals* (1926), also suggested that artists working in areas other than music seemed to look to music as an example of the progress that needed to occur in their own fields. "The recent emergence of a younger group of Negro artists, preponderantly literary, zealous to be racial, or to put it better, determined to be true to themselves, to look for their art material within rather than without," wrote Johnson, "got its first impulse, I believe, from the new evaluation of the Spirituals reached by the Negro himself." Johnson went on to explain that the sudden recognition among Negroes that their race had produced one of the finest forms of folk art in the world resulted in a consciousness of their inherent racial talents, which gave rise to a "new school of Negro artists."[21] So, although Floyd's book is an edited one, his introductory remarks about black music being the pathfinder of the Renaissance have been helpful to me in fashioning a central vision of the Renaissance.

There are several contemporary histories of the Renaissance that have a central vision of the movement, particularly Nathan Huggins's *Harlem Renaissance* (1971) and David Levering Lewis's *When Harlem Was in Vogue* (1984), but in these books we find that music is treated as being of relative unimportance and that the unifying vision of each book is that the Renaissance was a failure. Music is not completely ignored in their books, it simply is underestimated. In addition, Huggins and Lewis fail to understand that, just as the Renaissance in literature was a "classical" movement, so was the Renaissance in music a "classical movement"—that is, a Renaissance of black vernacular sources but classical forms. Ragtime, blues, and jazz were the wells to which the Renaissance artists went for the substance—the themes, rhythms, and "feel"—of their "high" art. This is true whether we are speaking of the musical composition or the novel, painting, or anthology of poetry or folklore.

I believe that the only way Huggins and Lewis could have concluded that the Renaissance was a failure is specifically by underestimating the importance of this Renaissance music, and the only way they could have done this after consulting the classic Renaissance texts (including Johnson's *The Autobiography of an Ex-Colored Man,* his preface to *The Second Book of Negro Spirituals,* and Locke's *The Negro and His Music*) would have been for them to have ignored all the clues to the contrary. In particular, they ignored the prophetic aspect of *The Autobiography,* which publisher Alfred A. Knopf recognized when he reissued the book in 1927, fifteen years after its initial publication by a Boston firm called Sherman, French and Company. Knopf's promotional material said, *"The Autobiography of an Ex-Colored Man* has, of course long been known and sought for as one of the principal source-books on the life of the Negro in America. . . . Not the least remarkable fact about it is that all of the truths postulated by him [Johnson] in 1912 still hold good in 1927, and most of his astonishing predictions have become realities."[22] With regard to music being an important theme in this prophetic work, Johnson revealed the obvious: "I have written a good deal on the subject of Negro music and its development. . . . I spoke of it in 'The Autobiography of an Ex-Colored Man.' . . . The Negro's gift of music has been almost entirely overlooked, except as a sort of side-show."[23]

By treating music as a sort of side show to the Renaissance, Huggins and Lewis miss important thematic connections that link W. E. B. Du Bois's *The Souls of Black Folk* (1903), Johnson's *The Autobiography of an Ex-Colored Man* (1912), and Locke's *The New Negro* (1925) and *The Negro and His Music* (1936). In his preface to *The Second Book of Negro Spirituals,* Johnson does not specify the source of the "new evaluation of the spirituals" which prompted the emergence of the "new school of Negro artists," but his protagonist in *The Autobiography* implied that it was Du Bois. In reflecting on his travel throughout rural Georgia collecting folk melodies and future compositional themes, the colored man in Johnson's novel explained that a strict imitation of white culture by colored artists would be taken by whites in a "comic-opera sense," but that Du Bois had demonstrated in *The Souls of Black Folk* that future Negro artists could create new art that depicts the life, ambitions, struggles, and passions of their race. In his essay titled "The Negro Spirituals" in *The New Negro,* Locke also made reference to Du Bois's comments on the spirituals in *The Souls of Black Folk.* Locke said the humble origin of these folk songs is too indelibly stamped upon them to be overlooked, but underneath the simplicity lies, as Du Bois had pointed out, said Locke, an "epic intensity" and "tragic profundity of emotional experience" for which the only historical analogue is the Psalms.[24]

By failing to give black music a more important place in their discussions of the Negro Renaissance, Huggins and Lewis overlooked an obvious and important link between Du Bois's book of 1903, Johnson's book of 1912, and Locke's books of 1925 and 1936: that the new school of black artists got their first impulse of self-conscious racialism from the new evaluation of the spirituals initiated by Du Bois. By missing this unseverable link between the aforementioned texts of 1903, 1912, 1925, and 1936, Huggins and Lewis maneuver around potential challenges to their periodization of the Renaissance, a periodization that has the Renaissance commencing approximately between 1917 and 1919 and ending approximately between 1930 and 1932. Had Huggins and Lewis pursued an understanding of "the primacy of music to the Renaissance philosophy and practice," they would have had to turn to the musicians who did "serious" and "famous work," such as Burleigh whose fame predates their time frame, and Dett and Still whose compositions burgeoned well beyond the 1930s.

My research on the music of the Negro Renaissance also presented the necessity of taking issue with Huggins and Lewis on several other points which have some baring on the conclusion I wish to reach with regard to the Renaissance being a success in part because of the contribution of black music. In particular, my wish to challenge the work of Huggins and Lewis is not simply because they omit serious consideration of music, in contrast to the intellectuals who helped shape the movement, but because they seem to misunderstand the Renaissance and thus conclude that it was a failure. In chapter 1, I challenge their opinions by defining the goal of the Renaissance artists and intellectuals (the "vindication of the Negro") and by defining the strategy by which they sought to and did successfully reach that goal (the "mastery of form"). In chapters 2 and 3, I use the philosophy and practice of Dett and Still, respectively, to show how musicians participated in the strategy to attain the goal of "vindication." After defining the

Renaissance philosophy and practice in chapter 1, and demonstrating how music fits within those parameters in chapters 2 and 3, I then challenge Huggins's and Lewis's periodization of the Renaissance in chapter 4. This is important because to expand the time frame of the Renaissance, as I wish to do, is to be able to look at the question of its success or failure from a perspective broader than that of these two historians. When I have completed my four chapters, I will have argued that the Negro Renaissance was no failure, and that music was an important part of its success.

This is my goal, but the road to that end should be equally valuable. On that road the reader should benefit from the personal correspondence of important Renaissance figures such as Alain Locke, James Weldon Johnson, R. Nathaniel Dett, William Grant Still, Zora Neale Hurston, Langston Hughes, and others, thus bringing to the fields of music and cultural studies information and insights previously unheard. So even if the reader disagrees with my conclusion about the periodization and success of the Renaissance, this historic movement should nonetheless come into clearer focus by the end.

On the other hand, although this book will be valuable to different people in different ways, it is still important to me to present an alternative picture of the Renaissance—the Renaissance as lengthier than the mere 1920s and the Renaissance as a success. In this regard, not only am I building upon the phenomenal work of Houston Baker, Jr., *Modernism and the Harlem Renaissance* (1987), but on views held by scholars with whom I have had conversations on this question. Convinced by Baker's arguments, I set out to say more, always willing, nonetheless, to alter my direction in midcourse should the data say otherwise. But the data did not, and herein I present it as objectively as I can.

Chapter I

A Power That Will Some Day
Be Applied to Higher Forms

I do not think it would be an exaggeration to say that in Europe the
United States is popularly known better by rag-time than by anything
else it has produced in a generation. In Paris they call it American music.
The newspapers have already told how the practice of intricate cake-
walk steps has taken up the time of European royalty and nobility. These
are lower forms of art, but they give evidence of a power that will some
day be applied to the higher forms.

—*The Autobiography of an Ex-Colored Man*

I

Nathan Huggins believes the Negro Renaissance was a failure because it
posited an inadequate new strategy as an answer to the old problem of racism. But if we restore music to its rightful place of recognition as having
given the first impulse to the "new school of Negro artists"—as having been
the pathmaker to the Negro Renaissance—and as having been an intricate
part of the Renaissance philosophy and practice, then our evaluation of the
New Negro's "serious" and "famous work" in music should prove that the
Renaissance was a resounding success. Even so, our first task in being able
to contest Huggins's claim that the Renaissance was a failure is to determine whether its goal in fact had anything to do with alleviating the old
problem of racism, and if it did, then what its strategy was to attain that
goal.

According to such Renaissance intellectuals as Alain Locke, Charles S. Johnson, and James Weldon Johnson, the principal impetus behind the Renaissance was quite simply to attain the "vindication of the Negro." It is true that black nationalists such as Marcus Garvey and his United Negro Improvement Association (UNIA) and Elijah Muhammed and his Nation of Islam also wanted the Negro vindicated. But they sought this through a black separatism and a recognition of black superiority within the black community. The strategy of Alain Locke, Charles Johnson, and James Weldon Johnson for attaining the goal of racial vindication was the debut of the New Negro (the Renaissance man and woman), whose new image would displace the image of the Old Negro in the world of the white majority. "The Old Negro, we must remember, was a creature of moral debate and historical controversy," wrote Locke. "His has been a stock figure perpetuated as an historical fiction partly in innocent sentimentalism, partly in deliberate reactionism. The Negro himself has contributed his share to this through a sort of protective social mimicry forced upon him by the adverse circumstances of dependence."[1]

The "moral debate" over the Old Negro was the subject of a 1923 article titled "Public Opinion and the Negro," published in *Opportunity* magazine by editor Charles S. Johnson. The stereotypical beliefs that whites created and perpetuated about the Negro being immoral, criminal, and mentally inferior, wrote Johnson, have helped fashion a fictitious being unlike any real Negro.[2] "These beliefs unchallenged not only magnify themselves and breed others, but react upon the Negro group, distorting its conduct. This distortion provokes in turn a sterner application of these beliefs and so on indefinitely, and with each step the isolation increases, each group building up its own myths and stiffening its own group morale. If the myths can be dissolved, if indeed the beliefs can be honestly questioned, many of our inhibitions to normal, rational and ethical conduct will be removed."[3] In order for the myths to be dissolved, according to James Weldon Johnson, Africa, the original home of all black peoples, would have to be vindicated as well. "Popular opinion has it that the Negro in Africa has been from time immemorial a savage. This is far from the truth. Such an opinion is possible only because there has been and still is an historical conspiracy against Africa which has successfully stripped the Negro race of all credit for what it contributed in past ages to the birth and growth of civilization."[4]

In another editorial, "Blackness and Whiteness," published in *Opportunity* in 1928, Charles S. Johnson gave a list of examples in which the color black was portrayed negatively and the color white positively in English literature. He followed this with some contemporary instances in which such Renaissance writers as Langston Hughes and Ann Spencer vindicated the Negro by treating blackness or darkness as positive and thereby challenging the traditional myths and beliefs about black people. He wrote, "The advent of Negroes to the field of letters promises the most salutary results in breaking up some of these long, and hoary associations."[5] The breaking up of some of these hoary associations is what Johnson was suggesting in an earlier editorial of 1926 titled "Welcoming the New Negro," in which he said the Negro was "changing his skin" before the eyes of whites[6]—no doubt a swooping down upon whites (to use Carl Diton's language) so they could not tell their heads from their feet. Akin to the protagonist in *The Autobiography of an Ex-Colored Man*, Charles Johnson was suggesting that the root of the race problem in America lay in the predominant racial myths about blacks, and that these racial myths could be undermined not by strictly imitating white culture but by depicting the life, ambitions, struggles, and passions of the Negro race within the "higher" classical musical forms. Indeed, James Weldon Johnson frequently made quite explicit the implicit point made in *The Autobiography*: that he saw a direct connection between the "creative powers" of blacks and the solution of the race problem.[7]

Thus, in claiming that the Negro Renaissance was a failure, Nathan Huggins fails to take into consideration an important historical factor that deeply concerned Charles Johnson, a factor that Locke acknowledged as early as 1915 in an essay titled "The Theoretical and Scientific Conceptions of Race."[8] Huggins fails to consider the fact that the racist racialism of nineteenth-century French intellectual Joseph Arthur de Gobineau, as documented in his *Essay on the Inequality of the Human Races* (1853), had followed black people into twentieth-century America. This racialist legacy left American whites with the notion that blacks had a biologically and ontologically distinct history, tradition, personality, and purpose, which together imprinted upon black culture such traits as emotionality (rather than intellectuality), sensuality (rather than rationality), and inferiority (rather than "superiority"). "So for generations," wrote Locke, "in the mind of America the Negro has been more a formula than a human being—a something to be argued about, condemned or defended, to be 'kept down,' or 'in his place,' or 'helped up,' to be worried with or worried over, harassed or patronized, a social bogey or a social burden."[9] Thus, again, the Negro "changing his skin" and becoming "new" before the eyes of whites, swooping down upon whites and vindicating the Negro, was the goal of the Renaissance; while debuting the New Negro, who would depict the life, ambitions, struggles, and passions of the race within the "higher" classical musical forms, was the strategy.

But the white patrons and critics of Negro Renaissance art tended to want the Old Negro—to them, the "real" Negro—to keep his old skin forever, so there was continuous tension between them and the Renaissance artists and intellectuals who wanted the New Negro debuted. With regard to the traditional use of dialect in the spirituals, for instance, the white critics and patrons, such as Carl Van Vechten and Charlotte Osgood Mason, were generally for it, and the new school of artists and intellectuals generally against it. Van Vechten insisted that the retention of dialect in the spirituals was of utmost importance to their successful rendering and that spirituals sung in grammatical English were the farthest removed from the "true spirit" of the folk originals. Van Vechten was therefore quite displeased with the efforts of certain black arrangers and performers who disregarded this "charming" aspect of the "native songs."[10] But typical of such whites, Van Vechten's notion of Negro dialect was more reminiscent of minstrelsy than reflective of reality, as one black writer to *The New York Amsterdam News* pointed out about Van Vechten's so-called Negro dialect in his novel, *Nigger Heaven* (1926): "Having lived nineteen years in Harlem, roamed all its streets unchaperoned, and been at home with all its varied human types, I can speak, I think, with some authority when I say that Van Vechten's dialect doesn't exist up here."[11]

Charlotte Mason was in agreement with Van Vechten on the question of dialect in Renaissance art and was disgusted that blacks were so pleased that James Weldon Johnson had written his poem, "The Creation," without it. She felt certain that there would come a day when blacks would be fully repentant because they could no longer hear the creation narrative in their natural tongue but only in the white man's English.[12] However, Johnson, as he explained in the preface to *God's Trombones* (1927), the book which contains "The Creation," intentionally omitted dialect because it traditionally had been the instrument of pathos and humor in stereotypical portrayals of blacks.[13] In other words, Johnson viewed the use of dialect as a means of maintaining the fictional portrayal of blacks as pathetic, happy-go-lucky, singing, shuffling, banjo-picking people who reside in log cabins amid fields of cotton or along the levees.[14] In this regard, Johnson was pleased to be able to say that "The Creation" had next to nothing of the "traditional plantation atmosphere" or the "artificial atmosphere of the jungle" in the words.[15]

Thus, Kelly Miller, the Howard University dean and columnist for *The New York Amsterdam News,* was correct that nostalgic whites (such as Van Vechten and Mason, who wanted dialect maintained in black art) refused to take black people seriously. Miller said, "but tell them about the Negro jockey, banjo player, prize fighter, minstrel, mimic, buck dancer, cabaret critics, jazz orchestra, singer of jubilee glees or Memphis blues, and they will only stop to hear, but linger to listen. They never tire of the dramatic portrayal of lowly life of the humble."[16] This is the reason Harold Preece, a white writer of an article published in *The Crisis* in 1936, concluded that there was no difference between the yokel who appreciated the minstrel show and Van Vechten's white Negrophiles who promoted the notion that Negroes could gain social acceptance on the basis of their unadulterated folk culture.[17]

So, there is only one obvious reason why Nathan Huggins would consider it a flaw on the part of the Renaissance Negro to feel a sense of dissatisfaction with the Old Negro, the created Negro of the white man.[18] He evidently misunderstood the Renaissance artists and intellectuals, whose dissatisfaction with the Old Negro was not self-hatred but merely displeasure with the myths and stereotypes that defined and enslaved black people.

II

Much like Langston Hughes and Ann Spencer, who treated blackness or darkness positively in their writings in order to challenge the traditional myths and stereotypes about their race, the musicians of the Renaissance were also self-consciously motivated to vindicate the Negro by displacing the Old Negro with the New. If there were any New Negroes of music who seemed to lack this self-conscious motivation, New Negroes whom Huggins could possibly make an example of in an effort to support his presumption that the Renaissance was a failure,[19] Harry T. Burleigh and Roland Hayes left many a racially conscious New Negro with the impression that they would prefer to be ex-colored men. However, I will demonstrate that even in the case of these two men, any notions that they did, or desired to, sell their birthrights for a mess of pottage were as erroneous as Huggins is about the New Negro being a general "sell out."

Upon an initial impression, Burleigh could easily appear to be a kind of self-conscious ex-colored man and therefore, to Huggins, a typical New

Negro who posited an inadequate new answer to the old problem of racism. Eva Jessye, a choral arranger and director and Renaissance artist like Dett and Hall Johnson, said some people believed Burleigh's snobbery was related to his desire to disclaim his racial heritage.[20] Zora Neale Hurston, a Renaissance artist and folklorist, said Burleigh had "less understanding of a sympathy for Negroes" than any other person she could imagine.[21] So it might seem, for Burleigh not only believed blacks should advance themselves through individual rather than political action,[22] but he never openly promoted black causes.[23] This may explain, for instance, why in 1916 he declined without explanation an invitation from Joel E. Spingarn (benefactor of the Spingarn medal) to attend a conference whose purpose was to discuss race relations and the promotion of worthy blacks.[24] Moreover, Burleigh's own grandson, James Hall, Jr., seemed to corroborate the speculations of Jessye and Hurston by admitting that Burleigh did not seem interested in addressing racial injustice but rather seemed "universal" and "strongly non-ethnic." Continued Hall, "I don't think that he viewed himself as a black man, even in his approach to the spirituals. I suspect that he thought of them as a very valid form of music, one having a certain important creativity for the world."[25]

With these portrayals of Burleigh it could easily appear that he was part and parcel of the anti-racialism popularized by Jean Toomer, who insisted that he saw himself and all citizens of the United States as Americans. Regretful that his novel, *Cane,* had typecast him as a racialist, Toomer said to James Weldon Johnson: "I aim to stress the fact that we all are Americans. I do not see things in terms of Negro, Anglo-Saxon, Jewish, and so on. As for me personally, I see myself as an American, simply an American." He said further that because he saw the art and literature of the United States as American rather than Negro or Anglo-Saxon, he therefore had to "withdraw from all things which emphasize or tend to emphasize racial or cultural divisions" and align himself with things which stress human commonalities.[26]

That Burleigh was evidently "strongly non-ethnic" might even explain for someone of Jessye's, Hurston's, or Huggins's purview why his Christian affiliation was with the Episcopal church. Booker T. Washington had said that if Negroes were anything but Baptist or Methodist then white Christians had been tampering with them,[27] the comment Hurston was evidently referencing when she spoke to James Weldon Johnson about "those among us who have been tampered with and consequently have gone Presbyterian or Episcopalian."[28] That Burleigh perhaps had been tampered with by whites would probably explain to contemporaries such as Hurston and historians such as Huggins why he became the first black chorister for the all-white congregation of St. George's Protestant Episcopal Church in New York; and how, especially since the white churches of New York had a history of discriminating against blacks, he came to remain at that white church as the only black chorister for fifty-two years. The minister of St. Matthew's Protestant Episcopal Church, a white parish in nearby Brooklyn, actually printed a notice in the church's Sunday program of September 15, 1929, which read: "The Episcopal Church provides churches for Negroes. Several of these churches are within easy reach of this locality. They are in need of the loyal support of all true Negro Churchmen, therefore the rector of this parish discourages the attendance or membership in this church of the members of that race."[29] While James Weldon Johnson, as secretary of the NAACP, wrote the bishop over the district, calling for the ouster of that minister, here was Burleigh in a denomination that segregated its congregations and in a parish in which he was the only black chorister and possibly the only black member.

Burleigh was not the first or the last Renaissance musician to refuse to participate in public or political racialism and thus to appear, in the favor of Huggins's negative view of the New Negro, to be positing an inadequate new answer to the old problem of racism. According to Delores Calvin, one of the editors of the black-owned Calvin's Syndicated News Service in New York, there were a number of such Negroes; and she considered Roland Hayes, Marian Anderson, and Portia White to be among them. Calvin told William Grant Still's wife, Verna Arvey, that she was disappointed to learn from an interview that the young contralto, Portia White, seemed to have no racial pride or ambitions, at least no ambitions other than self-centered ones. She said that when she asked White if she would like to sing with the Metropolitan Opera Company if the barriers that barred Negroes were ever broken down, White said she would like to sing opera but would never elbow her way in, that the doors would have to open naturally. Commented Calvin offhand, "We know she'll be waiting 100 years for those doors to open *naturally*!"[30]

The alleged accommodationism that Calvin saw in Hayes and that Jessye and Hurston saw in Burleigh, and that Huggins sees in all New Negroes,[31] was not unlike the accommodationism Du Bois saw in Booker T. Washington (with whom both Hayes and Burleigh traveled singing spirituals as duets during Washington's lecture tour of 1914). In the polemic between Washington's philosophy of industrial and agricultural education and Du Bois's philosophy of a "talented tenth" of the black population leading the black masses in their plight out of oppression and to intellectual maturity,

Hayes said he came down on Washington's side.[32] He described himself this way:

> Although I am not unsympathetic with pro-Negro lobbies, I do not expect that we shall be saved by law, I cannot believe that our most urgent need is the enactment of new laws by white legislators. At the risk of being called reactionary, I want to reiterate my faith that we shall be saved by our own work and not as wards of the Government. I feel about the Negro problem the way a missionary feels about the Christian religion. In the back of every missionary's mind, there is a dream of bringing all the world to Christ, but in practice he goes out after converts one by one. In the same way, we Negroes must reach the hearts of white folks singly. Every once in a while one of us may make a convert who, like the Emperor Constantine, will draw souls after him.[33]

When black journalist J. A. Rogers had a lengthy interview with Hayes in 1928 about his position on race politics, he sensed that this celebrated man of the concert stage was troubled by the probability that the people of his race misunderstood him. Rogers responded by saying that no sensible Negro should expect Hayes to spoil his role as an artist by getting involved in the politics of race at a level that should be left for writers and speakers to cover. "I assured him," continued Rogers in his newspaper column, "that at each appearance he was doing more to break down race prejudice than a large number of us together were able to do by writing and speaking." This was so, Rogers said to Hayes, even when he was not conscious of it. "I am conscious of it all the time," responded Hayes. "My people come first to me and I try to make every move count."[34]

Such artists as Hayes and Burleigh, who believed blacks could benefit from being accepted by whites one at a time as successful individuals, were not viewed favorably by Du Bois (nor by Huggins, who comes down on Du Bois's side in the Washington–Du Bois polemic). In this regard, Du Bois wrote:

> With the growing recognition of Negro artists in spite of the severe handicaps, one comforting thing is occurring to both white and black. They are whispering, "Here is a way out. Here is the real solution of the color problem. The recognition accorded Cullen, Hughes, Fauset, White and others shows there is no real color line. Keep quiet! Don't complain! Work! All will be well!"

I will not say that already this chorus amounts to a conspiracy. Perhaps I am naturally too suspicious. But I will say that there are today a surprising number of white people who are getting great satisfaction out of these younger Negro writers because they think it is going to stop agitation of the Negro question. They say, "What is the use of your fighting and complaining; do the great thing and the reward is there." And many colored people are all too eager to follow this advice; especially those who are weary of the eternal struggle along the color line, who are afraid to fight and to whom the money of philanthropists and the alluring publicity are subtle and deadly bribes. They say, "What is the use of fighting? Why not show simply what we deserve and let the reward come to us?"[35]

Despite the ranting of art purists, continued Du Bois, art is and must always be used for propaganda. He did not "care a damn," he concluded, for any art that was not so used, particularly when black art is silent while white art bombards society with propaganda.[36]

However, that Hayes and Burleigh were politically conservative like Washington does not mean they were not motivated by the impetus of the Negro Renaissance to vindicate the Negro. In fact, the pages of *The Crisis* and *Opportunity*, the two magazines that served as sources of creative and intellectual outlet for the Renaissance Negroes, had only positive words to say about both artists. In 1924, an opinion piece in *The Crisis*, published during the time Du Bois was editor, read: "For thirty years Harry Burleigh has been leading soloist of a leading New York church. For three hours last Sunday thousands of his admirers clamored without to enter that church already full to bursting in order to pay tribute to the man who is today the greatest American composer of songs. It was a fine sight. There was no element of American culture unrepresented."[37] Well over a decade later, enthusiasm for Burleigh's contribution to the Negro Renaissance had not waned, as evidenced in a 1938 editorial in *Opportunity*, an editorial that seemed unconcerned with Burleigh's long tenure as the lone black chorister at St. George's Episcopal Church:

Mr. Burleigh possesses all of the qualities which inspire emulation. A cultivated gentleman, aristocratic in the best sense of the term, gentle in manner and speech, possessed of natural dignity, it is no wonder to those who know him that for almost half a century he has been a member of the Choir of St. George's. Certainly there are few people who would deny that his association with this congregation has not been altogether a happy demonstration of the triumph of sheer ability and personality over the apprehensions of racial difference.[38]

So, while Du Bois did not "care a damn" for blacks of Burleigh's political disposition, neither was Burleigh the ex-colored man of James Weldon Johnson's novel. To the contrary, Burleigh's role as the only black chorister at St. George's did in fact open doors for blacks and help vindicate them. In 1930, at St. George's annual vesper service of spirituals, for instance, the singing of Burleigh's arranged spirituals by the parish choir and by Burleigh himself were joined by the reading of biblical scripture by Richard B. Harrison, the black actor who had offended whites by playing the role of God in the musical comedy *The Green Pastures*.[39] So Huggins, to fashion a polemic in order to make my point, might want to say: Look at Burleigh, the so-called New Negro, the only black chorister in an all-white parish and a member of a white denomination that segregates its congregations. But I wish to say: Yes, look at the New Negro Burleigh, and beside him is the black God reading the Bible before an all-white Episcopal parish, a most profound racial vindication, to be sure!

The importance of Burleigh as a Renaissance man is therefore identical to the importance of Hayes as, in the words of an opinion piece in *The Crisis*, an artist whose accomplishments served as propaganda for the benefit of the race:

> How many of us realize the tremendous propaganda of Roland Hayes? He was at Carnegie Hall last week. He sang with a firmness, control and sweetness that entranced thousands of the most sophisticated music-lovers of America. Black and white sat together in the orchestra. Applauding devotees lingered until the lights went out. He sang old eighteenth century songs; he sang Negro melodies; he sang . . . "as no living singer sings." Think what it means to every black child in the world to have this black man singing.[40]

William Pickens, field secretary for the NAACP and former professor and dean at Morgan College in Baltimore, similarly commented: "Ten thousand white people will go and hear Hayes or Robeson sing the Spiritual . . . , and so get a pleasing impression of the Negro as an artist and a man, for every one hundred whites that may turn out to hear the Negro argue or speak in the most logical way in his own behalf."[41]

James Weldon Johnson had been saying the same thing since at least 1912 in *The Autobiography*, but he made the point again in his 1923 commencement address at Hampton Institute. "We might argue in the abstract that the Negro possesses intellect, that he has high ideals, that his soul is sensitive to the most delicate nuances of spiritual reactions, and yet not convince those with whom we argue," he said to the Hampton students. "But the production of sublime music, of moving poetry, of noble literature, is that which was to be demonstrated."[42]

So, even if Du Bois were correct about such artists being "weary of the eternal struggle along the color line" and about them being "afraid to fight," and even if Huggins believes such artists provided an inadequate new answer to the old problem of racism, this did not prevent such artists from being symbols of the desired propaganda. Thus, even if they were personal failures with regard to an adequate new answer to the old race problem, that does not necessarily mean the entire Renaissance was a failure.

III

Throughout my discussion of Hayes and Burleigh, I have been tentative about their racial conservatism because it really could have been, unbeknownst to me, self-conscious racialism in masked form—that is, an instance of what literary scholar Houston Baker calls the "mastery of form." In his book *Modernism and the Harlem Renaissance* (1987), Baker defines this "mastery of form" as the skillful ability of a black artist or intellectual to sound or appear stereotypically "colored" when the person is really engaging in "self-conscious gamesmanship" in opposition to racism, the manipulation of minstrelsy's stereotypes in the quest for black liberation.[43] Baker cites Booker T. Washington as the prototypal example of the "mastery of form," as illustrated in Washington's Atlanta Exposition address of 1895:

> A white farmer tells Washington on the day before his Atlanta talk that he will have to please an audience composed of white northerners, white southerners, and blacks. "I am afraid," says the farmer, "that you have got yourself into a tight place." But Washington's speech is an overwhelming success with black and white alike. It includes tributes to northern philanthropy, gratitude to southern patriarchs, and prescriptions for Afro-American accommodation in an age of Jim Crow. It also includes the *sound* of

minstrelsy. . . . Scandal is the only designation for the appearance of such a *sound* (a chicken-thieving tonality) in the first address presented in the South by a black man considered a *national* leader. Extricating himself from a "tight place" and finding room for an authentic voice seem to occasion the scandalous for an Afro-American speaker.[44]

Baker explains that Washington went so far as to take up forms and sounds of minstrelsy in order to earn a national reputation and the resultant benefits for the black masses. He concludes about Washington, "He demonstrates in his manipulations of form that there *are* rhetorical possibilities for crafting a voice out of tight places."[45]

Since the early phase of the Renaissance was heavily reliant on the philanthropy of such whites as Carl Van Vechten and Charlotte Mason, who felt nostalgically that the Old Negro was the "real" Negro, it was necessary for the Renaissance artists to be (or appear to be) accommodative and sometimes even to give their benefactors the stereotypical sounds and images they expected while working clandestinely for the "vindication of the Negro." James Weldon Johnson understood the circumstances and knew that they required some sacrifice on the part of blacks. In *Negro Americans, What Now?* (1934) he wrote:

> We should establish and cultivate friendly interracial relations whenever we can do so without loss of self-respect. I do not put this on the grounds of brotherly love or any of the other humanitarian shibboleths; I put it squarely on the grounds of necessity and common sense. Here we are, caught in a trap of circumstances, a minority in the midst of a majority . . . ; we have got to escape from the trap, and escape depends largely on our ability to command and win the fair will, at least, and the good will, if possible, of that great majority.[46]

Johnson understood the importance of courting the white patron and publisher, and he played the game of "mastery" without sacrificing his self-respect. With regard to his avoidance of an artificial "jungle" atmosphere in poetry, for instance, Johnson said such left him "cold." "Such poems are generally not written out of any experience or genuine emotion," he told the young novelist Frank Yerby. "The majority of the poems harking back to Africa that our young poets write strike me as second hand, even as third hand, poetry. They are not based upon actual physical or spiritual experiences."[47] On the other hand, while Johnson evidently would have considered it self-denigrating to succumb to the demands of white patrons, publishers, and critics for the traditional sounds of the plantation or the minstrel stage, even though masking a thrust toward racial liberation, he was nonetheless engaging in the "mastery of form" with his *Autobiography,* which was a call for "renaissance" (a quiet revolution of vindication) masked as the autobiography of a real ex-colored man. This was Johnson's style of "mastery" and he could not, with a sense of self-respect, succumb to the articulation of "chicken-thieving" tonalities, even for the sake of deceiving whites.

While Johnson would have considered it self-denigrating to manipulate the sounds of the plantation or of minstrelsy for the purpose of maneuvering toward black liberation, other Renaissance Negroes, such as Locke, Hurston, and Hughes, engaged in "chicken-thieving" deception for varying lengths of time. Each of them gave Charlotte Mason the Negro (or African) primitivism she insisted should be expressed through their arts and letters in order to continue to benefit financially from her patronage, but to Hurston and Hughes the masking eventually became too miserable.

To mask for Mason was no easy task, for she felt that such talented blacks as Locke, Hurston, and Hughes had lost their natural primitivity and needed to be taught to recover and preserve it artistically. So, she catechized them—her "godchildren"—like a relentless tyrant. The route to the recovery of their primitive authenticity, she taught them, was through their relinquishment of the adulterated sexual impulses that whites violently imposed upon their race during slavery, and their return to the sexual impulses of primitive religion that had so powerfully linked their Africans ancestors to the Infinite.[48] This was the "original Negro quality" Mason saw not only in the blues, of which she owned numerous recordings,[49] but also in Hughes's anthology *The Weary Blues,* Claude McKay's novel *Home to Harlem,* and in Paul Robeson's concert renditions of the spirituals.

Hughes, McKay, and Robeson were, for a while anyway, blacks of the "original" quality, and Mason warned Locke that he and the rest of the Negro artists and intellectuals of the Renaissance had better follow suit. "By the time the Negroes have finished ruining their inheritance on this slippery pond of civilization there will not be any place where the white man has not divided the spoils of primitive African art, African music, all Africa's strength," she said. "If you would just sit yourself down before the mirror and look Alain Locke in the eye and tell him to hurry up mighty quick and realize that this civilization he is holding so fast to the coat tails of is already in the throes of death."[50] Mason was insistent that Locke "slough off" the weight of white culture and that he use his education only to clarify the primitive thoughts that surged through his being. He would as a consequence, she said, be blessed by the souls of the slaves of Africa who watch on from the beyond.[51] For him not to "slough off" the weight of white culture, including the white man's "churchanity" (as Mason called Christianity), was not only to put on "slavery's ball and chain" but to commit apostasy against her own spiritual laws.[52]

Mason also considered it apostasy for blacks to imitate the white man's conceit. She said to Locke, "I don't see why the Negroes, who despise the way white people do when they are conceited, take on the same condition themselves the minute anything of importance happens. This is really great unhappiness to me, that none of you are ready to be men and substantial creative men."[53] The protagonist in *The Autobiography of an Ex-Colored Man* understood very well that blacks who were viewed as imitating whites, and thus as "putting on airs," could cause whites to be irritated and disgusted: "I think that the white people somehow feel that coloured people who have education and money, who wear good clothes and live in comfortable houses, are 'putting on airs,' that they do these things for the sole purpose of 'spiting the white folks,' or are, at best, going through a sort of monkey-like imitation. Of course, such feelings can only cause irritation or breed disgust." This kind of transgression of the highest order is what caused Mason's deep disdain for quite a few black artists, including Hayes and Dett, and later Hughes, Hurston, and Robeson. Thus, it was often necessary for the New Negro—who, like Booker T. Washington, wished continued benefits from white philanthropy—to feign the personality of the Old Negro whom whites created and were comfortable with.

Robeson's renditions of the spirituals were for a time sufficiently primitive for Mason because he sang them with that deep voice without the edge of refinement that distinguished the renditions of Hayes. To illustrate the difference as whites heard it, poet Carl Sandburg remarked: "Hayes imitates white culture and uses methods from the white man's conservatories of music, so that when he sings a Negro spiritual the audience remarks, 'What technic; what a remarkable musical education he must have had!' When Paul Robeson sings spirituals, the remark is: 'That is the real thing—he has kept the best of himself and not allowed the schools to take it away from him!'"[54] For Mason this may have been true of Robeson for a while, but he eventually began to sound to her about as white as Hayes. What she desired of Robeson, and Hayes if he would ever succumb, was the kind of singing Hurston captured in her semidramatic musical, *The Great Day*, which the folklorist produced with Mason's financial help in December and

January of the 1931–32 winter. The performance of children's games, ballads, work songs, blues, street and club dances, and preaching, most of it dramatized, all of it derived from the four years of field work Hurston did under Mason's patronage, led one journalist to comment that if there was such a thing as "natural and unpremeditated art," then this was it.[55]

Hurston enjoyed gathering and documenting this folklore, putting into practice the study she did under anthropologist Franz Boas at Columbia University, so she would continue to tolerate and manipulate Mason until she could make it on her own. But Hughes, when unable to feign faith in the old woman any longer, broke with Mason. "She wanted me to be primitive and know and feel the intuitions of the primitive," recalled Hughes. "But, unfortunately, I did not feel the rhythms of the primitive surging through me, and so I could not live and write as though I did. I was only an American Negro—who had loved the surface of Africa and the rhythms of Africa—but I was not Africa. I was Chicago and Kansas City and Broadway and Harlem. And I was not what she wanted me to be."[56]

The fact is, none of Mason's "godchildren" were or could be what "Godmother" wanted them to be, for behind the old woman's insistence that blacks rediscover and utilize their native folk culture in their art was not a desire to see them racially vindicated and ultimately liberated. Rather, Mason desired to see her own race vindicated and divinized. She believed that the culture of the Anglo-Saxon was depleted of divine essence, that Anglo-Saxon culture in fact "sucks the life blood out of the soul of art that is being born in this civilization."[57] On the other hand, blacks were believed to possess that "life blood" and could therefore serve as an example for whites to follow—that is if blacks, in creating their art, would only be true to their so-called primitive impulses.[58] Mason also believed that the Anglo-Saxon culture of warfare was sucking the life out of life itself. Having lived through the catastrophe of whites killing whites in the First World War, a war that shattered the self-perception of the "civilized" white world, Mason believed that the spiritual power her race could learn from primitive peoples would enable whites to control world events without the necessity of destruction.[59]

Mason was greatly influenced in some of these views by Natalie Curtis's folkloric collection titled *The Indians' Book* (1907), a volume of songs, stories, and drawings by Indians that purports to reflect the inner life and soul of one of the noblest types of primitive man.[60] *The Indians' Book*, whose research Mason briefly participated in and might have helped finance, was Mason's bible, in that both the philosophy behind the research and the substance of the document became part of her teachings to the Renaissance

Negroes she patronized. Mason read stories from *The Indians' Book* to her "godchildren" when they visited her and eventually gave Locke an inscribed copy. Feigning sincerity, I believe, Locke informed Mason that he kept the book in a special place on the table next to his best reading-and-thinking chair and that he read the book when he found moments of solitude.[61] If such moments of solitude ever materialized and Locke had bothered to read the book's introduction, he would have heard reverberations of Mason's relentless lessons. Anglo-Saxons, though people of mechanical and inventive genius, the introduction says, lack the spontaneous creative impulse of primitive peoples, peoples who have the potential to make a lasting contribution to the culture of American civilization. "The primitive races are the child races," Curtis's introduction continued. "Who can tell us what may be their contribution to humanity when they are grown? And have they not even now something to give?"[62]

Actually, this ideation and language was not even new to Locke when he met Mason in the late 1920s, for the same had been articulated in the article that white philanthropist Albert C. Barnes wrote for Locke's edited collection of essays titled *The New Negro* (1925). In his article titled "Negro Art and America," Barnes said the primitive Negro race, with its folk art unharnessed by the white man's education and pseudoculture which stifle the soul, could be of tremendous civilizing value to America by helping whites return to their original spiritual endowment. Barnes believed this spiritual endowment was a source of primeval happiness that had been cut off from whites via their tendency to permit the mind to predominate over the spirit.[63] So, in the very pages of *The New Negro,* there was an echo of *The Indians' Book* and of the white patron and critic who believed Renaissance Negroes should know and feel and reflect in their art the intuitions and rhythms of the primitive surging through them.

While Hughes finally had had enough of Mason and her *Indians' Book,* Hurston, in order to keep the monetary allowance coming from Mason until she could make it on her own financially, continued to feign Old Negroness—like Booker T. Washington to the northern white philanthropy and the southern patriarchy. Hurston, feigning masterfully, made an art of manipulating Mason. She complimented the old woman with, "Next to Mahatma Gandhi you are the most spiritual person on earth";[64] and she regularly addressed Mason with such plaudits as "Darling, my mother-god" and "Darling Godmother, The Guard-mother who sits in the Twelfth Heaven and shapes the destinies of the primitives."[65] When Hurston knew Mason was displeased with her, she wrote "Godmother" saying: "you are the last word, no matter what I do or don't. I can neither be present when you sit in judgment, nor cry out under sentence. You cannot be wrong, for everything that I am, I am because you made me. You can smile upon me, and you can look off towards immensity and be equally right. You have been gracious, but you were following no law except your inclination."[66] As long as the country was in its great economic depression, Hurston would continue to permit Mason to smile upon her or look off into immensity, because, at least on one occasion, she needed new shoes. "One other item of expense, Godmother," she wrote. "I really need a pair of shoes. You remember that we discussed the matter in the Fall and agreed that I should own only one pair at a time. I brought a pair in mid-December and they have held up until now. My big toe is about to burst out of my right shoe and so I must do something about it."[67]

Hurston's "mastery of form"—her masterful masking of racial vindication with prescriptive accommodation—thus included the sound of blues complaintiveness: "I really need a pair of shoes." The tones of blues complaintiveness were also heard when Hurston told Mason that she often felt so discouraged that she could see no reason to live save for the fact that "Godmother" saw something of worth in her. "Thus often I have been just stumbling along with no other light for me except your faith," croons Hurston. "I had no lamp within myself."[68] Part of the blues tonalities included the sounds of minstrelsy (minstrelsy intended to deceive). For instance, Hurston's "chicken-thieving tonality" was evident in her conclusion to that crooning about "stumbling along." "Devotedly Your Pickaninny, Zora," she wrote.[69] In another letter to Mason, Hurston signed off with that same minstrel mess: "your black spasm, Zora."[70]

Hurston eventually excommunicated herself from Mason's "Twelfth Heaven," but Locke remained faithful to the old woman until the day she died, for there had evolved out of their relationship a mutual bond of affection. The protagonist in *The Autobiography of an Ex-Colored Man* understood this kind of relationship intimately, as had the book's author with regard to Carl Van Vechten. "I dreaded . . . breaking with my millionaire," the colored man of Johnson's *Autobiography* recalled. "Between this peculiar man and me there had grown a very strong bond of affection, backed up by a debt which each owed to the other. He had taken me from a terrible life in New York and, by giving me the opportunity of travelling and coming into contact with the people with whom he associated, had made me a polished man of the world." Of course, Johnson and Locke were already polished men of the world before they met their white friends. The point is, though, that had Locke ever decided to sever his relationship with Mason, he probably would have thought the same thoughts as Johnson's protagonist when he left his patron in Berlin to return home to the United States: "And so I separated from the man who was, all in all, the best friend I ever had, except my mother, the man who exerted the greatest influence ever brought into my life, except that exerted by my mother."

Despite the longevity of his relationship with Mason, and despite the affection he had for the old woman because she had treated him somewhat like a son, Locke left clues aplenty that he was to some extent engaged in the "mastery of form." He evidently felt justified in his minstrel act because he firmly believed blacks were deserving of white patronage, deserving because white racism had made the lives of blacks difficult as artists and intellectuals. "I wonder if people ever stop to think what impossible conditions America imposes on Negroes who want to live and express themselves finely and creatively!" he said to Mason. "Of course, you have always known, and have in so many cases tried to help take the pressure off a few."[71] There was a patronizing tone to these words, yet they hardly compare to the time Locke tried to convince Mason that he was becoming a "real" Negro just as she had always wished. After returning from a trip to the South, Locke reported to Mason that a sense of belonging had come over him while in that region, a sense of belonging which resulted from his new feeling of being "truly Negro" and part of the "real folk." Revealing contradictions and insincerity that suggest he was again playing the minstrel, Locke continued: "How fine they are even in their depravity and almost hopeless backwardness—for after all they all have a genuine joy in living and a direct simplicity and sincerity."[72]

We can also see Locke "extricating himself from a tight place" when he maneuvered to remain faithful to Mason while also remaining friends with the black artists whom the old woman had excommunicated. When Mason came to disdain Paul Robeson because he allegedly imitated the white man's conceit (namely, she could not get access to him in order to influence him) and because both she and Locke had disapproved of his chicken-thieving role in *Emperor Jones*, Locke found a way to defend the Renaissance man. He told Mason that while in New York in 1939 he had a long talk with Robeson and found that he had changed. He pointed out that Robeson had begun refusing roles that portrayed the Negro race negatively or at least was insisting on changes in movie scripts to meet his criticisms, including changes in the starring role in Roark Bradford's *John Henry*. With regard to the latter musical, Locke said to Mason: "He insists on the music being genuine folk songs arranged. That is real wisdom, isn't it?"[73]

Locke similarly defended Roland Hayes, whom he liked and respected for his immense contribution to the "vindication of the Negro," but whom Mason had long disregarded as someone who was ruining his inheritance on the slippery pond of civilization by singing "too white." In December 1937, Locke wrote Mason about the evening he had spent with Hayes, who had just been appointed as a coach in song interpretation at Boston University's School of Music. Locke told Mason that he felt Hayes had changed, grown spiritually, as evidenced in the lecture he had prepared to give before the entire School of Music at Boston. Trying to remain faithful to Hayes while also appeasing Mason, Locke transcribed almost two full handwritten pages of Hayes's lecture on the singing of German lieder just to demonstrate to Mason that Hayes's emphasis on the importance of spirituality reflected her teachings. Hayes was quoted as writing:

> Remember the importance of spirituality in lieder-singing. However, let no one confuse my reference to spirituality with orthodox church and religion. Spirituality is a prime substructure to lieder-singing—is relatively the same as sub-soil of earth to vegetation. Nature has made and arranged the sub-soil many inches below the earth's surface, and stores it with plant food and moisture to the nourishment of the grasses, flowers and tender roots which draw on these essences during periods when there is no rainfall. . . . In a like manner has Nature-God made the soul of man, stores it up with His Spirit, and gives man the god-like privilege to draw from it to keep his heart filled with that essence we call spirituality.

The excerpt continued, and Locke concluded by informing Mason that he and Hayes had spoken highly of her, and that he had indicated to Hayes how glad "Godmother" would be to hear these words because of her long-time desire that he would glean such insight.[74]

IV

So, Houston Baker's concept of the "mastery of form" renders significant clarity to an important dynamic of the Negro Renaissance during the period it was lorded over by philanthropic Negrophiles. Another conceptual clarification that renders valuable interpretation, one that can be understood as a particular expression of Baker's "mastery of form," is Locke's notion of the "mastery" of European forms of classical art, in which forms the indigenous sounds of black culture were to be encased. "The artistic problem of the Young Negro has not been so much that of acquiring the outer mastery of form and technique," wrote Locke, "as that of achieving an inner mastery of mood and spirit."[75] The accomplishment of this balance between an "outer mastery of form and technique" and an "inner mastery of mood and spirit" is what excited Locke about William Dawson's *Negro Folk Symphony* when it premièred under Leopold Stokowski's Philadelphia Symphony Orchestra in 1934. "It is the form and character of the Dawson symphony that makes it so significant and promising," said Locke. "It is classic in form but Negro in substance, it shows mastery or near-mastery of the terrific resources of the modern orchestra." Locke concluded, "Mr. Dawson has tried to make his music racial, without at the same time losing touch with the grand speech of the master tradition in music."[76]

The concept of classical form is easy enough to grasp, but what exactly is the inner "mood and spirit?" William Grant Still raised this question when he said that someone trying to isolate the Negro element in American folk, popular, and classical music might wonder how the Negro element could be identified, but everyone knowledgeable of Negro music would know beyond a doubt that a distinctive mood and spirit came from music created by Negroes.[77] When we look further into Still's writings to see what he is talking about with regard to the identifiable characteristics of black music, we find that the inner mood and spirit he alludes to derives from African rhythm. In an article fittingly titled "The Music of My Race," Still said he heard African rhythms not only in the spirituals and the blues but also in the Cuban rumba, the Brazilian samba, the Colombian bambuco, and the Haitian merengue. He concluded that in various countries Negro music took on different characteristics correlative to the different cultural heritages dominating there, such as the Spanish culture in Cuba, the French culture in Haiti, and the Anglo culture in North America.[78] Locke made a similar comment about African rhythm taking on different characteristics based on the culture in which it finds expression. He said African rhythm sprouted freshly and variously in the soils of myriad lands of the African New World:

> This racial mastery of rhythm is one characteristic that seems never to have been lost, whatever else was, and it has made and kept the Negro a musician by nature and a music-maker by instinct. When customs were lost and native cultures cut off in the

rude transplantings of slavery . . . , underneath all, rhythm memories and rhythmic skill persisted to fuse with and transform whatever new mode of expression the Negro took on. For just as music can be carried without words, so rhythm can be carried without the rest of the music system; so intimately and instinctively is it carried. From this mustard-seed the whole structure of music can sprout anew. From a kernel of rhythm, African music has sprouted in strange lands, spread out a rootage of folk-dance and folk song, and then gone through the whole cycle of complete musical expression as far as soil and cultural conditions have permitted.[79]

Locke's comment that rhythm can be carried intimately and instinctively was explained further when he said slavery robbed Africans of their ancestral gift of fine craftsmanship, but the artistic urges to do fine craftsmanship flowed into one of the only channels left open to Negroes—movement, speech, and song. The body itself, continued Locke, became the Negro's primary artistic instrument, the voice being the Negro's "greatest single artistic asset."[80] William Grant Still came to the same conclusion about the enslaved Africans having been robbed of their material possessions while yet maintaining inherent talents, particularly musical talents which included the centrality of African rhythm. He said that when the enslaved were brought to America from Africa they had no material possessions but only the talents they possessed inherently, and that in America there was a spontaneous outpouring of these talents which resulted in three types of Negro music being created on the plantations—the ring shout, the work song, and the spiritual.[81] R. Nathaniel Dett concurred that it was obviously rhythm that established the link between the music of the American Negro and his African forebears.[82] Moreover, since black music was the principal carrier of African rhythm, it appears to be this particular Africanism that explains Samuel Floyd's remark that music's role in the Renaissance was, in comparison to how it has been underestimated by scholars, "much more basic and important to the movement."[83] There is nothing more basic and important to the Renaissance than African rhythm. So, African rhythm provided the pulse and impulse for the African "mood and spirit" which was encased within an outer European "form and technique."

Locke had conceived of this two-tiered "mastery" in music composition as early as his 1910–11 academic year in Germany, about a year before James Weldon Johnson's novel was released and Johnson's protagonist spoke similarly of encasing the hopes, dreams, and aspirations of the Negro in the "higher" classical musical forms. Writing to Carl Diton, who was studying music elsewhere in Germany, Locke encouraged Diton to learn the "theory" (or "form and technique") of the German school of music composition but to keep aloof of the "idiom" (or "mood and spirit").[84] William Grant Still, who had been doing "serious" and "famous work" in composition since the early 1920s, explained that in all the years he had been composing he never stopped studying form and hoping to "master it," and he insisted that everyone who writes music should have a thorough grounding in the forms developed by the classicists. Referencing Renaissance sculptor and friend Sargent Johnson, Still said that every conscientious artist recognizes the importance of "good form" and that Johnson once remarked that he too was principally concerned with form. "A layman with no feeling for form could construct an adequate shed," continued Still, "but a palace calls for an architect. A composer should be a musical architect."[85]

Roland Hayes, despite what some of his peers thought of his nonpolitical racialism, perceived himself to be contributing to the "vindication of the Negro" via this two-tiered "mastery." "Before my time, white singers had too often been in the habit of burlesquing the spirituals with rolling eyes and heaving breast and shuffling feet, on the blasphemous assumption that they were singing comic songs," said Hayes. "It pleased me to believe that I was restoring the music of my race to the serious atmosphere of its origin, and helping to redeem it for the national culture."[86] Hayes would have felt the same about James Weldon Johnson's poetry in God's Trombones, according to Wilber P. Thirkield, a Methodist Episcopal bishop who knew Johnson's parents from the years he taught at Gammon Theological Seminary in Atlanta. Thirkield said to Johnson, "Your work has always been on a high level and you have fulfilled the great wish of my dear friend, Roland Hayes, who in an interview on his last visit to Chattanooga deplored the fact that so many Negro writers were devoid of lofty spiritual aims and had a tendency to be swept away in the current of a jazz age."[87]

According to Locke, Dett, Still, Hayes, and Johnson, the folk music of the rural Negro and the popular music of the urban Negro could not alone be the means toward achieving this racial vindication; for though these genres were "Negro in substance," they did not show the mastery of the resources of the modern orchestra. Racial vindication would come when Negro folk music was set in classical form by blacks, and ultimate vindication when set in the larger of the classical forms. Even though Dett tended to arrange the spirituals using smaller classical forms, he understood the rationale behind the necessity of black composers mastering the larger forms. He said:

> For nearly 30 years the development of Negro music was perhaps too dependent upon creations in the smaller forms; but because of the unusual nature of many of these, the art was pushed rapidly forward. Though one who makes pencil sketches on paper may achieve results every bit as perfect in their way as another who chisels similar figures from marble, there is little doubt as to which artist's name will be written higher in the hall of fame. Comparison of their status with that of other composers had impressed this fact upon Negro musicians, with the result that the last dozen years or so have witnessed a vigorous attack by them upon the larger forms. The conquest . . . has caused a sharp change in the public's attitude toward Negro work.[88]

Dett's benefactor, George Foster Peabody, agreed. Having read and appreciated Locke's *The New Negro*,[89] Peabody was convinced that the two-tiered "mastery" Locke espoused was a viable strategy for the Negro to contribute to the national culture.[90] With regard to Dett, Peabody spoke of this two-tiered "mastery" as "genuine art capacity" (the "mastery of form and technique") and "African rhythm" (the "mood and spirit"): "The Negro ten percent of our population has a definite service, I think, which it can render to the people of this country through its very genuine art capacity and the music of Dr. Dett, based on the African rhythm which is so important a factor in the Spirituals, really lifts one up."[91] Peabody would later, as I will detail in chapter 2, send Dett's Hampton Institute choir on a tour of Europe for the purpose of revealing Dett's "artistic consummation" of the use of "African themes" (the spirituals) in his "unique composition."[92]

The two-tiered mastery of "form and technique" and "mood and spirit" characterized the other arts of the Renaissance as well. For instance, Sterling Brown explained that in attempting to interpret Negro folk life in a manner different from the plantation-minstrel tradition, he sought to encase folk materials in suitable forms and never hesitated to use any poetic form or to create variations of the folk forms. "I have studiously sought folk life," he wrote to James Weldon Johnson, "and attempted to deal with it in fitting structures—structures such as the clipped line, the blues form, the refrain poem, etc.—all with my own variations."[93] Johnson wrote back to Brown saying he was in favor of turning the "raw stuff" of Negro folk culture into "conscious art." He said, "Coming down to my own experience, I never heard in my life any Negro preacher, old or young, announce a sermon that bore anything like the exact resemblance in 'God's Trombones.' Yet, I have always been glad to claim that the old plantation sermons were the sources of my inspiration."[94]

Indeed, Johnson did an excellent job of mastering the balance of the two-tiered "mastery" in *God's Trombones,* according to John Hurst, a bishop in the African Methodist Episcopal Church. "You essayed an uneasy task in writing expressive poetry on what to many is an odd theme," wrote Hurst with regard to Johnson's artistic challenge to the traditional portrayal of black preachers as ignorant or comic figures. Their true characteristics, especially their poetic imaginations, continued Hurst, were "deserving of placing them on a higher plane than the mimic phonograph records, the vaudeville stage and the after-dinner joke." Hurst added, "Anyone who reads 'God's Trombones' cannot but be impressed with their imagination. Why then should they not afford serious material for the poet?" He concluded, "You have presented to posterity, very ably, an old picture in a very beautiful new frame."[95] Wilber Thirkield, the Methodist Episcopal bishop presiding over the Chattanooga area, concurred. He told Johnson, "You caught the spirit and movement of the preacher of the olden days. I have heard that weird and pathetic intoning of the preacher as the congregation swayed to the rhythmic beat of his voice and then broke forth into a sing-song refrain. I can hear between the lines of the singularly typical sermons so vividly set forth in your verse, the intonations of his moving voice." Thirkield concluded, "Your poems are true to life."[96]

Presenting to posterity an old picture in a new frame was exactly what Dett and Hayes did in selecting the spirituals as "serious material" for performance—because the spirituals were deserving of being placed on a "higher plane" than the mimic phonograph records, the vaudeville stage, and the after-dinner joke. In fact, no reliance on the contesting positions of such artists as Hughes or Hurston can shore up an opposing argument, for these artists were themselves placing black folk materials on a "higher plane." For instance, while Hurston criticized black composers and concert artists for taking "good negro music" and turning it into "mediocre white sounds,"[97] she was actually engaged in the same two-tiered "mastery" when she used black folklore as the basis of her books—say, her novel, *Jonah's Gourd Vine* (1934). The "form and technique" required of writing a novel for Western publication and consumption is foreign to the "mood and spirit" of this material that had been originated and maintained in the African oral tradition. So, for Hurston to say that the arranged spirituals "fell so far below the folk-art level of Negroes"[98] was for her to say the same about any number of books she liked, including her own *Jonah's Gourd Vine* and Johnson's *God's Trombones*, a book she told Johnson she liked very much.[99] With regard to *Jonah's Gourd Vine*, Hurston certainly must have felt that she, like Johnson, had "essayed an uneasy task" in writing expressively on what to many was "an odd theme." At least Johnson thought so after reading the novel. About her "good story," which he felt to be well written, Johnson said: "You have greatly improved both in your grasp of life and in your technique,"[100]—that is, both in her "mastery of mood and spirit" and "mastery of form and technique."

With the mastery of "form and technique" and "mood and spirit" characterizing the new impetus in the arts and letters, the Harmon Foundation adopted the concept of two-tiered "mastery" as its criterion for awarding blacks the highly touted Harmon awards, which were established in 1926. The director of the foundation, Mary Beattie Brady, said the awards were an attempt "to stimulate the Negro artist to give a free expression of his own individuality and the artistic impulses of the Negro people developed with the highest technique." Stated once more, Brady said: "We wish to encourage new creations from Negro men and women moved by artistic impulses and to induce such aspiring artists to study and strive for perfection in expression of what they find in themselves and in their racial experience."[101] So, on the one hand Brady referred to black artists being free to express "the artistic impulses of the Negro people" and to express that substance they "find in themselves and in their racial experience"—"mastery of mood and spirit." On the other hand, she spoke of the need of black artists to develop these "impulses" with the "highest technique" and of their striving for "perfection in expression"—"mastery of form and technique." Sure enough, that year, 1928, Dett and Still, who had perfected this two-tiered "mastery," were among the winners of the Harmon award. Two years later, the advice Locke had given Diton about this two-tiered "mastery" (during the 1910–11 academic year when they were both studying in Germany) paid off when Diton won the Harmon award in composition.

So, considering the foregoing factors—Still's remark that the importance of "good form" is what allies the arts, Locke's notion of two-tiered "mastery," and the Harmon Foundation's criterion for rewarding black arts and letters—the Negro Renaissance can be generally characterized as an epoch in which art and letters with an inner-African "mood and spirit," derived significantly (if not principally) from the remnant of African rhythm, found expression in European "form and technique" and flourished for the purpose of providing an adequate new answer to the old problem of racism. This two-tiered "mastery" was a particular expression of Baker's "mastery of form" when it became a strategy for pacifying white expectations for Negro "mood and spirit" while simultaneously vindicating the Negro by demonstrating mastery of European "form and technique."

V

Despite the newness of the artistic style that Locke defined as the "outer mastery of form and technique" and the "inner mastery of mood and spirit," Kelly Miller argued that the New Negro was not new at all, that the New Negro was the same Old Negro who had merely been exposed to a new environment. This so-called New Negro, continued Miller in a 1930 newspaper column, came from various parts of the country and the West Indies, bringing with him "the faculties and foibles of the folk from which he springs" but finding in such cities as Harlem a different kind of environment in which he began to develop his peculiar genius. Miller concluded that because the New Negro was simply the Old Negro trying to take himself too seriously with artistic self-portrayal rooted in self-conscious racialism, he was a "fool."[102] One Harlem resident who read these remarks in Miller's column in *The New York Amsterdam News* wrote a letter of retort to the newspaper's editor, rightly pointing out that Miller gave a one-sided critique of some of the factors that contributed to the interest Negroes had been able to win in various respected fields of human endeavor.[103] Reverdy Ransom, an African Methodist Episcopal bishop, years earlier had reflected the writer's point in an original poem titled "The New Negro," which he published in the *Amsterdam News* in 1923. It is not that the New Negro is really old, Ransom's poem implied, but that the Old Negro is also new. Though the Negro is "old as the forests primeval," poeticized Ransom, he is nonetheless "new." Slavery and oppression made him stronger, the poem continued, chiseled him to form; now, as "the last reserve of God on earth," he bears "rich gifts to science, religion, poetry and song."[104]

In the polemic over whether the Renaissance Negro was new or still old, Nathan Huggins comes down on the side of Miller. Huggins complains that Renaissance Negroes, though they enjoyed black folk music and acknowledged its contribution to American culture, were unwilling to view this music as "serious" art of high culture—a provincialist attitude, concludes Huggins, which caused these blacks to edify the culture of their learning over the culture of their experience.[105] But because Huggins recognizes neither the Renaissance's goal of racial "vindication" nor its strategy of two-tiered artistic "mastery," he misunderstands the Renaissance artists and intellectuals. Locke simply said, for instance, that if Negro music was to fulfill its "best possibilities," then Negroes could not continue to be musical simply by nature but would have to be musical also by nurture. In order to attain their "highest musical success," wrote Locke, the Negro had to build a cadre of trained musicians who *first of all* knew and loved the folk music and *then* were able to develop it into "great classical music."[106]

This is exactly what James Weldon Johnson accomplished with his poeticized black sermons in *God's Trombones*. Based first on a love of the black sermonic tradition, he secondly developed the tradition in classic poetic form. Johnson's work simultaneously affirms the black religious tradition and contests the white stereotypes of the black preacher. This is what James W. Brown, pastor of New Mother AME Zion Church in Harlem, seemed to be saying to Johnson in a letter he wrote him after reading *God's Trombones*. Brown said that in those days when the church was being assailed and traditional black preaching was being eulogized as a lost art, Johnson's book came as both a protest and a defense not only for the black preacher of sixty years earlier but for the preacher of their day.[107]

But because Huggins insists that the Renaissance Negro edified the culture of his learning over the culture of his experience, he concludes that the New Negro was but a public relations promotion in that the Negro was really the same person all along, and that the Old Negro was simply carried within the bosom of the New.[108] In actuality Huggins is not saying anything that had not been said before, except that when William Pickens said it in his book titled *The New Negro* (1916), published when Pickens was a professor at Morgan College in Baltimore, he was not weighing in on Miller's and Huggins's side of the polemic. Said Pickens:

> The "new Negro" is not really new: he is the same Negro under new conditions and subjected to new demands. Those who regret the passing of the "old Negro" and picture the "new" as something very different, must remember that there is no sharp line of

demarcation between the old and the new in any growing organism like a germ, a plant or a race. The present generation of Negroes have received their chief heritage from the former and, in that, they are neither better nor worse, higher nor lower than the previous generation. But the present Negro is differently circumstanced and must be measured by different standards.[109]

Pickens alluded to the basic premise for the Renaissance strategy of "mastery" when he went on to say in the title essay of *The New Negro* that what most seriously hindered whites from having a wholesome opinion of the Negro was their familiarity with the Negro domestics who served them and the Negro criminals they read about in the newspapers, as well as their unfamiliarity with the values of the Negro middle class. Pickens concluded that any strategy for improving the country's race problem had to involve Negroes demonstrating to whites that they could master the form and technique of white culture but master it with a Negro difference.[110]

So, indeed the New Negro was a public relations promotion, the vogue of the New Negro did have to be sold to the public in terms that the masses could comprehend.[111] It had to be sold to the dominant overculture in a form whites could comprehend and respect so that the overculture could be ridded of its racialist fictions which had been holding blacks enthralled. In order to reach the intended goal of challenging these fictions, Locke believed there would have to be a certain amount of culture conformity on the part of blacks, the same degree of conformity requisite for any minority people wishing to survive amidst a different cultural majority.[112] Locke said:

> And now just a final word about what really is the goal of race progress and race adjustment. The thing which it must promote . . . is culture-citizenship. Now, culture-citizenship is something which is to be acquired through social assimilation, not necessarily physical assimilation. . . . Culture-citizenship must come in terms of group contribution to what becomes a joint civilization. That is where the consummation of the doctrine that I have just mentioned will be found, because it will enable us, and others who have the burden of social proof placed upon them, to qualify in terms not merely of imitation but of contribution.[113]

Locke's comment was made in 1917, five years after James Weldon Johnson's protagonist had articulated the notion in *The Autobiography*; and the point was repeated five years later, when Locke wrote:

Ultimately a people is judged by its capacity to contribute to culture. It is to be hoped that as we progressively acquire in this energetic democracy the common means of modern civilization, we shall justify ourselves more and more, individually and collectively, by the use of them to produce culture-goods and representative types of culture. And this, so peculiarly desirable under the present handicap of social disparagement and disesteem, must be for more than personal reasons the ambition and the achievement of our educated classes. If, as we all know, we must look to education largely to win our way, we must look largely to culture to win our just reward and recognition.[114]

Although Johnson had suggested the same in *The Autobiography*, he stated the point more directly in the commencement address he gave at Hampton Institute in 1923. In his address titled "The Larger Success," Johnson implored the black graduates of Hampton to use their education to help train the masses of their people: "This service has a definite end in view. It is the securing for yourselves and those for whom and among whom you will specifically work the status of full and unlimited American citizenship."[115] Part of what was preventing this citizenship of blacks in America, explained Johnson, was the fact that blacks were not fully employing the powers they already possessed:

> Perhaps our greatest God-given endowment is our emotionalism. . . . But this greatest power in our possession is being recklessly dissipated in loud laughter, boisterous dancing, and a general good time. . . . When we have learned to channel down our emotional power, to run it through a cylinder, it will be transformed into great music, poetry, literature, and drama. It will become an irresistible force in battering down many of the obstacles that now confront us.
>
> I spoke of our wonderful music as being the touchstone, the magic thing, by which the Negro can bridge all chasms. . . . It is through the arts that we may find the easiest approach to the solution of some of the most vital phases of our problem. It is the path of least friction. It is the plane on which all men are willing to meet and stand with us.[116]

Johnson concluded, "The status of the Negro in the United States is more a question of mental attitude toward the race than it is a question of actual conditions. . . . There is nothing that will do more to change this mental attitude and raise the status of the Negro than a demonstration by him of intellectual and esthetic parity through the production of literature and art."[117]

Johnson again explained this point in *Negro Americans, What Now?* when he said that the ignorance whites have about blacks, derived from the stereotypes created and perpetuated by dramatic and literary minstrelsy, constituted one of the greatest obstacles preventing blacks from acquiring equal citizenship.[118] "Now, just as these stereotypes were molded and circulated and perpetuated by literary and artistic processes, they must be broken up and replaced through the same means," wrote Johnson. "No other means can be as fully effective. Some of this work has already been done, but the greater portion remains to be done—and by Negro writers and artists."[119] In response to Jean Toomer, who said he wanted to "withdraw from all things which emphasize or tend to emphasize racial or cultural divisions" and to align himself with "things which stress the experiences, forms, and spirit we have in common,"[120] Johnson said: "In most of my writings I have stressed the truth that the work done by the colored creative artist is a part of our common, national culture, and that within the past decade it has begun to be so recognized."[121]

Neither Johnson nor Locke favored total assimilation as a solution to the race problem, but they did advocate blacks using the two-tiered "mastery" as a strategy for racial vindication. Once again, the protagonist in Johnson's novel articulated this strategy. The colored man felt certain that the root of the race problem lay in the attitudes of whites, attitudes that could be changed not by strictly imitating white culture but by depicting the life, ambitions, struggles, and passions of the Negro race within the "higher" classical musical forms. Huggins's failure to grasp this, along with his failure to see through the mask that Baker calls the "mastery of form," is what led the historian to criticize the New Negro for proclaiming a new race consciousness on the one hand while on the other hand imitating whites in dress and mannerisms and being enslaved to white forms and values.[122]

Contrary to Huggins's interpretation of the Renaissance artists, there were subtle clues that they were, like Booker T. Washington during his Atlanta Exposition address, crafting a voice out of tight places. First of all, every "inner" expression of African rhythm in Renaissance art, despite the "outer" appearance of white forms and values, constituted an unbalancing or de-symmetricizing of those forms and values and therefore a rejection of enslavement to them. If we listen closely enough, we can also hear the Renaissance artists articulating that unbalancing, such as when Dett insisted that arranging Negro folk song in European forms did not improve the folk song:

> In this connection it should be stated that controversies aris-ing from the discussion as to whether or not one ought to try "to improve" the folk song, (be it a Negro folk song or whatever its source,) are absurd. One might as well talk of "improving" a full grown tree or a rose blossom. We try to preserve the tree or the rose because of its beauty and worth. Either one, through the skill of man, may be made presently to disintegrate later to reappear in other creations of beauty and utility. Even so the folk song is rich in elements which may be the inspiration of new creations resem-bling the original as a desk resembles a tree—only in the nature of its material.[123]

Locke similarly articulated his rejection of enslavement to white forms and values by arguing that the European element in Negro art was not to take precedence over the African element. Huggins may recall that Locke said the challenge to the young Negro was not so much to acquire the "outer mastery of form and technique" as to achieve an "inner mastery of mood and spirit."[124] There needed to be, as Still also articulated it, a "balance" between these inner and outer elements. Composers needed to make an effort to balance the "intellectual approach" to music (the outer Europeanism) with the "emotional," which could be accomplished by blacks absorbing the folk materials of their culture into their "inner be-ing."[125] Thus, concluded Still, Negro music could actually be of value to larger musical works when fashioned into "organized form" by a composer who has the "underlying feeling" and develops it "through his intellect."[126]

That Locke, like Still, placed significant value on Renaissance artists ab-sorbing the black folk materials into their inner beings also goes to suggest that the Renaissance artists were not enslaved to white forms and values. In the article in which he said the problem of the young Negro was not so much the acquiring of the "outer mastery of form and technique" but the achieving of an "inner mastery of mood and spirit," Locke went on to say that though these artists are thoroughly modern and their Negro ideas "now wear the uniform of the age," their hearts yet "beat a little differently."[127] The hearts of both Dett and Still "beat a little differently" because the spiri-tuals had made an impression upon them as children. Just as the spirituals had made a lasting impression on James Weldon Johnson's fictional pro-tagonist who never forgot the "quaint songs" his mother used to sing, Dett and Still never forgot their maternal grandmothers singing the spirituals either. When Dett, as a student at Oberlin Conservatory of Music, heard a performance of the slow movement of Antonín Dvořák's "American Quartet," which contains quaint melodies from the spirituals, his heart beat differently. Suddenly it seemed that he was hearing the sweet voice of his long-departed grandmother calling across the years, and in a rush of emotion that stirred his spirit to its very heart, the meaning of these songs that had given her soul such peace was revealed to him.[128] Still must have had a similar heartfelt experience, for his maternal grandmother also used to sing spirituals all day long. Still also went with his mother to visit a rural church where he heard the congregation sing spirituals and saw them "shout" (dance). At the time the religious histrionics humored him, he recalled, but he later drew from the experience of having heard this authentic black music at its source.[129]

It was probably these experiences which planted a seed that would later lead Dett and Still back to the South like Johnson's protagonist, back to the South to collect black folk songs at their source. Concert soprano Dorothy Maynor once said of Dett, her teacher and mentor, that although he was born in Canada and raised over the border in New York, he still had a yearning to learn about Negro life in the South.[130] Maynor herself, and others such as Hayes, also spent time collecting black folk songs in the South. Hayes spent a substantial period of time studying African music too, a year and a half as of the time Locke met up with him in early 1936. Locke found that Hayes had acquired a surprising degree of technical knowledge about African music and that he had hopes of going to Africa for further study.[131]

So, if we view the Old Negro as the retention of an inner-Negro "mood and spirit"—not as the Old Negro proper but as the unadulterated essence of the Old Negro, which was being encased within an outer Europeanism (not to improve it but to preserve it)—then we can reject the idea that the Old Negro was carried within the bosom of the New as a kind of self-doubt and self-hate.[132] We can, moreover, interpret the Negro Renaissance as being successful in delivering what it claimed for itself—a new strategy and a re-imaged Negro. The consequence of this strategic re-imaging of blacks was what Locke described as white society's forced reckoning with a fundamentally changed Negro,[133] by which he evidently meant not only a Negro fundamentally different from the fictitious personage whites had fabricated and cultivated in their minstrel music and literature, but a Negro who had also mastered a requisite balance between an inner African "mood and spirit" and an outer European "form and technique." Locke concluded that,

"Subtly the conditions that are molding a New Negro are molding a new American attitude."[134]

Another success resulting from the two-tiered strategy of "mastery" was the molding of a new attitude among blacks themselves with regard to their folk heritage. Perhaps the self-doubt and self-hate was not, after all, found in the Renaissance artists and intellectuals (who at least believed their folk culture was worthy of "serious" development), but was in those blacks and ex-colored people who believed black folk culture was not so worthy. In this regard, Dett blamed the black minstrels for destroying not only their own initiative to do serious composition based on black folk themes, but also for destroying the initiative of other blacks by teaching them that their culture was only worthy of being laughed at.[135] The black minstrels and other popular musicians were also known for their reckless lifestyles, which left blacks (middle-class blacks in particular) with the impression that their musical culture was worthy of nothing but contempt. Still's own mother was among those who viewed black musicians as immoral vagabonds, such that she constantly made light of her son's desire to become a composer rather than a doctor. "Today I can see that she did what she did for my benefit," said Still, "yet even today it is hard for me to realize that the structure of Negro society at that time was such that even a woman of her vision could not understand that the kind of composer I meant to be was far different from her concept, nor would she or others of that period have envisioned an Afro-American attaining a position of prominence in the symphonic or operatic fields!"[136] So, the re-imaging of the Negro by Renaissance musicians not only resulted in a challenge to the racialist attitudes of whites but to the self-doubt and self-hate of those blacks and ex-colored people who had rejected their cultural heritage altogether.

VI

If Locke's efforts to re-image the Negro and mold a new American attitude via the two-tiered strategy of "mastery" really involved an element of self-doubt and self-hate, then the Renaissance intellectuals could have attempted to undermine the idea of race altogether by emphasizing the universality of humanity. But their efforts to bring about the "vindication of the Negro" did not include abandoning the concept of race. For instance, Locke clearly understood that much of the West's thinking about race had been pernicious and that there were those who therefore wanted to dispense with the notion; but, too, some of the most magnificent advancements made in arts and letters had taken their inspiration from the idioms of black heritage, and these advancements were contributing to the redemption of the false social and economic meanings of "race."[137] Although writing to this effect in 1915, Locke seemed to be speaking of what a decade later would be well known as the Negro Renaissance:

> Now there are too many . . . people in the world . . . who feel that race is so odious a term that it must be eradicated from our thinking and from our vocabulary. I believe that a word and an idea covering so indispensable, useful, and necessary a grouping in human society will never vanish, never be eradicated, and that the only possible way in which a change will come about will be through a substitution of better meanings for the meanings which are now so current under the term. Really when we come to face the issue, we see that some of the most constructive thinking that has been going on within the last two decades has been in terms of units and ideas which really are racial in their very conception. Some of the most magnificent movements which have been recently inaugurated in art and in letters have taken their inspiration from the expression of racial idiom and race life. And certainly in those fields there has been a certain amount of redemption of the false social and economic meanings that have made the term rather a byword of reproach. . . .
>
> Race as a unit of social thought is of permanent significance and of growing importance. It is not to be superseded except by some revised version of itself. . . . To redeem, to rescue, or to revise that thought and practice should be the aim of race theorists and those who want to educate people into better channels of group living.[138]

Thus, contrary to the accusations of self-hate in the New Negro, Locke was questioning why blacks would even want to dispense with the notion of race. First of all, he believed it was the culture, history, and experience of blacks that alone had the potential to cause whites to celebrate rather than hate them. We get a sense that this was viewed as a possibility during Locke's day in an article on Robeson published in a white newspaper during the winter of 1929–30. The writer said the triumphs of someone like Robeson brought honor not merely to himself but to his race. "It is well to familiarize ourselves with the incidents of a life like his in order to learn in fuller measure what the members of his race are capable of contributing," he wrote to his white audience. "Like Roland Hayes, like Countee Cullen and James Weldon Johnson, the poets, Paul Robeson . . . shows what gifts lie in a down-trodden race, and inspires whites, bigoted or indifferent, or supercilious, with greater respect and increased helpfulness for his race."[139] Secondly, with regard to his coveting the notion of race, Locke seemed to believe that once blacks were liberated from the predominating fictions about the Old Negro, then black culture would be able to emerge as one of the greatest cultures of Western civilization. What sweet vindication that would be, he seemed to be thinking.

Locke's wish not to sacrifice the magnificence of black cultural particularity for the hope of a nonracial universality, in part because of the success being met by Renaissance artists in building upon their unique heritage and vindicating their race, was an idea shared by other Renaissance Negroes as well. James Weldon Johnson, for instance, saw his people as "a gifted race, a race endowed with imagination, a sense of rhythm, and a sense of beauty; a race which should and will give to America and thereby to the world some of its greatest poets."[140] Even with regard to popular music, Johnson said: "What is now called American popular music is based entirely upon the rhythmic secular music of the Negro."[141] The desire not to sacrifice the magnificence of black cultural particularity for the hope of a nonracial universality was also the idea behind Johnson's comment in the preface of *The Book of American Negro Spirituals* (1925). Johnson said it "would have been" a most notable achievement if white settlers in America, faced with the struggle of conquering untamed nature and stirred with the hope of building a free nation, had created a body of folk song comparable to the Negro spirituals—it "would have been," he said—but such did not occur.[142] This wish not to sacrifice the magnificence of black cultural particularity for a nonracial universality was also the sentiment behind some of Johnson's passages in *The Autobiography of an Ex-Colored Man*. At the close of the book, for instance, Johnson's protagonist said that beside the gallant band of colored men who were making history and a race, he, "an ordinary successful white man," felt small and selfish.

The emergence of black culture as one of the greatest cultures of Western civilization would come not simply with black people's increased transgression of the societal color line, but only with their increased transgression of the essentialist color line—the presumed biological and ontological cleavage between whites and blacks. Supposedly evidenced by the alleged fact that whites were rational and intellectual and their music classical and that blacks were emotional and carnal and their music folk and popular, this essentialist color line would be undermined by Renaissance artists "up-lifting" their folk and popular musics to the level of the rational, the intel-lectual, and the classical. By masterfully encasing African "mood and spirit" within European "form and technique," the Renaissance Negroes of music (like the Renaissance Negroes of the other arts and letters) helped undermine the fictions and stereotypes that undergirded the essentialist color line.

By following this two-tiered strategy of "mastery," Hayes helped blacks begin transgressing the social color line. In a 1929 newspaper article titled "Collapsible Color Line," a journalist said that at Hayes's concerts the color line dissolves and whites and blacks sit elbow to elbow, and that there would be more of this before there would be less. "What is the meaning of it? Just what has happened here?" the journalist asked. "Something quite simple and very profound. . . . This people that we have wronged has found a way to conquer us; not by violence but by melody. In the face of a cultural tri-umph in this magnitude by the negro the pretense of white superiority will become more difficult to maintain."[143] But Hayes did not simply help blacks transgress the social color line by occasionally facilitating the integration of audiences. He helped them transgress the essentialist color line, the color line that delineated between blacks and whites in terms of alleged biological and ontological differences. Hayes recalled an instance of this transgression on an occasion when he performed at Carnegie Hall in New York:

> I received the most extraordinary letter. "Dear Mr. Hayes," my not very coherent correspondent began, "I want to apologize for hav-ing behaved like a cat."
>
> I called up a friend at the box office and asked him if he knew anything about the writer of that letter. He told me that a South-ern woman had come to him a day or two before the concert to protest against my appearance in Carnegie Hall. She seemed to be determined to hear me, however—my friend said he did not quite understand why—and she was furious because she could not buy a ticket at the last moment. She was informed that a dollar and a half would buy her the privilege of standing up at the back of the hall. That was the only alternative to missing the concert.
>
> "I wouldn't pay a dollar and a half to *sit down* and hear a nigger," the lady said, but pay she evidently did, because after the recital she looked up my friend and told him that she had changed her mind about me.
>
> "I stood behind the railing," she said, "and waited for the mon-ster to come in. When he came out on the platform, I turned my

back. I couldn't bear to look at him. It made me mad to see him standing there"—she must have taken a peek at me—"with his head bowed and his eyes closed and his hands folded." It appears that she had expected me to begin with some cacophonous blast, and the soft, lovely entry of Handel's "A Tender Creature" disarmed her, broke her down. Her conscience would not let her rest until she had made her *mea culpa* to my friend and me.[144]

In an award-winning essay published in *Opportunity* in 1925, Sterling Brown, the Howard University poet and friend of Locke, rendered an impressionistic piece on Hayes which captured the racial attitudes of whites attending a Hayes concert and the kind of transformation that transpired. The whites who were attending the fictional concert were of two types—those who were slightly contemptuous of blacks but felt that Hayes was an exception in that he had succeeded in the ways of whites, and those with self-conscious hostility who were also partly envious of Hayes.[145] Of the transformation of the racial attitudes of whites, Brown wrote:

Roland Hayes sings. And as he sings, things drop away, the uglier apparel of manhood slinks off, and the inescapable oneness of all becomes perceptible. Roland Hayes sings, and no centuries of fostered belief can change the brotherhood of white and black. Roland Hayes sings, and boundaries are but figments of imagination, and prejudice but insane mutterings. And what is real is a great fellowship of all in pain, a fellowship in hope. Roland Hayes sings, and for that singing moment, however brief, the world forgets its tyranny and its submissiveness.[146]

This is the phenomenal accomplishment of the Negro Renaissance. It is not simply that blacks and whites were able to sit elbow to elbow when listening to Hayes sing or to the performance of a Still symphony or a Dett oratorio. It is that the artistic strategy of two-tiered "mastery" forced the de-essentializing of the color line and that black culture could emerge to be one of the greatest cultures in the West. The Negro Renaissance was no failure, in other words, and black music was an important part of its success.

Chapter 2

Wild Dreams of Bringing Glory and Honor to the Negro Race

But the effect upon me of "Shiny's" speech was double; I not only shared the enthusiasm of his audience, but he imparted to me some of his own enthusiasm. I felt leap within me pride that I was coloured; and I began to form wild dreams of bringing glory and honour to the Negro race. For days I could talk of nothing else with my mother except my ambitions to be a great man, a great coloured man, to reflect credit on the race and gain fame for myself. It was not until years after that I formulated a definite and feasible plan for realizing my dreams.

—The Autobiography of an Ex-Colored Man

I

R. Nathaniel Dett had a keen sense that there existed in America not only a social and legal color line but an essentialist one. He intimated that the firm hold of this essentialist color line was helped by the proliferation of the theatrical and literary minstrelsy of the day, from which he believed whites received their only perceptions of blacks, perceptions of them as people of heightened emotion and feeble intelligence.[1] By song and story— popular theater, in particular—minstrelsy held the black preacher and his congregation up to ridicule in comic ditties, darkey ballads, and coon songs. Said Dett, "It is doubtful if anywhere in the world a race of people ever were so publicly derided in story, drama, and song as the Negro in America."[2] One reason this racial derision persisted, figured Dett, was that the "Negro racial mind" remained inaccessible to whites, due to the fact that between the races little substantive social intermingling transpired. Concluded Dett, "in spite of the Villards on the one hand and the Van Vechtens on the other the soul of the Negro remains an unsolved interrogation to a nation which boasts of its celerity of perception and infallibility of achievement."[3]

The racial dilemma of Dett's day was that the nineteenth-century racialism (a racist racialism) of Joseph Arthur de Gobineau and his European collaborators had followed European whites to America and that Gobineau's racialism played a part in reinforcing the distinctions whites (even liberal whites like Oswald Villard and Carl Van Vechten) made between the "real" Negro and the Westernized Negro. Dett partly blamed the perpetuation of this racialism on those whites who falsely believed they knew the true Negro. Having been to a Negro show, read a Negro novel (probably by a white author), seen a movie in which there were Negroes appearing (usually in serio-comic parts), or had a Negro cook, such whites, said Dett, believe they are at an advantage when it comes to understanding Negroes when they are really at a disadvantage because they cannot approach the Negro or his music with an open mind. Continued Dett, "being blinded or misled by preconceived ideas, they go far astray, not realizing that though they may be enthusiastically in motion, they are not necessarily arriving anywhere."[4]

That it was the "real" Negro around whom whites fashioned their theories of Negroness, and that whites counted on the Renaissance Negroes to remain faithful to their alleged inherent primitivity, was demonstrated to Dett on the evening of April 22, 1915, at Hampton Institute's forty-seventh anniversary celebration. The Hampton Choral Union, a community chorus of fifty voices which Dett directed, was performing arranged spirituals, and Dett felt certain that it was gratifying to the black community to see a black chorus directed by one of their own who was developing the musical resources of the race. Said Dett, "in the new style of presentation of their songs they felt, as was expressed by one of them in the words of a race song, that they were 'steppin' on higher groun'."[5] But the whites who attended the anniversary concert were disappointed, particularly the visitors who believed Hampton Institute had always emphasized the preservation and presentation of black music in its pure "primitive" state.[6] Evidently the visitors wanted the spirituals to be accompanied by swaying, hand-clapping, and foot-patting, said Dett, because it is their tradition to be amused by such behavior and because they have formed the bad habit of laughing at other people who are culturally different from themselves.[7]

The bad habit of whites always expecting blacks to be "real" and always wanting to laugh at them and their music, plus the lack of anything to laugh at on the occasion of the Choral Union's performance for Hampton's forty-seventh anniversary, was to Dett the reason the whites attending the concert were so disturbed—so disturbed, in fact, that an explanation of the program was necessary.[8] The task of explaining why the choir had programmed arranged spirituals was taken up by the chairman of the anniversary music committee, Robert Russa Moton (who would be selected to succeed Booker T. Washington as president of Tuskegee Institute at the end of that year). To make his point, Moton cited a comment by composer Will Marion Cook (Alain Locke's long-time father figure): "To sing works of development to which the composer gave thought and culture requires thought and culture. If you, admitting an inferior condition, fail to give to the child opportunity for breadth, which only comes from comprehensive development, just so far you have hindered his understanding, appreciation, and rendition of all masterpieces."[9] In defense of Dett's sophisticated arrangements and compositions based on the spirituals, some of which the Choral Union sang that memorable evening, Moton concluded that Negroes must be encouraged to show the potential their folk songs have for use as themes in anthems, oratorios, and operas.[10]

The distinction made between the "real" and Westernized Negro by the whites who attended Hampton's 1915 anniversary concert was a regular part of the music criticism Dett and the other Renaissance Negroes had to endure for at least another four decades. When the Hampton Institute choir performed under Dett's direction at Carnegie Hall in April 1928, for instance, Olin Downes, music critic for *The New York Times,* insisted that musical interpretation "more racial in quality" had been eclipsed by white musical influences.[11] Downes then commenced his racial theorizing, saying: "The negro's musical impulses are not those of the white. He is less restrained, and often more individual as well as spontaneous in his expression." Then Downes proceeded to theorize about the "real" spirituals: "Some negro spirituals are wildly dramatic. Often they have rhythms and phrase lengths which cut entirely free from white tradition. Many of them are rollicking rather than pathetic or tragic in expression." Since the spirituals that the Hampton choir rendered in Carnegie Hall were not of Downes's "real" kind, he then said of the performance: "Need last night's program have contained nothing but solemnly religious music? Could not certain of the harmonizations have been less formal, more exotic? For us there was too much evidence of the musical influence of the whites and not enough of the originality of the race which has given America the spirituals and the dance rhythms that have gone over the whole world." Finally, Downes, even after firming up racial difference, only hesitantly concluded that the choir performed excellently: "With these reservations, it must be said that the choir made an excellent showing."[12]

Nearly ten years later, in May 1937, Downes made a similar assessment of Dett's oratorio, *The Ordering of Moses,* which tells the biblical story of the passage of the Hebrews through the Red Sea using the spiritual "Go Down, Moses" as the musical thematic material. In his review of this première performance, Downes could not escape being fascinated by the exceptional accomplishments of Dett's career, by the success of the performance, and by the audience's warm reception of the composition. Downes even seemed to intuit a comprehension of the intent of Dett's "development" of the spiritual when he commented about his essay titled "The Emancipation of Negro Music" winning the Bowdoin Literary Prize at Harvard University in 1920 (actually "The Emancipation of Negro Music" was the first of four essays collectively titled "Negro Music"). Wrote Downes, "This essay is not known to the writer, but possibly the style of 'The Ordering of Moses' affords a clue to its pronouncements."[13] Yet, despite Dett's masterful accomplishments and Downes's intuited understanding that the oratorio exemplified the "emancipation of Negro music," Downes still felt the oratorio could have been musically more Negroid:

> Mr. Dett had reason to congratulate himself upon the effect of his music. It was carefully performed, though it must be said that . . . a wilder and more emotional treatment could have been given certain of the solos and recitatives done in the pale white fashion. And possibly for this reason, and despite the popular reaction, it seems to the present chronicler that while Mr. Dett has done well, he has not gone nearly far enough in striking the racial note in his music. . . .
>
> There is a deeper, greater and more powerful thing, in this same direction, for the Negro artist to do. There is still the question of the way which he is to find to do it, which cannot be the way of either imitation or emulation of another race's culture. "The Ordering of Moses," in so far as it was the expression of a Negro musician, triumphed. The weaknesses are those of a musician educated too well in a conventionalized mold.[14]

Similarly, Charlotte Mason (who was a private rather than public critic of Negro Renaissance art) felt Dett was too influenced by white culture and was therefore "letting the white man run him."[15] She had equally nega-tive feelings toward Roland Hayes because the same white influences were evident in his refined singing style. After having heard Hayes perform on one occasion, Mason said she was saddened because "he sang awfully well, like a white man."[16] That is to say, she continued, he sang "very badly" be-cause he had "no bottom in him."[17] After Mason heard Hayes sing again, she felt all the more certain about her first impression, which seemed to unleash the racism inherent in her racialism. She raved, "The whole audi-torium was full of little pickaninnies running up and down waving red flags with 'Dead' 'Dead' 'Dead' written on them! Of course, nearly all his audi-ence were fossilized beings and couldn't hear that he wasn't singing."[18]

Dett's benefactor, George Foster Peabody, was more reasonable and lib-eral than Mason, but his views were still deeply rooted in the Western ra-cialist tradition (racialism that was racist). Peabody was opposed to Negroes abandoning the spirituals in favor of what he believed was a complete imi-tation of the white man, but he also felt that Negroes should not be limited to traditional interpretations of the spiritual in that this would re-empha-size the tendency of educated Negroes to find them too recollective of sla-very. Wrote Peabody, "The unique merit of Dr. Dett is that he, alone, of all Negro musicians, as far as I know, has built so many compositions on the African tone or whatever may be the accurate phrase to determine the unique rhythmic and other qualities of the Spirituals."[19] At least Peabody believed this for a time, until one of Hampton's white administrators seemed to convince him of the contrary.[20]

Dett's own defense of his sophisticated compositional style reveals his strategy—maintaining in the arranged spiritual the peculiar African "mood and spirit" while also mastering the "form and technique" important to the debut of the New Negro. In this regard, Dett said:

> though American white people appear to love these songs, seem-ing never to tire of listening to them, and are very persistent in urging the Negro to "stick to them," yet they apparently have never entertained the idea of the universal use of the songs for religious worship. It is probable that the vast majority of others than those of the race itself would be mildly scandalized by even the suggestion of such a thing. Negroes are perfectly aware of this, and since American standards are after all white people's stan-dards, it is impossible for colored people to escape being affected by this adverse sentiment against their songs when considered from the standpoint of serious utility.

Wild Dreams of Bringing Glory and Honor to the Negro Race

It occurred to the writer that if a form of song were evolved which contained all the acceptable characteristics of Negro folk music and yet would compare favorably in poetic sentiment and musical expression with the best class of church music, it would be a means of solving this peculiar problem, for, being created out of native material, it would save to the Negro and his music all the peculiar and precious idioms, and as work of art would summon to its interpretation the best of his intellectual and emotional efforts. These principles being fundamental, the appeal would be as great to white people as to the colored people, while at that same time such composition would constitute the development of a natural resource.[21]

While Downes, in his reviews of Dett's music, stubbornly held to the prevailing white racialism of the day, a reviewer of a Hampton choir concert at Boston's Symphony Hall in March 1928 succumbed to the power of Dett's concurrent mastery of European "form and technique" and African "mood and spirit." Writing for *The Boston Globe*, the journalist stated that no choir in recent years had sung "with subtler or finer artistry," that this choir could rank alongside the best in the world, and that the choir, like Roland Hayes, had to be judged "with no thought of race distinction."[22] The reviewer similarly lauded Dorothy Maynor, one of the better soloists in the choir, who would go on to match Hayes in the two-tiered "mastery." As though uttering a prophecy, the reviewer said that the cultivation of naturally good voices did not always pay off but that Maynor's voice seemed promising for a philanthropist willing to gamble on paying for her musical education. "There is certainly a chance that she might become a great singer," the reviewer concluded, "something no experienced reviewer would prophesy of most girls with good voices."[23]

II

Dett's career was for Dorothy Maynor a paradigm of the two-tiered "mastery." With regard to the tier that was more difficult for a black man to master—the "form and technique"—Dett uniquely mastered the academic preparation of the trained European musician. Born in Drummondsville, Ontario, in 1882, he received in 1908 his bachelor of music degree in composition and piano from the Conservatory of Music at Oberlin College. Following his degree from Oberlin, he continued in the Western scholastic tradition by holding a number of faculty appointments, all of which were at historically black colleges as director of music: Lane College in Tennessee (1908–11), Lincoln Institute in Missouri (1911–13), Hampton Institute in Virginia (1913–32), and Bennett College in North Carolina (1937–42).

Just as he was beginning his teaching career at Hampton in 1913 as the first black director of music, Dett's choral composition, "Listen to the Lambs," tied with a work by Carl Diton for the first-place prize presented by the Music School Settlement for Colored People in New York. For an average man this would have been evidence enough of the excellence of his training, but Dett continued his academic preparation with intermittent graduate study at the American Conservatory of Music, Northwestern University, Columbia University, University of Pennsylvania, Harvard University, Oberlin College, and the Fontainebleau School in Paris. While at Harvard, Dett won the university's Francis Boote Music Award for his motet, "Don't Be Weary Traveller." He also won the Bowdoin Literary Prize for his four-part essay, "Negro Music," the same prize Alain Locke won in 1907, during his undergraduate years at Harvard, for his essay titled "Tennyson and His Literary Heritage."

Also while Dett was at Harvard, his benefactor, Peabody, planted an idea in him that would be nurtured with his benefaction until it burgeoned into fruition ten years later. After congratulating Dett for winning the Bowdoin Literary Prize, Peabody said with regard to the Negro in America and the colonial situation in Africa: "I hope that you feel that the year has given you larger command of yourself and strong grip on the situation to help your people. This is one of the most critical times in the world's history and the problem of the functioning of your race in our Democracy is one of the most serious of all times. In my opinion if there be a failure now in this Country in this respect, the two hundred and fifty million of your race in Africa will be paying the penalty for centuries perhaps."[24] Fitting in with Peabody's plan, it seems, Dett, by the early 1920s, had caught the attention of such Renaissance Negroes as James Weldon Johnson. When Johnson gave Hampton's commencement address for the class of 1923, he said that Negro folk music would one day be the source from which Negro composers draw in order to voice not only the essence of their race but the soul of the nation, and that Dett, in this regard, had already attracted the attention of the world's musicians.[25] By the late 1920s, Dett had become even more of a nationally recognized musician and scholar, having received honorary doctorates from Howard University in 1924 and Oberlin College in 1926, and having received the gold medal Harmon Foundation Award in 1927 for his creative achievements in music composition. Three years later, the

Hampton choir toured Europe, the fruition of the seed Peabody had planted in Dett's thoughts ten years earlier when he was studying at Harvard.

The career Dett had established via the strategy of the "mastery of form and technique"—the education, teaching career, the awards, and the public and academic accolades—had prepared him to make an impact on what Peabody told him a decade earlier was one of the most critical times in the world's history for the Negro race. Having used money from the Palmer Fund, which he administered, to send Dett to study music with Nadia Boulanger at the Fontainebleau School in Paris during the summer of 1929, Peabody was ready to see Dett's training and exceptional preparation of the Hampton choir debuted in Europe.[26] So Peabody used Palmer funds to send Hampton professor George Ketcham to Europe to look into details of management and cost for such a tour.[27] Ketcham returned with the endorsement of some of the most influential people of England and Belgium and reported to Peabody that if properly managed, the choir could have satisfactory results in terms of turning a profit and influencing European colonial policy.[28]

Charlotte Mason learned about the plans for the Hampton choir's tour of Europe through Locke, who heard it from Dett when the two men met on board a ship headed for Europe, Dett on his way to Paris to study at the Fontainebleau School, and Locke on his way to Europe for a tour at Mason's expense. Locke shared the news about the Hampton choir's tour with Mason in a letter, and Mason wrote back expressing her dismay. "I was disgusted that Dett had to be on the same vessel with you," Mason wrote to her "Dear Boy." "I know how annoying that was to you, and how balking to the whole Negro movement is this thing he is doing! He began well in his work but letting the white man run him, and ending now going to Europe taking a 'Dett Choir' and not a Negro choir is absolutely disastrous to establishing the Negroes [Negro's] real life where I have dreamed it can stand, a bulwark against loss to them."[29]

Actually, the European tour of Dett's choir would not at all be "balking" to the Negro Renaissance movement, but rather would be beneficial. Whether or not it was really annoying for Locke to have Dett as a shipmate, the fact is that the upcoming tour of the "Dett choir" (rather than a so-called "Negro choir") was quite in line with Locke's own notion of the "vindication of the Negro." Indeed, as Dett's choir performed in London, Antwerp, Brussels, The Hague, Rotterdam, Amsterdam, Paris, Hamburg, Berlin, Dresden, Vienna, Salzburg, Zurich, Lausanne, and Geneva, the choir brought about the most effective and timely choral debut of the New

Negro. It was effective because of the overall scholarly ambiance that Dett brought to the tour: He was "Dr. Dett" and his choir, originating from a Negro college, would be singing spirituals arranged by the choir director himself. The tour was timely, indeed more timely than the memorable tour of the Fisk Jubilee Singers a half-century earlier, because 1930 was a high point in the Negro Renaissance, a Renaissance which had gained international recognition.

Although Peabody had planned and was sponsoring this tour that he believed would be a most effective and timely musical debut of the New Negro in Europe, he nonetheless shared something in common with Mason, who disparaged the idea. Like Mason, Peabody's ultimate goal as a benefactor of the Renaissance Negro was not to attain "vindication" for the Negro. Mason's goal was, as I explained in chapter 1, to save the white race from losing its soul as well as its warfaring self-control (which it lost when it seemed nearly to have destroyed itself in World War I). Peabody's goal of revealing the "native African talent" in the spirituals and the consummation of this talent in Dett's composition based on African themes[30] was for Dett to demonstrate to Europe what Negroes were capable of accomplishing "under true leadership"—ultimately white leadership (since whites ran Hampton Institute and had trained and provided opportunities for Dett).[31] As Peabody put it to Hampton's principal, George Phenix, he was interested in "the application of democratic principles to the native people in the Colonies of Great Britain," which he thought could be brought about by the British educating the Africans of their colonies much like white-administered Hampton Institute was educating Negroes in America (as the choir tour intended to prove).[32] The result would be "the evolution of the African into modern civilization," a civilization of their own which would be more closely aligned with their alleged natural qualities.[33] So, Peabody's intent for the tour of the Hampton choir was to nurture in the Europeans, particularly those with colonial "possessions" in Africa, a better understanding and appreciation of blacks, and to demonstrate that the natural artistic skills of blacks could be developed with European benefaction through the kind of opportunity whites in America were affording them.[34]

On the other hand, Dett's goal for the tour was in kinship with the message James Weldon Johnson brought to Hampton Institute in 1923—the "vindication of the Negro"—and so he would have to find a voice in this tight situation of disagreement with the tour's benefactor. The kind of voice Dett would find was demonstrated in Brussels when the choir was given a tour of the Museum of the Belgian Congo and a look at its world-famous collection of African art.[35] One carved depiction of an African trying to protect his wife from a white slave catcher moved Dett to have his choir sing the spiritual "No More Auction Block for Me" before the museum officials and government heads connected with the colonies.[36] What subtle but sweet vindication that must have been.

It was, of course, Peabody's intent for the tour that became the official position of Hampton Institute. This official position was enunciated in the resolution passed by Hampton's Administrative Board on October 23, 1929, and then sent to the Board of Trustees for approval. The resolution read:

> The Administrative Board of Hampton Institute is fully conscious of the steady and untiring interest of members of the Board of Trustees in considering and promoting all projects which are for the advancement of colored races.
>
> Heretofore the interests of Hampton have been chiefly devoted to the Negro and Indian people of this country. Now an opportunity is presented to promote the interests of the Negros of Africa through influential white people of Europe who are interested in Colonial and Native affairs.
>
> Mr. George Foster Peabody has for a period of some years shown a particular interest in the development of music at Hampton Institute. He has encouraged the Music School. He has furthered the work of the Choir. It has been largely due to his interest that the Choir has been presented before large and important audiences.[37]

After the Board of Trustees approved the Administrative Board's resolution, they made it clear to the Italian businessman selected to manage the tour, Albert Morini, that the intent of the tour had to remain foremost in the planning and execution of it, and that he was to arrange at least fifteen concerts to be held in at least ten different cities and three different countries. "In order to carry out the educational purpose behind the trip," read the instructions to Morini, "it is expected that you will arrange concerts primarily in those countries which have political and educational interests in Africa, with a special effort to reach the interest of Great Britain."[38] A few days later, in the second week of the 1930 new year, Dett announced to his choir during its rehearsal time that a select group of choristers would be touring Europe in the spring, an announcement that was received with great enthusiasm.[39] There was even growing enthusiasm for the tour among the Hampton administrators, who felt privileged to be playing a part in the implementation of this history-making project.[40]

It was because of the official goals of the tour that John D. Rockefeller, Jr., joined the Palmer Fund in underwriting it.[41] But from the perspective of the Renaissance artists and intellectuals, whose goal was to bring about the "vindication of the Negro," these lofty notions of teaching the Europeans how to better manage the "African possessions" were starting the tour off on a problematic premise—the acceptance of European colonialism. Additionally, George Ketcham and assistant treasurer Robert Ogden Purves had ideas more closely aligned with Charlotte Mason's in terms of their views on how the spirituals should be performed during the tour. They believed the spirituals should be sung in the "original" way, unarranged, an opinion they shared with (and which may have influenced) Peabody.[42]

Dett did not outwardly contest the mounting opposition to his intention for the tour—his intention to vindicate the Negro by showcasing his sophisticated arrangements of the spirituals (his two-tiered "mastery"). He just unofficially and quietly pursued his own ideals, which were influenced by the philosophy and practice of the Negro Renaissance, ideals he heard James Weldon Johnson articulating in 1923 when Johnson gave Hampton Institute's commencement address. Although he once slipped and became hot-tempered with Phenix, Hampton's principal, as they discussed the tour,[43] he otherwise gave the impression that he would comply with the instructions given the choir and its chaperones in Phenix's "farewell talk," even though Ketcham (rather than himself) was given the ultimate authority during the tour. Having been informed by Phenix that everyone left the farewell talk in good spirits,[44] Ketcham, who was waiting to meet the choir in England, felt confident that Dett would cooperate with regard to the concert programming and that the tour would run smoothly.[45]

Contrariwise, Dett only feigned compliance with Phenix and Ketcham and with Peabody's colonialist intentions for the tour, much like Locke and Hurston only feigned compliance with Charlotte Mason's ideas about the purpose and necessity of complete primitivism in Negro Renaissance art. Unlike the whites, Dett was interested in the "vindication of the Negro." The conflicting intentions would make for some interesting dynamics during the tour—indeed, a classic master-slave dialectic.

III

We need only examine Dett's publications on the spirituals and his program notes for Hampton choir concerts to see that his views of the spirituals were often different from the views held by the white patrons and critics of the Negro Renaissance. Dett especially expressed concern about the appropriate development of the spirituals, development in the mode of what Locke called the "mastery of form and technique." Aware that the most appropriate rendition of any music results from a performer's understanding of the composer's intentions, and cognizant that the intentions of the creators of the spirituals were special because they were a people rather than individual composers,[46] Dett suggested that the key to the modern interpretation of the spirituals lay in the sincerity of the rendition, and not simply, we can deduce, in the degree of primitivity. "Folk songs are the records of the very heart throbs of man, which to read aright requires an almost divine insight," he wrote. "Such insight is dependent above all else on one quality absolutely essential to the true interpreter—Sincerity."[47] The antithesis of the "sincerity" requisite for the true interpreter of the spirituals was manifested by those who incorporated them into the Broadway musical revues, a setting Dett felt denigrated the spirituals.[48]

Though the spirituals needed no mannerisms or stage tricks to help them on their way,[49] Dett felt that his own compositions, despite his mastery of form and technique, were models of sincerity, for they were sincere in mood and spirit. He even felt this about his two orchestral works most exemplary of the "mastery of form and technique"—the motet *Chariot Jubilee* and the oratorio *The Ordering of Moses. Chariot Jubilee,* whose mood and spirit were derived from it being thematically based on the spiritual "Swing Low, Sweet Chariot," was first performed April 22, 1920, at Harvard University by the St. Cecilia Society of Boston. This was at the time Dett was a special student at Harvard during the 1919–20 academic year. The motet was performed again in May of the following year at Syracuse University's Annual Music Festival of Central New York. *The Ordering of Moses*, whose mood and spirit were derived from it being thematically based on the spiritual "Go Down, Moses," was Dett's 1932 master's thesis in music composition at the Eastman School of Music. One of the choristers who performed the piece when it premièred five years later, at the Cincinnati Music Festival in May 1937, indicated that it was the unanimous opinion of the choristers that the oratorio was the best piece of music they sang at the festival.[50]

To be sure, Dett's treatments of the spirituals were sincere, even though he encased the African "mood and spirit" within the "form and technique" of the European classicists. His reason for this two-tiered "mastery" was to preserve the music blacks previously disregarded due to the shame they felt toward the period of slavery out of which the music evolved.[51] It is in this regard that Dett drew a line of demarcation between Negro composers who imitated European music through and through and those (such as himself) who mastered the European "form and technique" while savoring the African "mood and spirit."[52] "Inasmuch as folk songs, regardless of locality, are made by people lacking scientific or academic culture," he wrote, "a chief characteristic of all such music is the preservation of certain oddities or even crudities of rhythm, melody, harmony, and words, the presence of which gives individuality to the music, and consequently is the means by which folk music is distinguishable from the more polished utterance of the art song."[53] In addition to the call-and-response pattern typical of the spirituals, Dett identified the frequent use of the pentatonic scale and above all the rhythm as the prominent elements that reveal the African roots of the spirituals. "Reincarnated and re-christened with each generation, as syncopation, ragtime, jazz, and swing," Dett said of rhythm, "the possibilities for development of this element seem endless."[54] Indeed, Dett developed this natural resource by adhering to the endless possibilities available to the composer using folk song as thematic material, possibilities that ranged from the supporting of the original folk tune by an accompaniment of simple chords to the creation of original compositions akin to the spirituals only in mood, spirit, and style.[55] It is in a median style—folk melodies set in elaborate European art forms—that Dett distinguished himself.

That the "inner" Africanism in Dett's arrangements of the spirituals was "sincerely" maintained even when encased in an "outer" Europeanism is duly evident in the acclaim Dett's choral performances received from mixed audiences in America and Europe. One such favorable review, a review of the choir's performance in Boston's Symphony Hall in 1929, appeared in *The Boston Evening Transcript*. The journalist wrote: "These listeners were not disappointed. . . . They enjoyed . . . the racial ardor that is often the most moving element in a concert by negro singers. Yet they might have observed an artistic and technical approach similar to that of other choirs—say the St. Olaf Lutheran Choir, for example. . . . The elements that differentiated this occasion from others of similar intent were the racial overtones and undertones observable in vocal timbres, rhythmic pulses and spiritual concentrations."[56] The ability to master "form and technique" (to an extent that permits comparison with the St. Olaf choir) while savoring the "racial ardor" of the spirituals was helped by the choir also evidencing its mastery of the European classics. This is suggested in a review of the choir's performance in the chamber music auditorium of the Library of Congress in 1927. Writing for the *Christian Advocate,* the journalist said:

When a Negro choir sings a French folk song so that the applause is spontaneous, dispelling the prevalent impression that the spirit of such a piece cannot be given full value by an American choir; when a cultured audience coming primarily to hear Negro singers in a program of Negro folk music is carried beyond the race aspects of its performance into the realm of a universal art knowing no color line, a lasting impression in musical annals has been made.[57]

Dett's "outer mastery of form and technique" and "inner mastery of mood and spirit" were bringing about the desired "vindication of the Negro" then, so Dett had good reason to ignore the white patrons and critics of the Negro Renaissance who, in their theorizing about the difference between the Westernized and "real" black person, questioned the sincerity or authenticity of his arrangements.

IV

The same month Dett's choir set off for their European tour, April 1930, an article titled "Your Negroid and Indian Behavior," by the Swiss psychologist C. G. Jung, was released in the United States. It was an article that must have revealed to any of the Renaissance Negroes who read it the importance and timeliness of the choir demonstrating its "mastery of form and technique," for Jung's theories not only added to the perpetuation of nineteenth-century racialism in twentieth-century America but revealed the extent to which that dated racialism was still alive in Europe. In the article, Jung said his impression of whites in America was that there was a "subtle difference" in their language, gestures, mentality, and movements which distinguished them from white Europeans.[58] He determined that the difference he observed was attributable to the cultural and psychological influences Negroes had on American whites: "Now what is more contagious than to live side by side with a rather primitive people? Go to Africa and see what happens. When the effect is so very obvious that you stumble over it, then you call it 'going black.'"[59] James Oppenheim, the American scholar, novelist, playwright, and poet, read the article and indicated to James Weldon Johnson that in his forthcoming book, *American Types: A Preface to Analytic Psychology* (1931),[60] he summarized as well as enlarged Jung's findings. He told Johnson that it was the Negro himself, and not simply

Negro art forms, that had "colored the white man." The white man had been colored by the Negro, said Oppenheim, in favor of the theory that the American was a "new race," just as the white man had "whitened" the Negro.[61]

In any case, Dett had good reason to proceed with his agenda of vindicating the Negro, despite the fact that the official intent of the European tour was to teach the white colonialists in Africa how most righteously to lord over their "possessions." Thus, he essentially ignored the letter George Phenix sent to catch him as he and his forty choristers were boarding the French steamer SS *De Grasse* in New York. "Dear Dr. Dett," the principal's letter began:

> I have been thinking a good deal since you were in my office the other day about the suggestion I made in regard to the singing of spirituals and the more I think of it the more I am convinced that my suggestion has merit. I am confirmed in this feeling by some things that have happened since.
>
> The other day after you were in my office one of our best colored people happened to be here and spoke about the Sunday evening concert in the most appreciative terms, but these words of appreciation were followed by a remark to the effect that there were no spirituals on the program, that they were so finished that their essential character had been lost. He expressed a wish that something might be done to retain the original quality of these songs. I have also heard recently that in Charleston, South Carolina, a group of white people have organized to sing Negro spirituals and to preserve them in their original form as folk songs.
>
> A folk song to be real must be sung as it is sung by the "folk." These folk songs can of course be harmonized differently and modified and the material they contain be utilized in the most sophisticated sort of compositions, but when this is done they have ceased to be folk songs. As sung by the choir a week ago, our spirituals were in a sense dè-spiritualized and it seems too bad that people on the other side should be given an erroneous idea of what these spirituals really are. As I intimated the other day, I believe if the choir could sing the spirituals without a conductor and in the same manner that they would sing them if they had come together by chance in South Carolina or some other place, that the contrast between them and the other songs on the program would be striking and would add to the dramatic value of the entire perfor-

mance. I hope very much you will give this suggestion full consideration and at least experiment with it somewhat in your early concerts.[62]

Phenix's request of Dett would not come to pass, for even during their transport to Europe, Dett would be reminded of the racialism that his artistic consummation of the spirituals had to challenge. From the time the SS *De Grasse* departed from New York on the morning of April 23, Dett saw that the Hampton choir not only provoked the curiosity of the white passengers but caused the release of a deluge of stereotypes. About this Dett wrote:

> "Islanders," was one comment; "A Negro show," was another; "Entertainers," was still another. But as the dress of the party was quiet, and none drank wine, spoke dialect, or indulged in gambling, these conjectures did not seem to be substantiated, and the mystery deepened. When it was further noted that these young people were reserved in their dancing, orderly at games, unobtrusive at meals, and friendly to strangers without making advances, curiosity overrode convention, and inquiries, amounting almost to demands, were made that we tell who and what we were, and wherefore and whither we were bound.
>
> "A choir from a Negro school?" "Then surely we would sing; perhaps someone would sing a solo. Let's see—'I'll Always Be in Love With You'—that's a pretty song, but 'Ole Man River' is better, don't you think—has more snap, and well, you know, it's more characteristic."
>
> When it became known that the choir's repertoire contained only classic music and that most of this was of a religious nature, wonder gave place to a sort of amused surprise, and it seemed for a while that by their refusal to sing jazz, the members of the Hampton Choir would ostracize themselves.[63]

When the choir finally gave the passengers a demonstration of their talents, the result was just as Dett wished it to be: increased interest and excitement over "the influences that made such things possible."[64] George Ketcham confirmed this, and more, in a letter back to Phenix. He said that when the ship landed in Plymouth, England, on May 1, and the choir had been given a gracious official welcome by the Lord Mayor of the city, a white woman from Newport News, Virginia, who had been initially startled to find Negroes aboard the ship, approached Dett to say how happy she was to see him receive such a welcome and to wish him and the choir well.[65]

That was one of Dett's small successes during the tour. But in this master-slave dialectic he had some digressions as well, one of which occurred when the Hampton choir fulfilled its engagement to sing at the tomb of British missionary David Livingstone. On May 4, the day the entourage had been driven from Plymouth to London, the choir, before some three thousand people, laid a wreath at Livingstone's tomb in the Westminster Abbey and sang Dett's arrangement of "Don't Be Weary Traveller," the spiritual requested by London well before the choir had even set sail for Europe.[66] Having the choir sing at Livingstone's tomb was intended to help advertise the London concert,[67] but several newspapers that reported on the event for the world watching from the west side of the Atlantic captured Dett and his choir in this compromising position. The caption heading an article in *The Colonist* of Victoria, British Columbia, read: "Descendants of Slaves Honored Africa's Friend."[68] One journalist, writing for *The Christian Science Monthly,* said: "For their part, the Hampton Institute students desired to lay a wreath of laurel on the tomb of David Livingstone . . . and with their songs to convey some of the gratitude which their race feels to the many Englishmen who have sought to guide them in their journey out of darkest Africa."[69] The racialism that undergirded the idea that there was a "darkest Africa" was what Dett's "mastery of form and technique" had been strategically aimed at countering, yet here it was being reported that his choir was "desiring" to convey "some of the gratitude their race feels" to the very man and men whose books—Livingstone's *Missionary Travels* (1857), as well as Henry Stanley's *How I Found Livingstone* (1872), and *In Darkest Africa* (1890)—were culprits in the cursing of African peoples in the West.

But even in this regressive moment when Peabody's aims for the European tour gained ground in the dialectic with Dett's intentions, it was by the grace of two American journalists with a hermeneutic inspired by the mood and spirit of the spirituals that Dett's position in this dialectic buoyed up from momentary submergence. In an article titled "Deserving," an editorialist for the *Musical Courier* quoted another editorial in *The New York Herald Tribune,* the latter saying:

> One hesitates to assess the significance of the incident for fear of failing to do it justice. Westminster Abbey is the Valhalla of a race which enslaved the ancestors of these boys and girls so reverently listened to. In capturing it, as they did, they were in a sense

paying off an old and bloody score, but in a coin such as revenge rarely employs.

Compare the quality of these Negro spirituals with that of the hymns current in the Anglo-Saxon world on either side of the Atlantic! Is a comparison possible? Then consider their source in the sufferings and humiliations of a slave existence! What these colored choristers were offering before the altar of the white master, in his sanctuary of sanctuaries, were flowers plucked from the Gethsemane he imposed, flowers so exquisite that he must bow his head in their presence and acknowledge his inability to gather their equal.

"Vengeance is mine, saith the Lord." Well, here it was in its divine form.[70]

After quoting this from *The New York Herald Tribune,* the editorialist for the *Musical Courier,* also inspired hermeneutically by the mood and spirit of the spirituals, then entered. He said that the latter comment came quite close to opening old sores but that it was nonetheless pertinent and interesting. The writer continued:

The Herald here gives the Anglo-Saxon world a slap that it most justly deserves. We Anglo-Saxons on both sides of the Atlantic ought to be thoroughly ashamed of ourselves for the sort of music we have introduced into our churches and the sort of music we ourselves are composing for use either inside or outside of the churches. If ever a race ought to wake up and see itself as it is, that race is the Anglo-Saxon—musically speaking. If the Herald editor aids us in the awakening we should be thankful to him.[71]

The idea that blacks, in reaching the heights of classical attainment once reserved for whites, were in a sense "paying off an old and bloody score" is an obsessive theme in the writing of a number of white critics of the Negro Renaissance, critics who recognized and ultimately could not prevent the "vindication" that the Renaissance artists were pursuing. About four and one-half years later a British journalist, reporting from New York for a London newspaper, was drawn to this same sentiment as he wrote on the Philadelphia Orchestra's performance of William Dawson's *Negro Folk Symphony* on November 20, 1934, at Carnegie Hall. After listing Dawson's impeccable educational credentials (like Downes did when reviewing Dett's oratorio) and after agonizing over whether Dawson made a success because of his natural abilities or because he was an atypical Negro (implicit in Downes's review as well), the journalist wrote:

> When the white men found that the Negroes were using their drums as signals of war—drum taps taken up again and again over a wide area, warning the black men of their foes—they took from the Negroes all their drums, thereby depriving them of their musical instruments. And now, today, in the person of William L. Dawson the Negroes have achieved their glorious revenge. In the rendering of his symphony most of the white man's musical instruments—violins, violas, cellos, horns, clarinets, oboes, trumpets, bells, chimes—were used. In his triumph at Carnegie Hall Dawson gained sweet revenge in its finest form.[72]

So Dett had good reason not to follow Phenix's suggestion to have the choir sing spirituals unconducted in the true folk manner during their tour of Europe. Without the choir's "outer mastery of form and technique" accompanying the "inner mastery of mood and spirit," Dett would have been unable to reap such "glorious revenge," unable to pay off that "old and bloody score" and vindicate the Negro.

Perhaps Ketcham was pricked by this "revenge" Dett was wreaking on Europe (and him), for he reported to Phenix every little instance in which Dett failed to comply with his authority, particularly Dett's neglect to comply with his and Morini's expectations for the programming of the concerts. Ketcham complained about Dett selecting his own compositions and arrangements as encores for the concert in London, saying to Phenix that Dett's "Ave Maria" did not go so well, and "I Couldn't Hear Nobody Pray" lacked exuberance. "Of course that is generally the trouble with Spirituals that are led by a man with a stick," Ketcham complained, "for they have got to be spontaneous group expressions to be real."[73] And Ketcham reported to Phenix that Morini wanted Dett to include some secular songs on a program but Dett insisted that religious music should not be intermixed with secular music.[74] Dett compromised on the issue, but a couple of days later Ketcham had something else to report. Eager to prove musical misjudgment on Dett's part, he told Phenix that in a review of one of the concerts, a music critic had given particular attention to the very two selections Dett wanted to omit from the program and had given hardly any attention to Dett's own works, other than to say that the choir liked to sing them.[75] And Ketcham reported that Morini had insisted that the program to be given in Antwerp and Amsterdam be tailored with the consideration that they were both great Jewish centers, to which Dett responded that he conducted a church choir and did not wish to make changes.[76] And Ketcham reported that in Paris, Dett closed the first half of a successful concert with his arrangement of "Don't Be Weary Traveller," which seemed to quiet the crowd, and that during the second half of the concert Dett programmed several of his longer works such that people soon began to leave the hall.[77]

While Ketcham felt that spirituals "led by a man with a stick" lacked exuberance and agreed with Phenix that Europeans should not be given an erroneous idea of what the spirituals really were, Dett was insistent on proving to Europeans that, as he put it to the media during the tour, the Negro is more than a minstrel and all Negroes are not Josephine Bakers.[78] Evidently the spirituals (arranged), rather than the secular songs Morini wanted mixed into the choir's programs, were the best proof. Had Dett succumbed to Phenix's wish and shown the Europeans the spirituals as sung spontaneously by the folk, he would not have been able to challenge the Europeans' essentialist notion that there was a "real" Negro who was emotional (rather than "rational") and inferior (rather than "superior"). Viewing the Hampton choir from this perspective suggests that their tour abroad accomplished something other than to show whites, as Peabody wished, how to be better overlords in their African colonies. Their tour facilitated encounters between whites and blacks with the consequence of having challenged the prevailing racialist thought.

V

Use of the two-tiered mastery of "form and technique" and "mood and spirit," we must conclude, comprised a magnificent maneuver by the Negro Renaissance artists, insofar as these artists were able in an age of Jim Crow to garner ingeniously a voice in tight places, a voice intended to counter the racist racialism created and long nurtured by whites. Given Dett's adeptness at balancing the outer Europeanism and inner Africanism, we can see why the overseas reviews of the choir's performances portrayed the students from Hampton in a way that significantly differed from the invented Negro of European racialism, the Negro of Gobineau's creation.

At the concert given in The Hague on May 9, for instance, the choir was well received and had to give three encores.[79] The review in The Hague's *Het vaderland* said, "I marvel first at the schooling, the exceptionally fine discipline, the ever-joyous tone sonorities and colors of such natural voices, and at the remarkable memory of the fine choir when not a page of music was used during the evening. It is beyond understanding how the effects were achieved, bringing forth the spiritual and the inner qualities. This is an exceptionally fine chorus."[80] Before a small but enthusiastic audience in Brussels, the choir gave another well-received performance, and between acts Dett was sent to the royal box to meet the queen.[81] The choir's schooling and discipline were recognized by the reviewer for Brussels' *La meuse,* who wrote: "From the standpoint of vocal technic the choir is perfect. It could easily teach many things to our own choruses. The queen was present at the concert and Dr. Dett was presented with a palm leaf by the Musique des Guides."[82]

The concert in Berlin on May 20 was evidently an even greater success,[83] for the reviewer for the *Tageblatt* said: "The program was a great success; after the first number idle curiosity was turned into genuine enthusiasm and appreciation. The artistic training of these singers is outstandingly remarkable. There is perfect tone balance."[84] To be so received in Berlin was especially significant since the tickets to the concert did not sell well due to the fact that the right-wing party was bitterly against all blacks.[85] Munich and several other German cities turned down offers to have the choir sing because they were still bitter toward the black troops on the Rhine River after the German surrender in 1918, so the choir's victorious performance in Berlin was all the more sweet.[86]

The recognition given to the choir's artistic training, discipline, and technique was important to Dett's settling of "an old and bloody score," but the effect of vindication would not have occurred if these Europeanisms had not been mastered with an African difference. In this respect, the reviewer of the concert on May 30, in Lausanne, France, writing for the *La feuille d'avis*, recognized both the formal and technical "mastery" of the choir and the music's "deeply moving" mood and spirit:

> The mixed choir from Hampton Institute was a wonderful revelation. Conducted with real artistry by Dr. Dett, a composer of high attainments, the choir offered a beautiful program with an art particularly expressive and human. There was absolute mastery of the most difficult passages, incomparable blending, beauty of subtle shading, marvelous discipline, all united into the finest cohesion. We can compare the Hampton choir with the best Russian choruses and it has something even more deeply moving in expression.[87]

The performance on May 14, in Paris's Théâtre des Champs Elysées, had a similar effect on Lewis D. Crenshaw, a former Virginian residing in

France. Crenshaw might or might not have been one of the black Americans, among them Countee Cullen, who had come backstage to congratulate the choir for its excellent performance.[88] In any case, the next day Crenshaw wrote Phenix a letter that seemed almost to have been written at Dett's request:

> As a former Virginian now residing in France, I cannot refrain from sending you a word of appreciation of the splendid concert given last night in Paris by the "Hampton Choir," which I had the pleasure to attend.
>
> I heartily congratulate Hampton Institute on having trained such a group of singers, who are certainly worthy ambassadors of your school.
>
> I and my family were entirely surrounded by French people and I can assure you that every number on the program gave them intense pleasure. I have heard "spiritual" songs for many years in various Southern States, but rarely have they made the impression that they did on me last night.
>
> We are particularly pleased with the two numbers composed by Nathaniel Dett "Listen to the Lambs," and "Let Us Cheer the Weary Traveller."[89]

Wishing to sound equally optimistic when Ketcham's frequent letters were giving him no reason to be, Phenix wrote back to Crenshaw saying:

The sole purpose was to counteract many unfortunate impressions which have been created by jazz artists, dancers, etc., who have in recent years invaded some parts of Europe. The hope back of the venture was that seeing and hearing a group of young people such as we sent over might influence the minds of those who are shaping the destinies of the natives in Africa to the advantage of these natives. From all newspaper accounts and from frequent cables which I have received I judge that the undertaking has been a distinct success. A cable the other day reported that in Dresden it was necessary to extinguish the lights in order to induce the audience to go home."[90]

The above French journalist's statement that the Hampton choir was a "wonderful revelation" and Crenshaw's statement that the choristers were "worthy ambassadors" of Hampton should be understood as referring to

Dett's masterful re-imaging of the Negro. That the choir's rendering of select European classics played a role as important as the arranged spirituals in Dett's capacity to traverse the essentialist color line is evident in the review that appeared in Geneva's *La tribune* following the choir's performance in Geneva on May 31 before an enthusiastic audience that filled the concert house.[91] The reviewer initially seemed trapped by his racialist presumptions and drawn to the mythic type of primitive Negro, but the choir's perfect rendering of classical works precluded his being able to give a stereotypically essentialist portrayal of the choristers. He wrote, "The 40 Negro Singers directed by Dr. Dett scored a truly triumphant success at the Grand theater. The chief impression carried away is that of deep conviction and faith. Many of the Negro songs are simple stories from the Bible, however, the choir also sang the Russian 'Kyrie Eleison' by Lvovsky to perfection. The ensemble is outstanding; the harmony, the attack, the articulation are absolutely faultless."[92]

The following extract from Vienna's *Der tag,* which reports on the choir's well-received May 23 concert that required several encores,[93] summarizes all that the foregoing reviews seem to have been indicating, and specifically what Dett was implying in stating that Negro music provides an important point of contact between the races. The journalist wrote, "And now that the Negro singers from the renowned Hampton Institute proceed in triumph through European concert halls they are not looked upon as foreigners but as interpreters of human experience common to mankind."[94] Based on such reviews, Peabody was happy with the results of the tour,[95] which he had hoped would show the Europeans with colonial possessions how better to educate their colonial subjects according to their natural abilities. Dett claimed victory as well, for he considered the triumph of the European tour to comprise what he called the "emancipation of Negro music"—that is, an unchaining of Negro music from a half-century of misunderstanding and low ideals set upon it by minstrelsy.[96]

For the moment, however, this lofty success eluded tangible results for blacks, not to mention that the success eluded results for Dett himself and the choir that his expertise helped nurture. Chorister Solomon Phillips was ominously foreseeing in this regard when he wrote in his diary during the tour, "Superiority Complex is going to ruin this choir one of these days if some few are not made to see light."[97] Those who conspired against Dett during the tour did not see the light and continued in their superiority complex to work against him until his resignation was requested in July 1931. The request came from Phenix's successor, Arthur Howe, who was carrying out the tenor of the trustees who had made the decision regarding Dett as early as the winter of 1930 (prior to Howe's election as Hampton's president).[98] Peabody explained to Dett that in asking for his resignation, the trustees were responding to his lack of cooperation with departmental associates and executive authority prior to Howe's election.[99] So, while no clear reason was given Dett for the request of his resignation, Peabody's comment seemed to suggest that *The Norfolk Journal and Guide*, the black-owned newspaper that had closely followed the careers of Dett and his choir, was correct in one of its speculations regarding the dismissal. The paper speculated that the request for Dett's resignation might have been related to the clash of personalities during the European tour: "In Europe he was importuned constantly by the white European managers to give [the] type of program not within keeping with his own ideas. He was attempting to show Europeans the ability of [the] Negro to sing any music, as well as his own, in developed and undeveloped forms."[100]

Perhaps the war against the stereotypical essentializing of blacks would be won in the long run and the Negro Renaissance would be a success (as I believe it was), but Dett had lost the battle against Ketcham and Morini. In addition to Ketcham's letters to Phenix during the tour, Morini eventually added several of his own letters, and all of these seemed to contribute to Dett's downfall. The day of the choir's last concert, June 4, two days before the departure of the entourage for home, Morini wrote administrator Robert Ogden Purves at Hampton to inform him that Dett had been a very difficult person to deal with in that he did exactly the opposite of every piece of advice he was given regarding the programming. "A cooperation with him was therefore absolutely impossible," said Morini; and he signed off promising a more detailed report to follow.[101] In the meantime, Purves wrote back saying that it was most upsetting to hear about the difficulties Morini had with Dett and that it was "very humiliating" to have had such behavior from someone connected with Hampton.[102]

Morini then followed up with the more detailed report he had promised. He said someone had complained to him after the Hampton choir's first concert in London that it was church music rather than Negro music that was being performed, which he interpreted as meaning Dett had too many of his own sophisticated arrangements on the program. Upon this warning, continued the letter to Purves, Ketcham was told that the choir's program had to be changed completely or else the entire tour would be a fiasco. Ketcham was cooperative, concluded Morini, but from that point on Dett either ruined the concerts or lessened their potential successes. "The consequence is that the tour was not very brilliant and that the success was always partly spoiled," he said.[103] Purves again wrote back saying that it was deeply regrettable to everyone at Hampton that the great opportunity the choir had was lost to some degree by Dett's obstinacy, selfishness, and meanness.[104] Wishing to slight Dett even more, a couple of months later Morini wrote to Ketcham asking if the Hampton choir could return to Europe the next year but under a different conductor,[105] to which Ketcham responded that had Dett behaved himself the choir's return might have been possible. Then Ketcham uttered words that forecasted Dett's fate at Hampton: "Dett is still with us. I am not free to say anything more except that the authorities at the school know the full story of the trip and this information was given not only by Don Davis and me but also by Miss Stewart and Mrs. Washington. The hand of fate often moves slowly."[106]

A month later Phenix died unexpectedly in an accident, but the hand of fate would still move on Dett under Phenix's successor, Arthur Howe. Dett might even have seen the hand of fate swinging around to unseat him when Howe ended up being elected to succeed Phenix, for he could remember giving Howe a "blessing out" a couple years earlier for segregating the commencement of the nurses. Dett refused to take part in the commencement ever again unless seating for blacks and whites would be equal.[107] Dett's conflicts with Howe continued after Howe became president, for Dett felt it necessary to go to the principal in order to fend off Ketcham's continued imposition on his musical expertise and authority as the director of music and of the choir. Ketcham had made up a musical program which had three consecutive pieces in a minor key, to which Dett responded angrily to Howe that it was musically unfitting. But there was more on Dett's mind, and he continued at length in his letter to Howe:

> There is another point to be considered in regard to this, which had previously escaped my attention. A visitor here on the grounds, in fact the manager of one of the larger New York bureaus, recently brought word of the criticism of Mr. Paul Robeson for his mixing of religious and non-religious Negro songs on his program which he recently gave in New York. You may not know it, but there has been for some years a very earnest effort on the part of the more serious minded musicians to differentiate the various classes of Negro music, and not have grouped together songs which are purely religious and those which have a secular trend—the idea being to emphasize the dignity of the religious element in Negro music. I have been one of the leaders in this movement, which has had the support of many of the best thinking musicians, as well as many others, of the country.

I have been successful in getting certain pieces recognized for their religious worth. Foremost among these is "Listen to the Lambs," which has been on the programs of the best churches in America. In the final group which Mr. Ketcham arranged, he puts "Listen to the Lambs," "Stan' Still Jordan," "Poor Mourner Got a Home," and "Let Us Cheer the Weary Traveller," all together. This is an arrangement which I have spent years fighting. "Poor Mourner Got a Home" is one of the kind of songs which is never used in regular church service. We would hardly use it in our own church service. And the humorous setting which Mr. Diton has given it removes it still further from the realm of religious significance.

For me to conduct a group of songs, the arrangement of which is absolutely opposed to what I conscientiously believe and have worked for in regard to Negro music, is to keep me in a continual state of embarrassment, as well as to hold me up to the ridicule of those who are acquainted with the effort I have been trying to make in Negro music.[108]

Dett added to his typed letter a handwritten postscript comprised of words perhaps reminiscent of the "blessing out" he gave Howe about his segregating the students at the commencement of the nurses in 1929. He wrote, "I am about sick with the mess and fuss of all this which is sapping my strength and my enthusiasm."[109]

That Dett's resignation was requested about a year before he could have retired with benefits, and that this dismissal was occurring when the country was in an economic depression and finding a job might have been difficult, suggests a certain perniciousness to the handling of the whole matter, the kind of perniciousness William Pickens noted with regard to the treatment of John Work at Fisk University about six years earlier:

John Work had served Fisk University for a generation before this little man was ever heard of at the institution. The influence and popularity of the brown man was evidently so great as to arouse the jealousy of the little white man who was brought into the institution as superior officer. We do not know what influence at first removed Work from leadership and membership in the "Fisk Singers," but we know it was a very evil influence that finally forced him out of the institution altogether. . . . After pursuing the "missionary ideals" for all of his sound life, he was kicked out by a newcomer—and like an old horse was allowed to find whatever pasturage he might find.[110]

Indeed, the handling of Dett and Work, both Renaissance artists responsible for the choral debut of the New Negro, reminds us of the perniciousness and the power of the whites who upheld the status quo Jim Crow and how difficult yet necessary it was for them to find a voice in those tight places.

Among the musicians Howe considered to replace Dett, with input from Peabody and Robert Russa Moton, were Harry T. Burleigh, Edward Boatner, and Clarence Cameron White. Peabody said rightly that Burleigh did not have the genius of Dett,[111] and the position went to White. White was a Renaissance Negro too, but he also did not have Dett's genius. So, had Dett been able to remain at Hampton, had he been free to carry out his strategy of "mastery" for vindicating the Negro, doing so in subsequent tours at home and abroad, he would have continued to contribute immensely to the New Negro's transgressing of the essentialist color line. Dett did not simply retire to a pasturage like an old horse, however. He went to the Eastman School of Music in 1931 and a year later culminated his many years of intermittent graduate work with a master's degree in music. The performance of his thesis, the oratorio he later titled *The Ordering of Moses,* was premièred five years later in 1937. It was a success for the Negro Renaissance not to be overlooked, even though William Grant Still for over a decade had been doing quite well in the symphonic field.

From 1937 to 1942, Dett was director of music at Bennett College in North Carolina, carrying on his work, but with success that was smaller in comparison to that of his Hampton years. Nonetheless, Dett left a legacy of continued success in such Hampton students as Charles Flax and Dorothy Maynor.

VI

Maynor admitted that Dett's influence on her was "the great Continental Divide that bisected my life."[112] Flax might have felt the same way, for he too was a chorister and soloist at the time of the 1930 European tour. He also traveled with Dett to fill concert engagements, during which he sang Dett's arrangements of spirituals to Dett's piano accompaniment. Flax later became a music instructor at Hampton, served for a long time as the school's director of the chapel choir, and founded in 1939 the Crusaders

Male Chorus, which performed throughout Virginia's Tidewater Area and along the eastern seaboard.

While Flax was a successful New Negro with a reputation that was more regional than national, Maynor's career as a concert soprano far surpassed his contributions to the Negro Renaissance and might have been even more important than the contributions of the Hampton choir or maybe even those of Paul Robeson and Roland Hayes. Hers might have been a more important racial vindication because she was a black woman, a point that was made in a 1936 editorial in *Opportunity* which congratulated Marian Anderson for her highly touted concertizing and her triumphant return to America from her European tour. The editorialist said that Anderson's "crashing the color line" had few parallels, for as difficult as it was for a Negro man to reach such heights, it was "infinitely more difficult for a Negro woman."[113] It was infinitely more difficult for a black woman because, as Charles S. Johnson wrote in a 1923 article for *Opportunity*, the Negro woman worked under the weight of pernicious myths. Johnson pointed out as an example the fact that a white American scholar had argued that less than three percent of Negro women were virtuous and that a German scientist had based his claims about Negro inferiority on his examination of a single Hottentot woman.[114] Indeed, in a way that the white racialist imagination had made concrete in their media descriptions of her, Maynor carried the mark of the Hottentot or Bushman African woman, whom nineteenth- and early twentieth-century Europeans had made into the ultimate symbol of supposed aberrant black female (and male) sexuality and into the symbol of a supposedly distinctly different black biology. This is why Maynor's artistic career was so important to the Negro Renaissance movement.

Part of the Maynor portfolio that enabled her to contest the European's racialist essentializing of her and of black people in general was, as was the case with Dett, her privileged upbringing and classical musical training. Born in Norfolk, Virginia, in 1910, Maynor began attending grade school at Hampton Institute when she was fourteen years old. She entered high school at Hampton in 1925, finished there in 1929, and entered Hampton's music department that year as a student of Dett. Her senior music recital, foreshadowing her professional recitals, included the European classics by the likes of Handel, Brahms, Schubert, and Verdi, and ended with a set of spirituals that included arrangements by Dett, Burleigh, and Clarence Cameron White. After graduating from Hampton in 1933 with a bachelor of science degree, she was given a scholarship to attend the Westminster

Choir School in Princeton, New Jersey, where she received a bachelor of science degree in conducting in 1935.

After one year of substituting for Charles Flax as the music instructor at Hampton Institute's grade school, Maynor moved to New York in the summer of 1936 and studied voice privately with the help of white philanthropy. She was preparing for her professional debut, which followed her "discovery" by Serge Koussevitzky, conductor of the Boston Symphony Orchestra. When a reporter for *The New York Times* interviewed her following her discovery by Koussevitzky, the journalist seemed hopeful to chronicle an instance of Negro excitability bordering on youthful arrogance. "I suppose your ambition is to make an even greater success with your New York recital this Fall," the journalist prodded. "My work has nothing to do with that kind of success," Maynor calmly responded. "I hope to represent this art of song as well as I can. That's about all I can say. To accomplish that, to be a worthy representative of the best music—one feels so very small when one thinks of it."[115] While there was in Maynor's response some of the expected humility of blacks, her thoughtful confidence nonetheless served to challenge the prevailing stereotypes.

Maynor's debut came in November 1939 at New York's Town Hall. Langston Hughes, Countee Cullen, Roland Hayes, Paul Robeson, and Clarence Cameron White were among the famous Renaissance artists present for her highly successful entry into the professional Renaissance world. Following the Town Hall debut, interviewers pursued Maynor, often inquiring about her race, which was believed to be partly Indian. She replied with that same thoughtful confidence masked by the expected black humility: "There's no purity in any race. Just say I'm plain Negro."[116] For a period of twenty-five years thereafter, Maynor, with a clear sense of who she was and the race she represented, performed in North America, South America, the Caribbean, Europe, and Australia. As she stood before such American orchestras as the New York Philharmonic, the Philadelphia Symphony Orchestra, the Boston Symphony Orchestra, the Chicago Symphony Orchestra, and the Cleveland Symphony Orchestra, she performed a highly respected repertoire that included German songs by such composers as Bach, Beethoven, Schumann, Schubert, and Brahms; French songs by such as Debussy, Milhaud, Poulenc, and Ravel; opera arias by such as Handel, Mozart, and Verdi; and spirituals arranged by such composers as Dett, Burleigh, Clarence Cameron White, and Edward Boatner.

Maynor's goal was more than to interpret as artistically as she could the musical masterpieces of the world; it was also to help vindicate the Negro. "I want to help the Negro achieve the important place in American life to which his talents and contributions entitle him," she once said.[117] As was true of the Hampton choir under Dett, Maynor's strategy for helping blacks achieve their deserving place in American life involved singing both the spirituals and the European classics. This was the strategy she picked up from such predecessors as Roland Hayes,[118] a strategy Locke approved of in the scheme of racial vindication. As Locke put it, "Mr. Hayes has given this racial material a balanced background by which it has commanded more respect. . . . 'I will never sing spirituals without classics, or classics without spirituals, for properly interpreted they are classics,'—this is Mr. Hayes' artistic platform—and he is right and will be eventually justified."[119]

That Maynor, like her predecessors Dett and Hayes, masterfully re-imaged the Negro into a New Negro, while yet maintaining the African musical qualities of the spirituals, is exemplified in audience and critical response to her performances. Some white critics rebelled against her unwillingness to reflect her mark of slavery with "authentic" renditions of the spirituals, but black audiences and concert reviewers did not seem restricted by the expectation of "natural" differences between the races. They seemed to recognize in Maynor's performances of the spirituals the authentic mood and spirit that distinguished this music, probably seeing in Maynor someone who knew the spirituals just as intimately as themselves. If black concert-goers had read any of the press about her, they probably knew she was raised the daughter of an African Methodist Episcopal minister and that she sang spirituals Sunday mornings in her father's church and Sunday afternoons when neighbors gathered at their parsonage. Thus, a concert review of 1939 that appeared in Norfolk's black newspaper, the *Journal and Guide*, just raved about Maynor's singing of the spirituals in a way that whites such as Olin Downes could not: "Her spirituals took the house also and, after a tumultuous applause, she sang 'Everytime I Feel the Spirit' and 'Were You There,' unaccompanied."[120]

A couple of months later, an editorial on Maynor appeared in *Opportunity*; and though the editorialist recognized that her repertoire was not "particularly Negroid," he was not critical of her racial renditions like Downes was. In fact, he praised Maynor for having proven that there were no racial limitations to musical interpretation, that through sustained study a Negro could attain not only technical mastery of European music but could attain understanding and feeling for it, alongside a mastery of and understanding and feeling for the music of her own race.[121] In 1947, the same paper reported on another recital Maynor gave in her hometown. The enthused writer insisted that the racial descriptive be omitted when referring to her accomplishments: "Dorothy Maynor is an artist. Leave out the adjective—just artist (period)." The writer went on to offer accolades for her renditions of German, Spanish, French, and English classics, as well as for her renditions of the spirituals. Of the latter the writer said, "Few, if any single singer we've heard, can surpass her in interpreting this contribution of the race to the nation's culture."[122]

Conversely, white critics and benefactors of the Negro Renaissance could not seem to prevent the subjectivity of their racialist beliefs from trying to pass as objective and rational criticism. Downes, still the music critic for *The New York Times,* repudiated renditions of the spirituals that did not reflect the "real" Negro with his "natural" emotivity, sensuality, and inferiority. When he reviewed Maynor's professional debut at New York's Town Hall, he could find no flaw in her renditions of the European classics: "She proved that she had virtually everything needed by a great artist—the superb voice, one of the finest that the public can hear today; exceptional musicianship and accuracy of intonation; emotional intensity, communicative power." But about her renditions of the spirituals he had much critical to say: "It was inevitable that Miss Maynor would be asked to sing a group of Negro spirituals. Two of these, including the second 'By and By,' she did beautifully. But her voice, singular as it may seem, is not the ideal voice for Negro spirituals. It has not in sufficient degree the negroid coloring."[123] The next year Maynor gave another recital in New York's Town Hall and Downes again praised her European renditions but criticized her singing of the spirituals:

> There came the inevitable group of Negro spirituals apparently expected by the public when a Negro of either sex sings. As a rule, Negro spirituals sung in recitals are sung with an artiness that is discouraging. They lose their folk quality; they become self-conscious, theatrical, whereas no more sincere and inspired music has ever been written. Miss Maynor is to us refined to the point of self-consciousness when she sings these songs. Nor did we enjoy Nathaniel Dett's finicking and artificial arrangements, made for Miss Maynor, of the two spirituals, one with an echo effect at the end which is anything but congruous with the true nature of the music. The singing, without accompaniment, of the spirituals, "Swing Low, Sweet Chariot" and "They Crucified My Lord" were tonally among the most beautiful accomplishments of the evening. But it was conventionalized singing, and the melodic quirks bestowed upon the melody of "Swing Low, Sweet Chariot" did not make that haunting melody more irresistible than it is.[124]

Despite Maynor's general success in challenging the white-constructed mythologies of blackness, despite her lack of errors of the magnitude of the Hampton choir's honoring of Livingstone, the white racialist beliefs of mid-century were not easily redeemed. The day after her New York debut in 1939, a reporter named Michel Mok interviewed her for *The New York Post* and commented stereotypically about her "childlike humility" and her having "the glow and shy gayety of a jungle bird."[125] Mok, we see, imposed a difference, and the image he chose—Negroes as equivalent to children—permitted him and his white readership to feel secure in their racial "superiority" again. It permitted them to feel secure because the stereotypical image restored the moral imbalance in favor of what Gobineau called the "adult" white race. Mok continued in the mode reminiscent of the colonial literature of Livingstone and Stanley and the local color fiction of Twain and Faulkner: "There's sun in her skin of gold-powdered tan, in her melting deep-brown eyes, in her slightly husky sing-song speaking voice, in her smile that reminds you of a child bewildered by too many toys and sweets on Christmas morning."[126] Similarly, the December 1939 issue of *Life* magazine featured a photograph of Paul Robeson sitting with Maynor at the reception following her Town Hall debut, under which the caption read: "Paul Robeson, baritone, heard Dorothy Maynor. So did Roland Hayes, tenor. Marian Anderson sent a wire. These Negro singers would make an unsurpassed quartet."[127] Again, the writer imposed a difference, and the image chosen—the "Negro quartet," a four-person faceless monolith possibly reminiscent of minstrel performances—again permitted whites to feel secure in the idea of "natural" racial differences.

This *Life* magazine article, to proceed further, was suspect for far more villainous reasons. It said of Maynor at one point, "She is 4 ft. 10 in. tall, weighs 145 lb. In operatic arias, she stands in conventional fashion, hands folded in front. But when she comes to spirituals, she leans elbow on piano, jounces her chunky body up and down as she sings" (a photograph of her heavy bust line "jouncing" is provided in the magazine). Immediately following this description is another photograph that shows Maynor from the posterior. She is bent over, taking a bow, and her buttocks are protruding. So, the white readership of *Life* had now seen Maynor jouncing her breasts up and down and bowing with her buttocks protruding.[128] These images, whether or not intentionally (or consciously) stereotypical and pernicious, could not help but conjure up the nineteenth-century European icon par excellence of the black person: the buttocks (and large breasts) of the famous female Hottentot of nineteenth-century Paris, Sarah Bartmann.

By publishing these photographs of Maynor jouncing and bending and by describing her height and build as they had, the writers of the *Life* article were conveying to the sexualized imagination of mid-century racialist whites Maynor's likeness to the "Hottentot Venus." The link between the images is inescapable, since representations of the physiognomy of the Hottentot woman enters the twentieth century in such art as Pablo Picasso's *Olympia* (1901), and since Bartmann's buttocks and genitalia remain to this day on display in the Musée de l'homme in Paris.

Given this history and the continued racialist claims during Maynor's day about black sexuality, we should not overlook this probable symbolism when such publications as *Newsweek* and *The New York Post* began articles on Maynor by describing her as "a short and plump Negro woman."[129] Neither should we overlook the supporting evidence—the similar need *The Boston Herald* had to consult an anthropologist for racial theorizing following Maynor's successful New York debut. The *Herald* article read, "Prof. Earnest A. Hooton, the Harvard anthropologist, believes we should recognize—rather than overlook—distinguishing racial traits, and when they are beneficial, as in the case of the Negro's affinity for music, encourage them."[130] This, by the way, was the very same message George Foster Peabody wanted to convey to Europeans, especially those with "African possessions," in sponsoring the 1930 European tour of the Hampton choir.

I contend that Maynor's successful "mastery of form and technique" ("mastery" with a black musical difference) was all the more an event of far-reaching racial significance given the fact that she was "a short and plump Negro woman." Racial mythologies do not die easily, but I believe the attenuation of the customary view of the "real" Negro and specifically Maynor's and Dett's contribution to that attenuation, was, for instance, what paved the way for Maynor to sing for the inaugural ceremonies for President Harry S. Truman in 1948, and more importantly to be asked to sing the national anthem at the inauguration of President Dwight D. Eisenhower on January 20, 1953, the first black person ever to have sung the national anthem for a presidential inauguration. The last time Maynor was at the White House was in 1930, when the Hampton choir stopped to give a performance on the afternoon of April 21 as it headed to New York to board ship for Europe. The choir lined up on the steps on the side of the White House facing the monument in the distance and sang "O Hear the Lambs" to President Herbert Hoover and his special guests on the White House lawn, after which the president gave a half-salute and disappeared inside.[131] But would Hoover have ever imagined that one of the Negro youths in that choir that he saluted with disinterest would one day be singing the national anthem for a presidential inauguration, or that one day moral suasion along with violent rebellion would oust the European colonialists from Africa? What sweet vindication for the Negro Renaissance.

Alain L. Locke. Photograph courtesy of the Alain Locke Papers,
Moorland-Spingarn Research Center, Howard University.

Carl R. Diton.
Photograph courtesy of
the Black Sacred Music
Collection, Hampton
University Archives.

Roland Hayes.
Photograph courtesy of
the Black Sacred Music
Collection, Hampton
University Archives.

Marian Anderson. Photograph courtesy of the H. Councill Trenholm
Papers, Moorland-Spingarn Research Center, Howard University.

R. Nathaniel
Dett. Photograph
courtesy of the
R. Nathaniel Dett
Papers, Hampton
University
Archives.

R. Nathaniel Dett
and the Hampton
Institute Choir
during their
European tour of
1930. Photograph
courtesy of the
Music Collection,
Hampton
University
Archives.

William Grant Still showing W. C. Handy the theme music commissioned for the 1939–40 New York World's Fair. Photograph courtesy of Judith Anne Still.

William Grant Still.
Photograph courtesy of
Judith Anne Still.

Dorothy Maynor.
Photograph courtesy
of the Music
Collection, Hampton
University Archives

Chapter 3

The Terrible Handicap of Working as a Negro Composer

My boy, you are by blood, by appearance, by education, and by tastes a
white man. Now, why do you want to throw your life away amidst the
poverty and ignorance, in the hopeless struggle, of the black people
of the United States? Then look at the terrible handicap you are placing
on yourself by going home and working as a Negro composer; you
can never be able to get the hearing for your work which it might
deserve. I doubt that even a white musician of recognized ability
could succeed there by working on the theory that American music
should be based on Negro themes.

—*The Autobiography of an Ex-Colored Man*

I

What Dett did for the spirituals by developing in classical forms this folk
music reflective of human suffering and religious ecstasy, William Grant
Still did for the blues; and Still faced the very same opposition to this "development" that his older colleague did. There was a time, as Still explained, when certain whites held to the belief that every Negro musician
should only create and perform popular music. If the thought ever entered
their minds that a Negro musician might aspire to the artistic heights of
Beethoven and Mozart, he continued, they resolutely pushed the thought
aside.[1] Sounding much like the protagonist in *The Autobiography of an Ex-
Colored Man*, who believed whites would redeem their racism upon learn-

ing of the serious work of blacks such as himself, Still said: "It is true that some people incline to 'stereotype' a Negro composer, expecting him to follow certain lines, for no sounder reason than that those lines were followed in the past. But I have pioneered fields previously closed to members of my race, and have found that most people can be won over if they are convinced of one's sincerity."[2]

Convincing black people of the worthiness of their indigenous culture was just as difficult, for there was a time when blacks, burdened by the memories of slavery and its aftermath, thought it would be impossible for a black musician to succeed in the area of composing "serious music."[3] Among those blacks who were evidently burdened by the aftermath of slavery, to the degree that it was difficult to conceive of blacks composing serious music, was Still's mother, who bitterly opposed the music profession and preferred that her son become a medical doctor. To discourage him from his aspirations, she painted dire portrayals of the "down-at-the-heel" type of black musician who was disparaged in the "respectable" black community.[4] Coming from a "respectable" background himself, Dett understood that in those days black music was generally associated with ragtime, which was a music intended for dance or to ridicule blacks. In those days, continued Dett, to talk about Negro music to respectable Negroes was to embarrass them since the public's attitude toward it was generally contemptuous.[5] But Dett's choral works and Still's symphonic works began to change the perception of the general public and blacks themselves toward black music. For instance, when Still's symphonic work, *Darker America,* was performed in New York City's Aeolian Hall on November 28, 1926, and favorably reviewed, his mother finally understood and was satisfied that her son had envisioned a higher musical occupation.[6] "Although she had opposed my career in music," Still recalled, "she finally understood that music meant to me all the things she had been teaching me: a creative, serious accomplishment worthy of study and high devotion as well as sacrifice. She knew at last that the ideals which she had passed on to me during my boyhood in Arkansas had borne worthy fruit."[7]

Still acknowledged that none of his accomplishments would have been possible had it not been for the example set by Samuel Coleridge-Taylor, Harry T. Burleigh, Clarence Cameron White, and Dett, all of whom were role models who helped open the door of opportunity for the "serious" black composers of his generation.[8] Still viewed Coleridge-Taylor, a black English composer, as someone who won the respect of all the world and provided many black American composers with the incentive to pursue their dream of writing "serious" music.[9] Still was not greatly impressed with

Dett's orchestral writing, but he nonetheless felt Dett was an outstanding choral composer,[10] one who deserved credit for being among the first black musicians to be recognized as a "serious composer" in general musical circles.[11] On the one hand, while Still recognized the importance of Coleridge-Taylor and Dett as musical forerunners, Hale Smith, Ulysses Kay, and other younger black composers in turn recognized that Still's accomplishments had made it easier for them to practice their trade with fewer obstacles.[12] For instance, Hale Smith, writing to Still in 1964 to express his appreciation for him "opening the door" for his younger generation, said he had been contemplating the idea of sending Still the score of one of his compositions as an expression of his esteem for Still's work and as an acknowledgment that the younger black musicians would be having a far more difficult time if Still and others like him had not cleared the way. "In my opinion," wrote Smith, "one of the most important of your contributions has borne fruit in the sense that we who are following no longer need fear the implied image of inferiority in the expressions 'Negro Composer', etc."[13] This is exactly what Still accomplished with regard to his mother and it is what the Renaissance Negro sought to and did accomplish in vindicating the Negro with regard to the idea of the "Negro poet" or the "Negro novelist" or the "Negro sculptor." Feeling good about the role he played in the transformation of the long-time negative perceptions the general public had of black music, Still wrote back to Smith thanking him for his kind letter.[14]

Passing on his strategy of the two-tiered "mastery" that Locke termed the "mastery of form and technique" and "mastery of mood and spirit," and the goal that Locke called the "vindication of the Negro," Still advised younger black musicians, who themselves could help eliminate the image of inferiority in the expression "Negro composer," to take advantage of every educational opportunity. By studying at the best schools under the finest teachers and building reputations based on solid achievement, in the years to come the whole world would look up to them as "worthwhile, cultured citizens and artists."[15] In his own words, Still was speaking of these young artists attaining what Locke termed "culture citizenship."

Still had certainly pursued "culture citizenship." Although he never completed his final semester at Wilberforce University, which he entered in 1911 as a biology student in preparation for a career in medicine,[16] he subsequently received training in music composition, theory, and violin at Oberlin Conservatory of Music during the 1917–18 academic year. Later he studied privately in 1922 with George W. Chadwick of the New England Conservatory of Music, the composer under whom black composer

Florence Price graduated at the Conservatory in 1906. At the time performing in Eubie Blake's original orchestra for the 1921–22 production of the Broadway hit *Shuffle Along*, Still carried on his compositional study with Chadwick during the three summer months of 1922 when the musical comedy was playing in Boston. The next year in New York, he began several years of private study with avant-garde composer Edgard Varèse, who came to the United States from France in 1916 and became an avid promoter of modern music. Though Still eventually expressed adamant disregard for avant-garde music and returned to a neo-Romantic style of composition, he credited Varèse for helping expand his compositional grammar.

While it was from his formal study at Oberlin and later with Chadwick and Varèse that Still acquired his "mastery of form and technique," it was from his professional experiences as a performer and arranger of black music that he acquired his "mastery of mood and spirit." In addition to playing oboe in and arranging for Eubie Blake's orchestra for the 1921–22 production of *Shuffle Along*,[17] Still played oboe and cello in and arranged for W. C. Handy's band, and later arranged blues and jazz scores for the bands of Don Voorhees, Sophie Tucker, Artie Shaw, Willard Robison, and Paul Whiteman. For Whiteman's orchestra, Still composed approximately 104 orchestrations, ranging from simple dance tunes to rather sophisticated works.[18] At other points in his career, Still conducted for the Black Swan Recording Company, directed and arranged for the Deep River Hour that aired over the radio network of the Columbia Broadcasting System (CBS), and composed for Warner Brothers Films in Hollywood. Writing commercial orchestrations enabled him to experiment with different combinations of instrumental sound and hear the results quickly, which allowed him, in his "serious" composition, to draw from a catalog of orchestral techniques and tonal colors that far surpassed what he felt he could have gathered through formal training.[19] Although the genres of commercial music that Still worked with during these professional experiences were not, in his own estimation, the epitome of Renaissance art (because they were popular rather than classical), these were the genres of music from which he drew in order to infuse his "serious" (classical) works with the black or African "mood and spirit."

So, with his "mastery of form and technique"—"mastery" with a masterful black or African difference—Still confidently overcame many of the racial barriers that had long relegated the Old Negro to ancillary positions in American society. Still was credited with being the first Negro to compose a symphony that was performed by a prominent symphonic orchestra, the *Afro-American Symphony* (1931), which premièred on October 29, 1931, under the direction of Howard Hanson at the Eastman School of Music. One of the eight operas Still composed, *Troubled Island* (1941), was credited as being the first opera by a Negro to be staged by a major opera company, the New York City Opera Company, which premièred the work on March 31, 1949. Additionally, Still was recognized as the first Negro to conduct an all-white radio orchestra (the "Deep River" program on WOR), a major American symphony orchestra (the Los Angeles Philharmonic in 1936), and a major symphony orchestra in the deep South (the New Orleans Philharmonic in 1955).

Still's "firsts" and those of other black artists were widely reported in the black newspapers because it was by these markers that the progress of the New Negro toward racial parity was measured. Still explained, "In all categories—singers, instrumentalists, conductors, and composers—the story has been the same through the years. At first there were none, just aspiring musicians. Now there are many. Progress has been made through a series of firsts, this or that person being the 'first Negro' to do this or that, to perform here or there, or to gain one or another honor."[20] Because of his achievements and longevity as a recognized composer of "serious" music and his having paved the way for a younger generation of black composers with his many "firsts" which opened doors previously closed, Still became known as the dean of Negro composers.

Perhaps the greatest "first" Still ever dreamed of—a first that would have facilitated the voicing of the joys, sorrows, hopes, and ambitions of the Negro in the "higher" musical forms had it been realized—was the formation of a national Negro symphony orchestra. This orchestra would have been the musical correlation to the national Negro theater that Locke dreamed of in 1927, where black playwrights and actors would "interpret the soul of their people in a way to win the attention and admiration of the world."[21] The national Negro symphony orchestra was identical to the orchestra earlier conceived of by Edmund Jenkins, the South Carolina–born black composer and musician who trained at the Royal Academy of Music in London and eventually settled in Paris. In the winter of 1923–24, Jenkins came to the United States with high hopes of founding a black orchestra alongside a school of music for blacks, both of which he intended to rival the best schools and orchestras built by Europeans, but his dreams were met by the resistance of those whites whose prerogative for the New Negro was for him to remain Old.[22]

A conductor named Ignatz Waghalter, who had immigrated to the United States from Germany, evidently ran into the same obstacles. In 1937, he wrote James Weldon Johnson and told him that he wanted to form and conduct a Negro symphony orchestra which would devote itself entirely to the performance of the music of the European masters. He said he was surprised to find that there was no such organization given that Negroes were "by nature" endowed with musical gifts.[23] Johnson responded enthusiastically, "The realization of such an idea is something I have dreamed of for a number of years. With all of the Negro's undoubted musical endowment there is no question that such an organization would be of immense value and would, I believe, be a success. You therefore have my heartiest endorsement of the idea and I am ready and willing to do anything that I can to formulate a plan for carrying it out."[24] At Johnson's suggestion, Waghalter consulted with Walter White, secretary of the NAACP, who suggested a board of directors comprised of William Dawson, Roland Hayes, Marian Anderson, Paul Robeson, and Duke Ellington.[25] But Johnson had told Waghalter that the requisite money to initiate such an orchestra would have to be raised by a board of whites, such as Deems Taylor and Carl Van Vechten.[26] When Waghalter returned to White for further consultation, White sent him to William Lawrence, who had organized a symphony in Harlem about a year earlier under the auspices of the Works Progress Administration.[27]

In his article titled "A Negro Symphony Orchestra," published in *Opportunity* in 1939, Still said he imagined that the musicians constituting a national Negro symphony orchestra would have jazz training, which would enhance their virtuosity and thus enable them to execute passages that were generally difficult for musicians trained only in the European school of performance.[28] If there could have been formed a Negro symphony orchestra "so fine," as Still put it, that it would rank with and perhaps even surpass the best orchestras in the world,[29] then such, according to the way the Renaissance Negro thought, would have helped vindicate their race. Reflecting the high artistic ideals of Locke as well as Locke's moral ideals that permit a black racialism that is not racist or racially exclusive, Still went on to say:

> The conductor should be a Negro. Most of the soloists should be colored. But we must also look forward to the time when the orchestra itself will be such a splendid organization that world-famous soloists, irrespective of race, will deem it an honor to appear with it; and when a renowned guest conductor may enjoy working with it.
>
> Since so many artistic white people have been generous enough to play and sing Negro music, a Negro organization should be equally broad. It should specialize not alone in Negro music

but in *American music*. Inevitably, following this policy, during the course of a single season, all fine Negro symphonic works will have been given an auspicious hearing, and more of our talented younger composers will have been inspired to compose more in that medium when they are assured of an audience. Well-balanced and interesting programs of purely American music could be arranged, and the result should be a lesson to a few of our contemporary conductors who are so eager to foist European culture on the American public while ignoring or belittling the fact that we are now developing a splendid culture of our own!

Eventually, a fine Negro Symphony Orchestra could make money. Under the proper management, it could tour the United States and Canada, then all the Latin American countries, and finally Europe. People might regard it at first as a novelty and would patronize it solely for that reason. Soon, as they realized its dignified purpose and appreciated its quality, they would attend just for the sake of the fine music they would hear, for this orchestra should be in no sense a blatant, barbaric group, nor should it be prim and proper, with false ideas of what constitutes real musical worth. This orchestra should be sincere, individually and collectively. It should be highly idealistic. And I repeat *it must be good.*[30]

Still's idea of a national Negro symphony orchestra never came to fruition, but his many other "firsts" summed up to be an important contribution to the "vindication of the Negro." Additionally, even before the first of his many "firsts," Still had won a Harmon Award in 1928, an award granted annually by the Department of Race Relations in the Federal Council of the Churches of Christ in America for the year's most significant contributions to black culture. As I explained in chapter 1, the criterion for the granting of the Harmon awards was essentially a concurrent "mastery" of what Locke called "form and technique" and "mood and spirit." According to the director of the Harmon Foundation, the awards were an attempt to stimulate the Negro artist to take "his own individuality and the artistic impulses of the Negro people" (the "mood and spirit") and develop them with the "highest technique" ("mastery of form and technique"). It is this very "mastery of form and technique" with a black or African difference that brought Still, the Great Depression notwithstanding, wide recognition and subsequent awards. He received a Guggenheim Fellowship in 1934 and again in 1938, and a Rosenwald Fellowship in 1939 and 1940. On the Guggenheim Fellowship he composed his first completed opera, *Blue Steel*; on the Rosenwald Fellowship a ballet titled *Miss Sally's Party* and a piano composition titled *Seven Traceries*. Of Still's many prize-winning pieces, the best known are *Festive Overture* (1944), which won the Jubilee Season Award from the Cincinnati Symphony Orchestra in 1944; and his piece for symphonic band, *To You America* (1951), which won the George Washington Honor Medal from the Freedom's Foundation in 1953.

As a result of his increased national recognition, to which his prestigious awards and fellowships contributed, Still received numerous compositional commissions. In 1936, the Columbia Broadcasting System (CBS) commissioned him to write *Lenox Avenue*, an orchestral work (later converted into a ballet) which was performed over the CBS radio network in 1937. While it was a masterpiece of classic "form and technique," Locke also found it to be one of Still's most "racially typical" compositions.[31] A year after the radio premier of this piece, Still was commissioned to write the theme music for the 1939–40 New York World's Fair (published in 1939 under the title *Rising Tide*). Subsequently his *Poem for Orchestra* was commissioned in 1944 by Erich Leinsdorf, conductor of the Cleveland Orchestra. Later, his *Romance* (1954) for alto saxophone and piano (eventually arranged for saxophone and orchestra) was written to fill a 1951 commission from the well-known concert saxophonist Sigurd Rascher. When Rascher made his commission he told Still that he knew of his works, as every educated musician did, and that he frequently thought that Still would be one who could compose something for the saxophone that would be truly in the nature and style of the instrument. "I am convinced," he said, "that a composition from your hand would meet with very considerable interest, wherever performed."[32] These commissions were evidence of Still's ongoing inroads to what Locke called "culture citizenship" and thus the ongoing success of the Negro Renaissance. As Still put it, "we have not done too badly in public esteem, and the fact that some of us are winning prizes, earning commissions and having our works played by symphony orchestras all over the world is in itself recognition of the fact that the public is coming to accept us for what we are."[33]

These and others of Still's accomplishments in the professional music world were eventually recognized by the academic world as well, first when he received the honorary Master of Music degree from Wilberforce University in 1936, and subsequently when he received a total of eight honorary doctorates: from Howard University in 1941, Oberlin College in 1947,

Bates College in 1954, University of Arkansas in 1971, Pepperdine University in 1973, New England Conservatory of Music in 1973, Peabody Institute of Music in 1974, and University of Southern California in 1975.

II

Still's approximately one hundred compositions, which so inspired Hale Smith and other black composers of younger generations, include symphonies, operas, ballets, orchestral works for chorus or solo voice, works for band, choir, piano, voice, and chamber pieces for winds or strings. All of these compositions fall into what Still identified as three stylistic periods, the first of which consists of his student works composed under the influence of French composer Edgard Varèse, with whom he studied in New York from 1923 to 1925. These works include his orchestral pieces titled *From the Land of Dreams* (1924), *Darker America* (1925), and *From the Journal of a Wanderer* (1925). *From the Land of Dreams* was performed in New York City on February 8, 1925, at a concert sponsored by the International Composers' Guild, which Varèse and harpist Carlos Salzedo established in New York in 1921. The performance of *Darker America* was sponsored by the same organization but performed at Aeolian Hall in New York City on November 28, 1926. *From the Journal of a Wanderer* was first performed by the Chicago Symphony Orchestra at the North Shore Festival in 1926.

Although Still would later look back on this stylistic period as his "growing period" and would prefer that only his later, more mature works be performed,[34] the compositions of this period contributed to the momentum of the Negro Renaissance, which was just then beginning to gain national recognition. For instance, in his review of *Darker America*, Olin Downes wrote for *The New York Times*: "The best music last night was that of 'Darker America,' even though Mr. Still, himself a negro composer, is inclined to add Mr. Varèse's harmonic ideas to his own treatment of negroid intervals and melodic phrases." Downes concluded, "This music . . . has direction and feeling in it, qualities usually lacking in contemporaneous music."[35] Locke did not place the works of Still's first compositional phase beyond the pale of the Negro Renaissance, but he did comment a decade later that as Still's composition matured, the folk idiom increasingly appeared, thus tempering his earlier ultramodernistic style.[36]

Still's second stylistic period, which succeeded his years of study with Varèse, extended from 1925 through 1934, a period during which he spent most of his time living in Harlem. Still said of this period, which commenced the year Locke's *The New Negro* was published, that the mid-1920s had to arrive before he committed himself to Negro music.[37] Sounding as though he were recalling *The Autobiography of an Ex-Colored Man* and the decision of its protagonist to depict the life, ambitions, struggles, and passions of the Negro race within the "higher" classical musical forms, Still said: "I had chosen a definite goal, namely, to elevate Negro musical idioms to a position of dignity and effectiveness in the fields of symphonic and operatic music."[38]

The works of this second stylistic period were the ones that especially fit in with the New Negro musical philosophy of capturing the life, ambitions, struggles, and passions of the Negro race within the "higher" musical forms. They include *Sahdji* (1930), an African ballet for mixed chorus, bass soloist, and orchestra; *Afro-American Symphony* (1931), a traditional four-movement symphony; *A Deserted Plantation* (1933), a three-movement suite for orchestra; *Ebon Chronicle* (1933), an orchestral poem; and *Blue Steel* (1934), a ballet for orchestra, soloists, and chorus. These works, especially *Afro-American Symphony*, were some of the first to help Still attain broad national and international recognition as an American composer.

According to Locke, *Sahdji* was one of the first "vindications" of the "serious use" of an African background and idiom and was an early step toward the development of Negro ballet, which was realized by Katherine Dunham's dance troupe.[39] The text was based on a play by Richard Bruce Nugent, at the time a young Harlem littérateur of about nineteen years old. With some minor editorial modifications, Locke included it in *The New Negro* (1925); but it was when co-editing *Plays of Negro Life* (1927), in which he and co-editor Montgomery Gregory included Nugent's work, that Locke thought of the possibilities of *Sahdji* becoming a ballet. Locke suggested that Nugent expand the piece for that purpose, came up with the idea of an African chanter, and looked up fifty or sixty African proverbs from which Nugent selected those that were interwoven into the text for the ballet.

Increasing the ante for the potential vindication this production could wreak, Locke wanted to be sure the ballet would be set by a black composer rather than by any of the white composers who were "haunting" Harlem for new finds in the newly popular black materials. He originally thought of the African composer Ballanta Taylor, whom Dett's benefactor, George Foster Peabody, had written him about. But he finally selected Still and was persistent in getting him to compose the work. Twice Still sent the manuscript back to Locke saying he could not do it. The first time, Locke mailed it back with a plea that Still continue. The second time, he sent it back by registered mail with no comment at all.[40] With initial hesitance, because of the technical difficulties surrounding the huge cast, Still agreed to compose the work.[41] The ballet premièred under Howard Hanson on May 22, 1931, the last day of the five-day Festival of American Music at the Eastman School of Music.

Locke was unable to attend the première of the ballet, for he felt it would have been too expensive for him to stop by New York City to pick up Nugent and take him to Rochester and then return him home, not to mention the cost of probably having to buy Nugent some clothes, since the last time Locke saw the struggling young writer he looked almost like a tramp.[42] A couple days later, Locke read Olin Downes's review of the première in *The New York Times*. Titillated by the musical "primitivism," Downes wrote: "Mr. Still is a composer of marked talent. Before this, his symphonic score, 'Darker America,' by reason of its exotic color and its emotional vigor, had commended him. The ballet 'Sahdji' is fully as racial in content as the former work, and it appears clearer and not less rich in style." Downes continued, "It is not Negro music diluted with conventions of the white, nor yet is it cast in the forms of negroid expression which has also become conventional. Mr. Still does not indulge in Harlem jazz, but harks back to more primitive sources for brutal, persistent and barbaric rhythms."[43]

Locke told Mason that though the ballet may not be "simple as a primitive thing should be," he was sure it would at least pave the way for something "more truly African."[44] Two days later he wrote to Mason again, repeating his comment about Still's neo-primitivism: "So the ballet was really a great success—and I believe it will be some satisfaction to you—in spite of its not being truly primitive or presented by Negroes for themselves. Still it is a half-way step toward that real goal. If only Still, who really has great talent, could be simplified. I do wish I could have heard his music, to be able to gauge his further possibilities."[45] As I explained in chapter 1, these critical words were for Mason's appeasement only, for Locke later wrote in *Opportunity* that this "colossally elaborate" ballet was proof of Still's "mastery of large technical resources."[46] Thus, during these years of the economic depression when Mason was discouraged because Negro artists were not being true to what she considered their natural primitivity,[47] Locke's faith held out and so did the Renaissance.

Having contributed to the completion of one important act of vindication with the performance of *Sahdji*, Locke next had thoughts of writing a libretto for a black opera.[48] Later he would suggest to Still that the two of them collaborate on a pantomime ballet on Uncle Remus,[49] which would have a chorus in "real African fable style," genuine racial props, and African rhythms.[50] Neither idea, the opera or the ballet, came to fruition, and Locke and Still were never to collaborate; but they remained friends and Locke later arranged other collaborations for Still.

While in 1931 race relations at home and abroad was a depressing topic and the economic depression was deepening, the Renaissance was just beginning to take off for Still. A little over five months after *Sahdji* was premièred on May 22, his most famous work, *Afro-American Symphony,* premièred on October 29 under Howard Hanson at the Eastman School of Music. The many compliments Still received following performances of this popular work, which eventually premièred in France, England, Germany, Belgium, Finland, and Australia, resembled the one he received from his lifelong friend, songwriter Eubie Blake: "I just heard your 'Afro American Symphony' and let me tell how proud I am to say I know you. It was beautiful."[51] Indeed, Blake, like many other blacks of the 1930s and beyond, was proud of the New Negro and prideful that this image of the Negro as a normal American was being presented to the world.

Long before writing this symphony, Still had recognized the musical value of the blues and decided to use a blues melody as the basis for a symphony. When he was ready to begin the work, he decided to create his own melodic theme in a blues idiom rather than employ an extant blues melody.[52] He explained:

> Some forms of Jazz are cheap, monotonous. No one can be blamed for scorning them. But there are also forms of Jazz that are valuable additions to music, forms upon which great symphonies can be built. The Blues, for instance, a purely Negroid and secular expression, are not trivial, despite the homely sentiments of their texts. The pathos of their melodies bespeaks the sincere anguish of lonely hearts. . . .
>
> The entire *Afro-American Symphony* was based on a Blues theme (original with the composer, not borrowed from folk sources), inverted, enlarged and altered as the occasion demanded. Obligingly it assumed a different character in each movement of the symphony, until finally it had expressed many moods. The *Afro-American Symphony* thus demonstrated the inherent dignity of this apparently banal Negroid musical expression.[53]

Still's esteem for the black folk genres he would elevate "to a position of dignity and effectiveness" was evidenced in an article on the spirituals and the blues he wrote for *The New York Amsterdam News* in 1940. There is no evidence in his remarks that his intent to "elevate" this music was indicative of a clandestine contempt for it or for the common folk who created it. To the contrary, Still viewed himself as fulfilling the wishes of his forebears who wished for the advancement of their children and the race as a whole. Wrote Still:

> Nowadays the history of Negro music, chronicled by able musicologists, is available to every student who wishes to visit his public library. There he may learn dates, names of all important composers and interpreters, musical instruments, and the technical details concerning the Negro's contribution to American music on the whole. But what of the ideals, the spirit behind this contribution?
>
> Back of all this musical accomplishment stand our parents, grandparents and great-grandparents, themselves uneducated, but possessed of an overwhelming desire for the advancement of the race and of their own offspring in particular. These are the people, unnamed in histories of music, who sacrificed everything to the attainment of their ideals. These are the people who were close to the creation of spirituals and of blues, which rank among the finest forms of folk music.
>
> These are the people who were strong enough to express in music their joys and sorrows, and to whom God was a living reality. They expressed the drama of the Bible in terms of pure musical beauty, and who shall say that it was not this same quality of unswerving faith that has served to advance the race and bring it safely through its dark hours of adversity?[54]

Still's high regard for the musical legacy of his forebears was not only evidenced in his occasional verbatim use of folk melodies but also in the detailed attention he gave to creating his own melodies in a folk style.

Attempting to demonstrate the inherent dignity of this simple folk music as an act of racial vindication, Still incorporated inflections, instrumentation, forms, and techniques of orchestration reminiscent of the jazz-blues idiom. In the first movement he employs a muted trumpet executing the syncopated blues theme. The syncopation, muted trumpet, and twelve-bar blues form evoke a jazz-blues "feel," as does the use of call and response and portamento (or the "slide" technique), both of which were transferred into black instrumental idioms from the blues and jazz vocal idioms. Still also makes extensive use of double-bass pizzicato in a manner generally used in jazz and known as the "walking bass." In the third movement he employs the tenor banjo, an instrument used in country blues and New Orleans jazz, which Still said he included for the effect of "local color."[55]

In 1934, three years after the première of *Afro-American Symphony*, Still moved to Los Angeles, where he began his third stylistic period and collaborated on several musical projects with Verna Arvey, a Jewish concert pianist and journalist who became his wife five years later. This period, lasting from 1934 to the time of his death in 1978, began the same year that Locke considered the second generation of Renaissance artists to have begun. Still had mastered the "form and technique" and the "mood and spirit" and was now reaching a point where musically he could speak in whatever stylistic idiom was appropriate to the particular subject being addressed. Consequently, it was a period during which Still became increasingly dismayed by those whites, the music critics among them, who wanted the New Negro to remain Old—those whites who supported Negroes working within the musical idioms of the spirituals and jazz but cast "definite aspersions" on black composers trying to rise to a higher compositional level.[56] Clarence Cameron White was reminded of this when he showed the completed score of his opera to a white musician of note. He told James Weldon Johnson that the white musician's first comment was, "Splendid, but you haven't made it funny." White remarked to Johnson, "this gave me an insight into the working of that mind which thinks the Negro must be a 'comic' in any situation."[57]

Still insisted that a subtle but deliberate effort was being made by people like Downes to prevent Negroes from reaping too much glory and that this was being done by attempting to stereotype Negro artists and keep them composing folk music or jazz.[58] Still felt that Negro bands should not be typecast and neither should he. "Many people have been willing to accept a Negro composer who arranges Spirituals, or who idealizes folk tunes," he said. "There are few who will concede his ability as a craftsman when he plows into the field of abstract music."[59] This made Downes, from Still's purview, no better than those white club managers who wanted Negro bands always to play a jungle style of jazz while preferring to hire white bands to play the "sweet" commercial style when the black bands could play that style just as well.[60] Still understood this problem as not simply a domestic one but a global one. That many whites were coming to regard stereotypical portrayals of Negroes as authentic would not help good race relations in this country or in foreign countries.[61] "In short," he concluded, "we would like to see the Negro presented to the world and to America as a normal American."[62]

Among Still's works of this third period are *Three Visions* (1936), a piano suite; *Festive Overture* (1944), for orchestra; *Songs of Separation* (1949), piano-accompanied vocal setting of poems by Arna Bontemps, Countee Cullen, Paul Laurence Dunbar, Langston Hughes, and Philippe-Thoby Marcellin (of Haiti); and *To You America* (1951), for symphonic band. Some of the works in this period that resemble those of the second period in depicting the life, ambitions, struggles, and passions of the Negro race within the "higher" musical forms are the works conductor Leopold Stokowski was referring to when, in 1937, he told Still how important it was that his music had the spirit of both Africa and America in it: "I think it would be good for the public to realize how great is your achievement, and that while you are in every way an American, you are of African origin and that your music is a fusing of African ancestral powers in you with your American birth and environment."[63] Stokowski, who had conducted a number of Still's works over the years, went on to identify the qualities of the "Negro character" that he admired and believed could contribute to American music in the United States and abroad. They were emotional intensity, electrifying rhythm, depth of expression, humor, ecstasy, and impulsiveness.[64]

The works to which Stokowski might have been referring are *Symphony in G Minor* (1937), Still's second symphony; *Lenox Avenue* (1937), a ballet depicting life in Harlem (scenario by Verna Arvey), set for orchestra, chorus, and piano soloist; *And They Lynched Him on a Tree* (1940), for two choruses, contralto soloist, narrator, and orchestra, based on a text by Katherine Garrison Chapin; *Troubled Island* (1941), an opera in three acts (libretto by Langston Hughes), set for orchestra, chorus, eight soloists, and ballet; *In Memoriam: The Colored Soldiers Who Died for Democracy* (1943), for orchestra; and *Suite for Violin and Piano* (1943), based upon works by three Renaissance artists: Richmond Barthe's sculpture titled "African Dancer," Sargent Johnson's painting titled "Mother and Child," and Augusta Savage's sculpture titled "Gamin." In the latter composition, for instance, Still, in an attempt to capture the characteristic of improvisation, which is so basic to folk and popular music of African origin, treated some melodic material in an improvisational manner. Delores Calvin, theatrical editor and secretary of the black-owned Calvin's Newspaper Service, heard the piece and liked it, she said, because its themes and musical development were "so typically Negroid." The melodies were so realistic, she explained, that the sad one made her cry.[65]

Critical response to Still's *Symphony in G Minor,* which was performed by the San Diego Symphony Orchestra under the composer's own baton, perfectly illustrates how, in all of the foregoing compositions of Still's third period, the two-tiered mastery of "form and technique" and "mood and spirit" was intended to work on its hearers by conveying both the rational and the emotional and thereby to undermine the racial essentialism of white fabrication. A reviewer for the San Diego *Tribune,* caught in this web of "mastery," wrote: "Integrity of craftsmanship, as well as the thought and feel and feeling of this very quiet, modest man, left its imprint upon his music, so that his impulse to portray his race, the Negro, as it is today, was clearly perceived in his symphony. We missed the rather wild frenzy which frequently characterizes Negro music, but recognized the new philosophy and temper of the Negro today, a 'desire to give to humanity the best that their African heritage has given them.'"[66]

During this period, Still also began to glean international attention, due in part to performances of his compositions in Europe by the black orchestra conductor Rudolph Dunbar, a native of Guiana who studied music in the United States at the Institute of Musical Art in New York before settling in Europe for further study and a career in conducting. Dunbar, who conducted various of Still's works in England, France, and Germany, gave an entire program of Still's compositions in Paris at the Théâtre des Champs Elysées on November 19, 1945.[67] These and other accomplishments of Still's third period led such concert singers as Roland Hayes, Lillian Evanti, and Mattiwilda Dobbs to write the composer requesting original vocal works which they wished to feature in their concertizing around the country and Europe. Although Marian Anderson was inaccessible to him, even at Dett's attempted mediation,[68] Still continued to receive encouraging plaudits from such distinguished friends as Locke, Handy, and Blake, all of whom kept in regular contact.

III

All the black musical styles and elements that Still intentionally incorporated into his compositions in order to "master" the African "mood and spirit" underscore his definition of Negro music as music that must have some of the rhythmic, melodic, or harmonic characteristics that are typical of Negro music as it is known.[69] This was a definition that avoided essentializing blacks in the tradition of the white patrons and critics of the Renaissance; but Still, like Locke, sometimes seemed to contradict his cultural definition of black music and sound rather essentialist. This is illustrated in one of his essays in which he said the Negro musician could not help but exemplify "to a certain extent" his African heritage. "No matter how academic his training or how straightlaced his view," wrote Still, "*something* of that exotic background will be heard in the music he writes."[70] Locke had argued the same point over a decade earlier when he claimed that "race expression" did not have to be deliberate to be vital, that at its best it never is deliberate. "This was the case with our instinctive and quite matchless folk-art," wrote Locke, "and begins to be the same again as we approach *cultural* maturity in a phase of art that promises now to be fully representative."[71] But we must take seriously Still's phrase "to a certain extent." His comment that "to a certain extent" the Negro composer would always reflect "something" of his African heritage actually helps us understand the entire statement as nonessentialist.

Still's qualifying words "to a certain extent" and "something" also help us understand as nonessentialist his remark a few years later that there is something so fundamentally Negroid about genuine Negro music that no white musician could imitate it: "No matter how extravagant the claims made for white imitations, how pleasing they may be as music, or how much similarity there is in their external aspects, they are at best only imitations."[72] These white imitations would always be superficial, Still believed, despite any external musical features that sounded indigenous, for these imitations would always lack a fundamental and indescribable quality that only Negroes possessed.[73] That "something," as Still described it in his article on the spirituals and the blues for *The New York Amsterdam News,* was the spirit of the ancestors who "possessed an overwhelming desire for the advancement of the race."[74] So, contrary to what is generally presumed about the New Negro, Still was not succumbing to the essentialism of white racialism when he made a comment that intimated that Darius Milhaud's music was at best only an imitation. With probable reference to Milhaud's *La Création du Monde* (1924), a ballet on an African theme in which the French composer attempted to incorporate jazz, Still said he could not fathom why anyone in the world would think of Milhaud and him "in the same breath."[75]

Still was equally nonessentialist and nonimitative of white racialism when he similarly criticized George Gershwin's opera, *Porgy and Bess.* Still remarked to Langston Hughes that Laszlo Halasz, the conductor who was supposed to direct *Troubled Island* for the New York City Opera Company, wanted their opera to be conducted by Alexander Smallens, probably because Smallens had previously conducted *Porgy and Bess.* Still said to

Hughes that he did not want their opera to be seen as being in the same "class" as Gershwin's opera, adding, with regard to Smallens: "He need not think that he can do Still just because he knows how to play Gershwin!"[76] Still was also thinking that no one ought to believe that Gershwin, because of the success of *Porgy and Bess*, was an outstanding exponent or interpreter of Negro folk music; and he said as much in a letter he wrote to an editor of a Hollywood periodical. The editor had commented in print that Still had endorsed Gershwin as being one of the outstanding exponents of Negro folk music, and Still insisted on a retraction, explaining to the editor that he had never made the statement and did not consider it to be true.[77]

Still's implicit point, that Gershwin (and white composers in general) could only "imitate" black music, was made a little more explicit by his wife in a reproachful letter to Dwight D. Eisenhower pursuant to the president's public remark about Gershwin's opera being a force to bring understanding between the races. Arvey wrote to the president:

> As one who has admired many of your actions and statements during recent months, it is with the greatest regret that I write to let you know that many of us cannot agree with your estimate of "Porgy and Bess" as a force to bring understanding between people. Those colored Americans who are striving to advance so that their country can be proud of their achievements and of their loyalty do not feel that this production represents them fairly. And I am sure that many of our Southern friends who are working for brotherhood and inter-racial understanding would not approve of it in that light either.[78]

Had Arvey known Still and his works of his first compositional period, she might have said the same thing to Carl Van Vechten after reading his introduction to the 1927 edition of James Weldon Johnson's *Autobiography of an Ex-Colored Man*. Van Vechten had written, "So the young hero of this Autobiography determines to develop the popular music of his people into a more serious form, thus foreseeing by twelve years the creation of The Rhapsody in Blue by George Gershwin."[79]

By way of reference to Hall Johnson, the black choral director who performed with Still in Eubie Blake's original *Shuffle Along* orchestra, it can be shown further that Renaissance artists often sounded as though they were essentializing blacks when that was not the case. In a 1936 review of Gershwin's *Porgy and Bess*, Johnson detailed why white composers failed to understand and therefore express the authenticity of black culture. It is clear that Johnson considered the key to creating authentic black music to be intimate knowledge of the culture and not an inherent and distinct biology, ontology, and history. He wrote:

> A good Negro opera, however, must be not only good opera but must be written in an authentic Negro musical language and sung and acted in a characteristic Negro style. Perhaps it is Mr. Gershwin's fault if he has not written a good opera, but he can hardly be blamed if he has not quite satisfied our notion of what a good Negro opera should be. This would require more time and application than any composer not a specialist in this line could be expected to put into it. The informing spirit of Negro music is not to be caught and understood merely by listening to the tunes and Mr. Gershwin's much-publicized visits to Charleston for local color do not amount even to a matriculation in the preparatory-school that he needed for his work. Nothing can be more misleading, especially to an alien musician, than a *few* visits to Negro revivals and funerals. Here one encounters the "outside" at its most external. The obvious sights and sounds are only the foam which has no meaning without the beer. And here let it be said that it is not the color nor the aloofness of the white investigator which keeps him on the outside. It is the powerful tang and thrill of the "foam" which excites him prematurely and makes him rush away too soon,—to write books and music on a subject of which he has not even begun to scratch the surface. It is to be regretted that the whites who have remained longer and learned more seem to count no serious musicians among their number.
>
> Mr. Gershwin has at his command, however, a certain Negroid flavor which has lent piquancy to some of his earlier compositions and which shows up to occasional advantage in his opera. But, while we agree that a composition in a definite racial vein must not necessarily reek in every single measure with that particular style, still we feel that, in a work of the proportions of *Porgy and Bess,* there should be more than just an occasional flavor.[80]

Johnson went on to say that *Porgy and Bess* was not a Negro opera but was Gershwin's idea of what a Negro opera should be.[81] He concluded his article by remarking:

It is possible, and not improbable, that an injection of genuine Negro folk-culture may be good for the anaemia of the American theatre. If so, who will prove it? Only we who sowed the seed can know the full and potent secret of the flower. The fact that others try to master it and fail (while we are making up our minds what to do with it), should not fill us with resentment, but with pride and fresh determination. With the greatest patience and the best of intentions, all they can ever grasp is—a handful of leaves.[82]

That it is only those who sowed the seed who can know the full secret of the flower was the point maestro Rudolph Dunbar was making to Still following one of his many European performances of *Afro-American Symphony*. He said a pianist, who had performed a Beethoven concerto under his baton that evening, later commented favorably on Still's piece: "Fine work that Grant Still Symphony; I like it very much; that is what Gershwin wanted to say when he wrote the Rhapsody in Blue." Dunbar said he found it remarkable that the pianist had made the comment because he had been saying the very same thing in various lectures he had given on Still's work.[83] In fact, the following month, in his next correspondence with Still, Dunbar stated the point about the symphony as though it were his original thought: "I'm happy to be the first conductor to introduce it in a public performance in England. It is going to take the place of Rhapsody in Blue. That is what Gershwin wanted to say when he wrote Rhapsody in Blue, but he didn't know how to express himself in that idiom at that time."[84]

The more we look at what Still's contemporaries of the Negro Renaissance had to say about whites trying to compose or perform black music, the more it becomes clear that their criticisms do not lay in the racist essentialism of their oppressors but in the fact that whites dabbled in black culture only long enough to imitate (or steal) the external characteristics of black art. Zora Neale Hurston, an acquaintance of the Stills, commented to this effect, stating that whites wrongly think Negroes are easily imitated, when, contrariwise, she had never seen a white performance of Negro music that was entirely realistic. "And God only knows what the world has suffered from the white damsels who try to sing Blues," she added.[85] Thus, there was a consensus among Still and many of his Renaissance contemporaries that only black musicians had the cultural and experiential capacity to create and perform genuine black music.

Blacks in America had this capacity because they tended to be raised in segregated black communities and therefore within a black cultural and experiential environment. Therefore, Still also believed that black composers who would just be honest with themselves would naturally compose black music without consciously striving to do so. Black composers who were not honest with themselves—the black composers who averted a self-conscious racialism—would not necessarily produce Negro music. "In order to be Negro music," Still insisted, "music has to have some of the characteristics of Negro music. You can't just have a black putting something down on paper and have it become black music."[86] What was Still's philosophical stance, then? Did he, in the early part of his career, believe that all music written by all Negro composers naturally exuded a certain racial character, while in later years believing that specific attention must be given to express that "exotic background?" The answer may be the former but with the qualification of a slightly revised version of the latter, namely that the "specific attention" black composers had to render to their art to derive black music was simply their being "honest" with themselves—honest about their experiences and their roots in black and African cultures.

Despite Still's belief that black composers should be honest with themselves and his quest to build an American music on the historical base of black music, Still did not believe black music idioms should be forced on black composers. He himself wished to and did pay homage to the "unnamed in histories of music" who were close to the creation of the spirituals and the blues, but he did not wish to be limited artistically to arranging folk music, as he felt Dett more or less was. He indicated that in no uncertain terms his own regard for Negro folk music was high but that there were times he resented the increasing attention being given Negro folk creations since this tended to result in a demand that other Negro composers "hew closely to the line established by the folk."[87] Arvey made her husband's point more bluntly in a letter to black music critic Nora Holt, but she just as well could have been speaking to Charlotte Mason or Carl Van Vechten: "Some people . . . are still emphasizing *Negro, Negro, Negro*—which is all good, except that they stop there. They don't go into the big, important field—which we must go into, if we are to play a part in making America a land where all of us will be brothers."[88] Many of the Renaissance artists felt this way. When a white man told Claude McKay that with his talent he had a wonderful opportunity to write poetry with Negro rhythms in it, McKay retorted defensively that he had as much right to the literary heritage of Shakespeare, Keats, Wordsworth, and Milton as the white man did.[89]

Still's impulse toward integration and his resistance to being musically "segregated" was communicated to several concert singers who requested arrangements of black folk songs from him. In 1943 Roland Hayes wrote Still requesting some music from the one he called "the first great composer of our group." He requested an arrangement of spirituals for orchestra and voice or possibly an original composition of characteristically Negro origin—not jazz, he clarified, "but something of highly religious and spiritual content."[90] Still responded immediately; and after suggesting some of his compositions that were not Negroid in the way Hayes probably expected, he stated his position: "Just as you have identified yourself with music to the extent that people think of you primarily as a great musician rather than as a racial singer, so I believe it is possible for the Negro composer to develop as an artist rather than as a racial product, although none of us want to forsake our heritage entirely. This heritage can and does form a wonderful basis for everything we do."[91]

That Still wanted to expand beyond the limitations of the racial terrain in the pursuit of "culture citizenship," but was not interested in forsaking his racial heritage because it formed the aesthetic basis of his composing, helps us understand his comment three years later to black concert soprano Hortense Love. Love had written Still requesting some arrangements of spirituals and possibly Haitian folk songs or even an original art song of Negroid character which she could perform during her concertizing, for she had just been contracted to give a series of concerts at major universities which had specifically requested her to render folk music peculiar to her race.[92] Still responded as though he were vicariously battling the essentialist stereotypes of blacks by Olin Downes and his likes. He told Love that she was free to consider his book of six spirituals published by W. C. Handy's company but that he preferred that she perform his art songs. "I feel that today too much emphasis is placed on Negro folk music which, although beautiful," he wrote, "is certainly not the Negro's only contribution to music."[93] In this regard, Still must have been pleased to hear from black concert soprano Mattiwilda Dobbs that in her concerts in Sweden she had been performing both his arranged spirituals and his arias from *Troubled Island*.[94]

Still's friend and one-time collaborator, Renaissance littérateur Arna Bontemps, agreed with Still's New Negro philosophy and told him so. "In your last letter you said something that I strongly approve [of]. You mentioned not letting the Negro element get out of proportion in your work. In fact, I'm coming to think that whatever we put into composition of our Negro background might better be allowed to creep in subconsciously. Otherwise we are bound and enslaved, trying to write in this or that manner because it is the fitting thing for a Negro artist to do. I think a good many

Negro artists are beginning to feel the effects of standing on one foot in order to hold a pose."[95] Around the same time James Baldwin wrote to Locke from Paris at the beginning of his writing career, saying that he was trying to break out of the literary typecasting of Negroes: "I'm sick, in a way, of being continually expected to write about Negroes and am afraid of the easy success such a road can possibly offer."[96]

Still also knew about having to stand on one foot in order to hold a pose—namely that it was an uncomfortable position to be in. He resigned from the position of music supervisor for the hit film *Stormy Weather* (1943) because of such discomfort—particularly the stereotyping on the part of his superiors:

> Late in 1942 I was approached to act as Supervisor of Music on the Fox all-colored film called "Stormy Weather," then titled "Thanks, Pal." I was told that the film had a very high purpose, and that it would employ some of our finest colored artists. That was the original plan. However, when I came to the studio the music director, Al Newman, began a systematic plan to discard every bit of work I did and to ignore my suggestions, on one pretext or another. . . . Naturally, I did not approve of Newman's ideas that in order to be authentic, Negro music had to be crude and Negro dancing had to be sexy. I knew from experience that those are the sorts of misconceptions that help to breed misconceptions in other people's minds and indirectly influence the lives of our thirteen million people.[97]

Still continued with his criticism of those white film executives who insisted on maintaining the stereotype of Negro music:

> Consequently each musical director has decided what Negro music should be in films and, right or wrong, he will stick to it. Unfortunately, in the majority of cases, no account is taken of the richness and variety of Negro music, music that ranges from an untutored folk expression to the most sophisticated symphonic forms. Invariably the type of music selected to represent the colored man is the folky sort, or the jazz element and all too often this is performed crudely in an effort to give what is amusingly termed "authenticity." A Negro choral director told me that film people always criticized her choruses on the ground that they were "too refined." Yet she employed colored people, singing Negro

The Terrible Handicap of Working as a Negro Composer

music without affectation. Colored people now wonder why, if there must be a "stereotype," why not a "stereotype" based on the best in Negro life and all its art-phases?[98]

In this regard Still stood opposed to the views of the white patrons and critics of the Renaissance, who were folk purists who insisted that all composed black music remain close to its folk roots. Tracing the source of this problematic position to the time of minstrelsy, Still said:

> To an extent, the Negro has always been influenced by the set standard of what the white man expects him to do. This, in music, has not been easy to evade. At the outset, it was expected that the Negro artist be a clown, and that he thus help to relieve the boredom of his audiences. Then the Fisk Jubilee Singers made it known that Spirituals were a dignified addition to the concert stage. Henceforward, all colored singers were supposed to sing Spirituals as a matter of course; all colored composers worthy of the name were supposed to transcribe and arrange them. Again, it took intelligent pioneering to get out of that rut—to show that we do admire and love our own Spirituals, yet that we are capable of interpreting other music more than "acceptably" and that our composers can create music in the abstract for the world to enjoy.[99]

Although Still fought against racial stereotypes, including the notion that black composers must "hew closely to the line established by the folk," he did not oppose "segregated" concerts of "serious" Negro music, such as the concert of his music that Rudolph Dunbar conducted at the Théâtre des Champs Elysées in Paris in 1945. Similarly, when in 1946 Dunbar, with Still's help, had been contracted to make his American debut conducting "serious" black music at the Hollywood Bowl, Still was very supportive of the "Negro culture night" being planned. On the other hand, P. L. Prattis, executive editor of *The Pittsburgh Courier*, who was helping to organize Dunbar's visit to the United States, was fearful of an all-Negro program. He said he did not want Dunbar "narrowly grooved into a Negro performer of things Negro."[100] Still told Prattis he disagreed.[101] In fact, both he and his wife were very disappointed when Dorothy Maynor, who had been invited to sing on the program, said she would only sing two French arias, two German songs, and a song each by Samuel Coleridge-Taylor and Richard Hageman. This seemed to be the kind of point Locke was making about the ambitious and well-trained black artist who sensed the threat of being isolated in a musical ghetto.[102] This was in fact Arvey's assessment of Maynor, that she probably believed the all-Negro program would "segregate" her. Arvey wrote:

> But to what lengths are we going to let our fear of segregation lead us? This was going to be something done on a very high cultural plane, and if everyone is so eager to give all-Negro concerts of Jazz, why shouldn't we show the world once, when some big white organization like this is willing to finance it, what colored people can accomplish in the higher brackets? In other words, will we let our fear of segregation make us ashamed that we are colored? My husband is afraid of segregation when it involves a nasty stereotype, but he feels that a program of this sort could do a great deal of good.[103]

The length to which blacks could let the fear of segregation lead them is the length to which Jean Toomer took it in deciding to "withdraw from all things which emphasize or tend to emphasize racial or cultural divisions," a remark he made to James Weldon Johnson when Johnson asked Toomer to contribute some of his poetry to the anthology he was compiling, *The Book of American Negro Poetry*.[104] This actually was not the length to which Maynor intended to go, however; for, true to "form," she was at least planning to perform one song by the black English composer, Samuel Coleridge-Taylor. In fact, the strategy used by Hayes, Dett, Maynor, and most other New Negroes of the concert stage, was the strategy that dominated that evening of August 22, 1946. It was a "Negro culture night," indeed, but it did not end up being an "all-Negro" concert in the "higher brackets." Still's *Afro-American Symphony* was featured, but Dunbar also conducted a work by American composer William Schuman. Similarly, William Gillespie sang "Old Man River" as well as a Franz Schubert song. The black group called the Luvenia Nash Singers, filling in for Maynor whose mother had recently died, sang a series of spirituals as well as an excerpt from an Italian opera.

The Renaissance strategy of the "mastery of form" had not changed, then. Akin to the programs of the Hampton choir (under Dett), Roland Hayes, Maynor, and Dunbar in Europe, the classical works from the pens of black composers were always strategically rendered alongside the classical works of the European greats as a means of pushing for "culture citizenship." A reporter for *The California Eagle*, a black Los Angeles paper, concluded: "It was an auspicious event in the enlightening of the world to the artistry of Negroes in the concert field."[105]

<h1 style="text-align:center">IV</h1>

Perhaps the composition that best illustrates the debut of the second-generation Renaissance composer—the New Negro composer who could write in whatever style was appropriate for the occasion, avoid being held to a musical ghetto, and still reflect his racial heritage without forcing it—was the theme music Still was commissioned to write for the 1939–40 New York World's Fair. In this event of racial vindication was an illustration of Dett's comment that though the artist who makes pencil sketches may be every bit as artistic as the one who sculpts marble, it is the latter artist who uses the larger media whose name will be more highly regarded.[106] Indeed it was so, for while Harry T. Burleigh rendered a program of spirituals at the fair's Temple of Religion, Still, by virtue of the fact that he was a symphonist, wreaked the greater "vindication" by being commissioned to write the fair's theme music, an accomplishment of importance to the New Negro movement which was reported in both *Opportunity* and *The Crisis*.[107]

The "vindication" wreaked by this event was all the sweeter because the committee that selected Still to be the composer of the fair's theme music did not even know he was black. The all-white committee listened to anonymous recordings of compositions and agreed unanimously that the composer of *Lenox Avenue* and *From a Deserted Plantation*, whoever he was, seemed to be the most capable of expressing musically the tone of the theme exhibit. That composer turned out to be Still, and the letter of commission came to him early in 1938 from the chairman of the theme committee, Robert Kohn:

> On behalf of the Board of Design of the New York World's Fair 1939 I am writing to ask you whether you would be interested in composing some music for us. The assignment we are considering is an interesting one, and I believe it would afford an excellent opportunity for a composer to write an effective score.
>
> Here is the idea in brief: The theme of the Fair, "Building the World of Tomorrow," is to be architecturally expressed in the Theme Building, which consists of an obelisk and a globe, or perisphere, 180 feet in diameter. Inside the perisphere there will

be an exhibit presenting part of the theme in dramatic form illustrating the prevailing interdependence of all people in the modern world. . . .

An original score must be written for this Theme Exhibit, and while the music will be of short duration (about six minutes), it will occupy an important position at the very key-point of the entire Fair.[108]

Still would be paid $400 when a rough draft of the score was completed, at which time his expenses to New York would be covered for a consultation. An additional $1,400 would be paid to him when the work was finished.

Still scribbled a note to himself on Kohn's letter which was to be shared with Kohn regarding the musical idiom he deemed appropriate for the theme music—one of a rather "universal character" that is modern in harmonic structure but not extreme. Still immediately wrote back to Kohn enthusiastically accepting the offer and sharing his ideas regarding how best to capture the spirit of human interdependence. Kohn responded, "Your idea of using a universal musical idiom, rather than one that expresses only one or two of our national elements, seems a sound one. So does your thought of making it 'modern in harmonic structure but not ultra-modern.'"[109]

The music Still was to compose would comprise the background music for the "World of Tomorrow" exhibit created by Henry Dreyfuss. The exhibit would be a continuous show, each cycle lasting the six minutes it took for approximately eight hundred visitors at a time to be carried around and down the sphere on two revolving ring-shaped platforms. What the visitors would see on their ride would be *the* modern industrial city named "Democracity," which would be modeled by a team of architects and engineers.[110] What they would hear would be a symphonic poem with a choral finale written by a New Negro, a Renaissance man. "It seems to me that this must be the first time, musically speaking, that a colored man has ever been asked to write something extremely important that does not necessarily have to be Negroid," Still wrote back in response to Locke's note of congratulations, "and I must admit that I can't help but be proud of the distinction, and I only hope that I can do well enough to live up to expectations."[111]

While Still must have enjoyed the challenge of composing in a "universal musical idiom" in an effort to capture the spirit of human interdependence, he continued in his third compositional period to pay homage to the folk culture of his ancestors by arranging spirituals. In 1937 he published *Twelve Negro Spirituals* for voice and piano, in 1961 *Three Rhythmic Spirituals* for mixed chorus and band, and in 1963 *Folk Suite for Band*. None of these works included spirituals arranged in hymnic form as though they were Christian hymns, for Still considered the hymnic style to be unbecoming to the spirituals.[112] Rather, he chose to enrich the spirituals with colorful harmonies so they would constitute a new musical experience for his listeners. In addition to composing these "serious" musical settings for the spirituals, Still composed "serious" settings for the folk songs of African peoples elsewhere in the world—Peru, Brazil, Mexico, Argentina, Jamaica, and Haiti, as well as for the folk songs of Louisiana Creoles and Native Americans. His use of this diversity of folk material is illustrated in his four chamber pieces titled *Folk Suite* (1962) and his four string quartets titled *Little Folk Suite* (1968).

Still may have refused to have all of his compositions "hew closely to the line established by the folk," but much of his musical output naturally contained some expression of his racial heritage. Furthermore, Still's self-conscious racialism did not manifest itself only in his use of folk tunes, but also in his thematizing of political issues relevant to black people. These works of Still's third compositional period, Renaissance works beyond the pale of the 1920s vogue of the Negro, can be understood as running parallel to the protest literature of Richard Wright, Chester B. Himes, Ralph Ellison, and James Baldwin, which also postdated 1934. One of these works from Still's pen was *And They Lynched Him on a Tree* (1940), an oratorio based on a ballad of the same title by Katherine Garrison Chapin, who was the secretary to the nearly blind Charlotte Mason. If anything could cause a black composer to be "too narrowly grooved" and typecasted as a radical (a communist) like Paul Robeson and Du Bois, it was Chapin's poem, for this work far surpassed the subtlety of Dett's "mastery of form" in *The Ordering of Moses* or when, during the 1930 European tour, he had his choir sing "No More Auction Block for Me" before officials of Belgium's colonial government. At the time Still set Chapin's ballad, southern white vigilantes were still wreaking the "white death" upon black men and boys who were alleged to have sexually assaulted white women, and the United States Congress still had not passed an anti-lynching bill.

It was Locke who brought the controversial poem to the attention of Still. He told Still that the poem was an epic indictment against lynching by way of pure poetry rather than propaganda and that he was the ideal composer.[113] Still agreed to do the work and he set the poem for orchestra, narrator, contralto soloist, and two choruses—one black and one white (Chapin's suggestion).[114] Chapin, in turn, was excited that Still was setting her poem. Having brought the score with her from New York upon a visit to Still's home in Los Angeles while she and her husband were out west, Chapin felt strongly that as artists she and Still "spoke the same language." She told him, "I have great hopes that the objective for which we are both striving will sing and grow in your being until it bursts forth spontaneously in music that will move people, so that it will stir something in their better selves, not because of propaganda, but because it is great music."[115] Several weeks later Chapin wrote to Still again, saying: "To put into great music a protest against lynching is a fine patriotic thing for an American composer to be doing right now!"[116] When Still's score was completed, Chapin brought a copy to Locke for him to see. Locke found it to be beautifully written and was struck by Still's inscription at the end of the score: "With humble thanks to God, the source of inspiration."[117]

Well before the piece was actually completed, negotiations were being made for the composition to be conducted by Artur Rodzinski and his New York Philharmonic-Symphony. But after the second Great World War had broken out, Rodzinski became disillusioned to the point of nearly giving up the idea of performing the piece because of its depressing topic. With Chapin's encouragement, however, he conceded to go on with its performance.[118] Three weeks before the première, Locke wrote a lengthy letter to Charlotte Mason, commenting that on the day of the performance they would witness "one of the few real vindications of the Negro." He continued:

> This comes just at a time when it is necessary to tell America what is wrong with democracy. I do hope that Mrs. Roosevelt will be there. She already knows of course, but in some way I cannot but think it is meant to drive the realization straight to her heart, and through her to the President, who now has the chance, if he will seize it, of being the second Abraham Lincoln, and of really saving American democracy.
>
> Lincoln is so often criticized for saying he put union first and the abolition of slavery next. Had he lived to guide the Reconstruction, he would have shown what that meant by doing real justice to the South, and thus making the position of the Negro safer. Now if Roosevelt really means to defend America, he must fight for his program internally—and that and only that will bolster the nation to its proper defense from external enemies. Hitler is a real scourge of God, and I hope the lesson will be learned to the extermination of imperialism and all forms of human exploitation.[119]

The Terrible Handicap of Working as a Negro Composer

Still's *And They Lynched Him on a Tree* was premièred by the New York Philharmonic-Symphony on June 24, 1940, during a concert devoted to the theme of democracy. The concert included a performance of Roy Harris's *Challenge 1940*, which was textually based on excerpts from the Preamble to the United States Constitution; and John Latouche's and Earl Robinson's *Ballad for America*, sung by Paul Robeson, who premièred the piece over the radio the previous year. The soloist for the "lynching piece" was Louise Burge, a music alumnus of Howard University, whom Locke wanted to sing the part. Still and his wife listened to a radio broadcast of the performance because they were unable to afford the expense of traveling across country to New York, but Locke was among the thirteen thousand people in the audience at Lewisohn Stadium.

In private Locke told Still that the piece was wonderful and destined to be an American classic.[120] His public assessment of the performance, documented in a review he published in *Opportunity*, was that the performance, in giving a crisis-ridden American democracy a much-needed heroic challenge, expanded the composition's particular theme of Negro tragedy into an inspiring plea for a more complete democracy.[121] Mason read Locke's essay in *Opportunity* and expressed her satisfaction that lynching had been dealt a blow. "You know Alain how this horror of lynching has been raging through my mind for more than forty years and how I have never stopped working on it." Regarding Still and Chapin having created this work together (he being black and she being white), Mason said further to Locke: "this combination establishes a point of view on democracy that has never been put before the world until this hour."[122]

While Rodzinski was initially unsure about performing the piece because of its "depressing topic," Leopold Stokowski, then conductor of the National Broadcasting Company (NBC) Symphony Orchestra, was put in the position of nearly having to perform the work over NBC's opposition.[123] Even after agreeing to broadcast the piece, according to Chapin, NBC was still frightened of the subject.[124] The broadcast went on, however, airing April 14, 1942, and the performance was a great success. Stokowski's assessment of the composition was that it was one of Still's greatest works.[125] The press's report was that the composition was being called by many "the most powerful utterance since *Uncle Tom's Cabin*."[126] That was a fitting comment given the explicitly critical nature of the work, for James Weldon Johnson had said the same thing about W. E. B. Du Bois's *The Souls of Black Folk*.[127]

Next, Still collaborated with Chapin on *Plain-Chant for America*, a poem that reaffirms American democracy and patriotic faith in America's future, which Still set for baritone soloist and orchestra. Still was originally planning to write a suite for the New York Philharmonic-Orchestra centennial but remembered he had Chapin's poem, which he felt had to be set and performed. Even though he had completed the suite for the New York Philharmonic, Still convinced conductor John Barbirolli to take the *Plain-Chant* instead. Excited about the work's importance, Still invited Locke to its premier on October 22, 1941, and Locke wrote back that he would not miss it. Locke said, "It is a most significant thing—quite symbolic really—both in the nature of the collaboration and the spiritual significance of the universal appeal, above race, to common denominator democracy."[128] Mason had nothing but confidence, she told Locke, that Still was a "very great creative musician" and would develop the work into a "broader expression" than would be possible with the one baritone voice, as beautiful as she believed that would be. She said further to Locke that she wished she had the money to push Still.[129] It is good that Mason did not have the money to patronize him, for Still developed the work as he alone saw fit, unhampered by anyone's requirements. Evidently the one baritone voice was sufficient, for Locke commented to Still that he really liked the composition—its words, design, and melodic themes—and that Burleigh, who was sitting with him, also liked the piece a lot.[130]

Still's requiem, *In Memoriam: The Colored Soldiers Who Died for Democracy* (1943), also showed this Renaissance artist to be well-connected with the experiences and issues of blacks in America without having to "hew closely to the line established by the folk." The piece was commissioned in 1943 by the League of Composers to be performed by the New York Philharmonic-Orchestra and aired over the CBS radio network. The letter of commission informed Still that he was one of twenty composers being invited to write a patriotic work for orchestra three to five minutes in length for the purpose of integrating the music of "serious" composers with the aims and feelings of the war days.[131] Still viewed this as an opportunity to pay tribute to the black soldiers fighting and dying for democracy,[132] yet he insisted that it was the "human need" that impelled him to write the piece and not any political interest.[133]

Although the requiem had no text or program, it did help accomplish Still's ideal of contributing to interracial understanding and thereby the "vindication of the Negro," perhaps even more so than the "lynching piece." Chapin herself could hardly find the words to tell Still how much she liked the composition. "How beautifully fine music can say what needs to be said these days," she said.[134] Not only could Still feel pleased with the fact that the critics had given the work high acclaim and that he had received many calls from people who were enchanted with its performance,[135] but also because some white Americans were deeply touched by the composition's message. One such person was a woman of Syracuse, New York, who wrote Still a letter of gratitude after hearing the broadcast performance, a letter that so evidenced the attainment of racial "vindication" that Still released it to the syndicated black press. The letter began with the salutation "Dear Sir":

> I have just listened to your symphonic tribute called "In Memoriam: The Colored Soldiers Who Died for Democracy" played by the Boston Symphony Orchestra. I wish I might convey to you the thrilling gratification which I felt in the thought that an American had produced so fine a composition. . . .
>
> Your composition was dedicated to the boys of your race who have given their lives for their country; the gratitude of their fellow-Americans belongs to these boys in equal measure. And I trust that those who return may indeed find a democracy of tolerance and unity—an America, with liberty and justice for all.[136]

An act of vindication, indeed; but liberty and justice for all certainly would not be reached before Still could get an opera performed, he must have been thinking. To get one of his operas performed would accomplish the ultimate "vindication" that Locke had dreamed of ever since the performance of *Sadhji* in 1931. Clarence Cameron White had the same thing in mind for his opera, *Ouanga*. In a letter to James Weldon Johnson, congratulating him on the publication of *Negro Americans, What Now?*, which he had just finished reading, White said: "I am especially interested in your expressions about overcoming the stereotype ideas of what we can and should do. I think you know that one thought was back of the writing of my opera; i.e. giving our qualified singers and actors a vehicle by which they might show their gifts in a field quite apart from the accepted American idea of the Negro and comedy on the stage." White continued, "I have no illusions that 'Ouanga' is a masterpiece, but it does, I believe, represent a step forward in what I might term a racial expression."[137] Johnson wrote back to White thanking him for his note of congratulations and saying: "It gratifies me that you picked out what I think to be the strongest idea in the book—the breaking down of stereotyped ideas through a means of artistic agencies. Each time a Negro writes a great poem, a fine novel, or composes a noble piece of music, or paints a great picture, he is helping to smash the stereotypes."[138]

Unlike concert contralto Portia White, whom Delores Calvin criticized for wanting to wait for the doors of the Metropolitan Opera Company to open naturally to blacks,[139] Still tried to elbow his way in, knowing that otherwise he would be waiting a hundred years for those doors to open naturally. Despite his efforts to get in, however, Still repeatedly failed with the Metropolitan. On one occasion, he said in a letter of 1939 to Robert Kohn, chairman of the committee that commissioned him to write the theme music for the 1939–40 New York World's Fair, that he suspected that his opera *Troubled Island* was rejected by the Metropolitan Opera Company on account of his color.[140] He had already had *Blue Steel*, his first opera, rejected by the opera company a few years earlier.[141] Now, following a standard review of *Troubled Island,* another had been rejected.[142] Kohn made some inquiries through a friend associated with the opera company, so he said, and reported to Still that his conclusion about racism was unfounded. He claimed that the examination of his opera was made by someone who did not even know him or that he was a Negro. Even if it had been known, Kohn said confidently, "it would have made no difference." Drawing to a close, Kohn said admonishingly: "Under the circumstances I hardly think that it would serve any purpose to press the matter further. After all, artistic judgment is a thing that cannot be debated or argued about."[143] Carl Van Vechten was not any more helpful or insightful. He told Arna Bontemps, who relayed the message to Still, that there would be significant production problems with his opera, pointing out the difficulties and costs of adding such a work to the schedule of the Metropolitan Opera Company.[144]

After Still's *Southern Interlude* lost in a contest sponsored by the Metropolitan in 1946, a contest that would have almost guaranteed a performance of the opera, Still thought to himself that racism had again struck. He believed this to be a conclusion that was not "fanciful" but inevitable based on numerous evidences.[145] Naturally his wife understood the obstacles her husband faced as a black man in white America and concurred with him that there really existed people of influence who considered opera-writing too high an artistic endeavor for a Negro.[146] One man who agreed with Arvey and publicized his views was Dick Campbell, former singer in Harlem and Los Angeles speakeasies and Broadway performer who later organized a number of black theater groups. In an article published just prior to the première of *Troubled Island* by the New York City Opera Company in 1949, Campbell asked rhetorically: "How long will the hard-pressed Met continue to by-pass Negro artists, and yet have the crust to make a radio plea for funds from the 'general public' which includes nearly twenty million Americans of color? How long will this august institution subscribe to the policy of Constitution Hall? How long will it continue to bring hundreds of slightly talented mediocre aliens of Axis countries to its roster in preference to those whose heritage is deeply rooted in the building of America?"[147] It would be almost a decade before a Negro artist would even be admitted to sing with the Metropolitan. That person was Marian Anderson, who in January 1955 sang a role in a Verdi opera.

When it was first published in New York's newspapers in 1944 that Still's opera was to première under the New York City Opera Company, Still was fast at work getting the chorus, orchestra, and solo parts completed. Arvey told Locke that if the production would go according to the present plans, it would be the most important accomplishment for Negro culture that had ever been attempted at home or abroad. Of her husband she said, with reference to librettist Langston Hughes: "He is not only going to show the world that Negroes can sing such music, but that Negroes can create such music, and such fine poetry."[148] That important event of racial "vindication" would have to wait for several years, however, since the attempt to raise funds to underwrite the opera failed. Thus, by the time *Troubled Island* was about to première in March 1949, a rather worried Still had been waiting thirty-seven years for this occasion—the première of an opera from his pen.[149] The performance of *Troubled Island* was certainly a fulfillment of Locke's petition over two decades earlier for blacks "to create serious drama that gives classic development to folk spirit and materials" and thereby to undermine the false stereotypes of Negroes.[150]

Still was present for the opera's première and thought it was a great success. However, when the critics were rather unflattering in their reviews, Still thought to himself that the cause had certainly been the racial prejudice of whites who were still resisting the onslaught of the New Negro.[151] The white American composer, Paul Creston, seemed to be one of those whites—relieved, it seemed, at Still's failure to make a hit; for he concluded a letter to Arvey saying rather flippantly about the première of her husband's opera: "Better luck next time."[152] There would be no next time, for luck was not what Still believed he needed. Better racial conditions, an acceptance of the New Negro, was what he believed he needed. The decades to come were to promise nothing more that might change Still's perception regarding racism in America: In 1960 the Metropolitan Opera Company rejected his opera titled *Costaso*,[153] and in 1964 *Highway 1, U.S.A.*[154] Thus the year 1949 was to prove to be the climactic point in the opera-writing career of a Renaissance man who had dreamed of writing opera ever since he was a youth.

Notwithstanding this one small failure, if we can even call it that, the Negro Renaissance was a success. Like Dett who, after a successful choir tour of Europe in 1930, lost the battle to keep his job at Hampton Institute but won the war in contributing significantly to the "vindication of the Negro"; so did Still lose the battle, with regard to his opera-writing career, yet win the war via his many important "firsts." The success of the Negro Renaissance is evidenced by the fact that Still's accomplishments made it easier for black composers of the younger generation to practice their trade without needing to fear, as Hale Smith had put it, the implied image of inferiority in the expression "Negro composer." Additionally, because of Still's two-tiered "mastery" and his resistance to those who opposed this New Negroness, his compositions helped chip away at the social and essentialist color line. So, because of his achievements and longevity as a recognized composer of "serious" music and his having paved the way for the younger generations of black composers with his many "firsts," Still was an important Renaissance man who contributed to the "vindication of the Negro." The Renaissance was no failure, then, and music was an important part of its success.

Chapter 4

A Problem Which Could Be Solved by the Simple Rules of Justice

So, when the white race assumes as a hypothesis that it is the main object of creation and that all things else are merely subsidiary to its well-being, sophism, subterfuge, perversion of conscience, arrogance, injustice, oppression, cruelty, sacrifice of human blood all are required to maintain the position and its dealings with other races become indeed a problem, a problem which, if based on a hypothesis of common humanity, could be solved by the simple rules of justice.

—*The Autobiography of an Ex-Colored Man*

I

Now that I have argued that black music, in terms of the philosophy of some of its creators and performers and in terms of the actual product, belongs not at the periphery but at the center of discussion about the Negro Renaissance, I will bring another interpreter of the Renaissance back into the discussion—Houston Baker. Baker's *Modernism and the Harlem Renaissance* (1987) will help me further contest the several scholars who argue that the Renaissance failed, particularly historians Nathan Huggins and David Levering Lewis. Baker's criticism of Huggins is that to begin an account of the Renaissance with the question of why it failed is naturally going to result in a negative account: "To ask *why* the renaissance failed is to agree, at the very outset, that the twenties did not have profoundly beneficial effects for areas of Afro-American discourse that we have only recently begun to explore in depth."[1] To Baker's dismay, Huggins, by the end of his book, concludes that the Renaissance failed because of its inability to produce a modern art that was not "provincial," a word Baker takes to mean "old-fashioned" or "moribound."[2] Huggins says forthrightly that when the 1930s commenced, the Renaissance had ended and the creation of the New Negro had failed.[3] By this he necessarily means failure not only in Harlem but in such cities as Philadelphia, Washington, Atlanta, Chicago, and Nashville—cities that in 1929, the year of the stock market crash, Locke identified as having joined the cultural awakening of the Renaissance.[4]

Although Huggins's verdict is an echo of Harold Cruse's verdict four years earlier in *The Crisis of the Negro Intellectual* (1967),[5] it is Huggins who first sets down a protracted argument in a specific study on the Renaissance. According to Huggins, the Negro Renaissance started around 1919 and burgeoned in the mid-1920s, only to be squelched by the Great Depression, which brought the movement to an end by 1931. Huggins says the Depression abruptly caused people to concentrate on the essentials of living rather than on the aesthetics of black culture, which resulted in the end of the "promoted culture" of the Renaissance.[6]

David Levering Lewis dates the Renaissance from around 1919 to 1932, having drawn the same conclusion as Huggins regarding the devastation of the country's economic crisis. In the final chapter of his book, *When Harlem Was in Vogue* (1984), Lewis says the Depression accelerated the inevitable failure of the Renaissance as a positive social force.[7] His choice of a chapter title, "It's Dead Now," is recollective of an article of 1942 in *Opportunity*, in which the Trinidadian-born novelist and essayist Frank Hercules wrote, "the Negro Renaissance, already growing old, died a violent death at the hands of the World Market in 1929."[8] But my thesis has been that to bring such "serious" black musicians as Dett, Still, Hayes, and Maynor into the center of discussion about the Negro Renaissance allows this movement to take on a breadth of time and measure of success that shows it to have extended well beyond the beginning of the Great Depression, as well as beyond the 1930s, 1940s, and 1950s; for in the 1930s, the fruits of the training and experience of these musicians and many others were just beginning to blossom. This extended periodization also leads us to turn an eye back on black literature, literature published during and beyond the Great Depression, to see if it was really bereft of value as a social force. I will look at that later literature through Locke's eyes in a moment.

First I want to say that, given the obvious musical successes of the 1930s, 1940s, and 1950s, it is quite odd to find scholars who have written on the music of the Renaissance also concluding that the Renaissance failed—the only possible explanation being that they have accepted Huggins's and Lewis's conclusions, even though both historians underestimate the importance of music in their discussions of the movement. For instance, Martin Blum comes to the same conclusion as Huggins in his article of 1974, "Black Music: Pathmaker of the Harlem Renaissance." After arguing briefly but insightfully that black music enjoyed a prophetic and practical role in the Renaissance as catalyst, contributor, and beneficiary, Blum concludes rather abruptly that the Renaissance ended with the coming of the Depression, a mere decade after he says the movement began.[9] Samuel Floyd, in the introduction to his edited book of 1990, *Black Music in the Harlem Renaissance*, also agrees with Huggins and Lewis that the Great Depression brought an end to the Renaissance and thus concludes: "It also happened that the Renaissance ended before composers could fully develop their skills."[10]

Baker is helpful in the task of countering Huggins's contention that Renaissance literature was "moribund" rather than modern. He identifies and defines two successful "discursive strategies" Renaissance artists and intellectuals used to reproach the racism of whites. The first, the "mastery of form" (to repeat the definition I gave in chapter 1), comprised a mastery of an ability to sound stereotypically "colored" when what the artist or intellectual was really doing was manipulating the stereotypes whites had of blacks, including the nonsensical stereotypes of minstrelsy, for the purpose of liberating blacks.[11] Baker cites as the prototypal example, as I explained in chapter 1, Booker T. Washington's Atlanta Exposition address.

A musical equivalent of this "mastery" in Washington's address is R. Nathaniel Dett's "Mammy," one of the four pieces in his piano suite of 1912, *Magnolia*. On the one hand, the image of the mammy fits comfortably into the stereotypical views that whites, southern whites in particular, had of blacks, which explains why music scholar George Pullen Jackson, a typical white southerner of Dett's day, seemed enamored by Dett's "Mammy." After hearing the piece performed by Dett at a recital at Fisk University in 1923, Jackson waxed emotional in a newspaper review, saying: "the determined applause that compelled Mr. Dett to halt the trend of his *Magnolia Suite* to repeat that unspeakably soulful poem-without-words, 'Mammy,' was proof conclusion that his hearers had had an experience of rare beauty."[12] The racial stereotype surrounding the mammy and the lush sounds that evoked nostalgic images of the Old South and the Old Negro enamored Jackson, but Dett was also re-imaging the mammy in sophisticated art (via his "mastery of form and technique") which had as one of its goals the "vindication of the Negro." Dett demonstrated in this composition, as in the concertizing of the Hampton choir, that in an age of Jim Crow there were rhetorical possibilities for forging out a voice in tight places.

Dett's "Mammy" represents the antithesis of the second "discursive strategy" which Baker terms the "deformation of mastery"—the straightforward debunking of white people's racist racialism.[13] Baker says the spirituals, as repositories for an African cultural spirit untainted by European forms and folly, are examples of this "creative deformation."[14] A musical instance of this "deformation" was Paul Robeson's concert debut at the Greenwich Village Theatre in New York in 1925, on which program Robeson sang only spirituals—the first concert of its kind (which Robeson repeated the following year in the city's Town Hall). This deformative act was in a sense akin to Antonio Salemme sculpting in bronze a full-size nude Robeson, which he titled "The Spiritual" (1926). The sculpture was so deforming, in fact, that the art alliance of Philadelphia refused to allow it to be exhibited in the city. The problem was not the nudity, figured Kelly Miller, but specifically Negro nudity—in other words, Miller explained, not prudery but race prejudice.[15] The disposition of "creative deformation" was also expressed in Duke Ellington's comment in 1944 that, "Jazz, swing, jive, and every other musical phenomenon of American musical life are as much an art medium as are the most profound works of the famous composers. . . . [To] attempt to elevate the status of the jazz musician by forcing the level of his best work into comparisons with classical music is to deny him his rightful share of originality."[16]

Thus, in terms of Locke's two-tiered "mastery"—"mastery of form and technique" and "mastery of mood and spirit"—the latter mastery (of "mood and spirit") was by itself a particular expression of Baker's "deformation of mastery." So, in summary, when Locke's two-tiered "mastery" became a strategy for meeting white expectations for certain traditional Negro sounds or "mood and spirit," while vindicating the Negro by allowing black artists to demonstrate a mastery of European "form and technique" and thereby increasingly gain "culture citizenship, it was a particular expression of what Baker calls "mastery of form." When the "mastery of form and technique" was pushed aside in favor of an unencumbered "mastery of mood and spirit," this comprised a particular expression of what Baker calls "deformation of mastery" or "creative deformation."

Not to deform creatively but instead to engage in "creative mastery" was, as I have been arguing, a strategy towards "paying off an old and bloody score" or attaining racial vindication. But this strategy could also leave one feeling like Countee Cullen felt when he wrote his most famous poem of the Renaissance, "Heritage." Cullen poeticized about his "dark blood" being "damned within" while he squirms like a baited worm as the "primal measures" of Africa's "unremittant beat" drip through his body which cries out for him to "strip." Not to "strip" or deform could also leave such New Negroes as Eva Jesseye and Zora Neale Hurston, as I illustrated in chapter 1, with the notion that Harry T. Burleigh was an Old Negro—a kind of self-conscious ex-colored man who therefore posited an inadequate new answer to the old problem of racism.

Jesseye's and Hurston's response to Burleigh was certainly, in this regard, Benjamin Stolberg's response to Dett's handling of the 1930 European tour of the Hampton choir. Following Dett's account of the tour in *The Crisis,* fittingly titled "A Musical Invasion of Europe," Stolberg, a German-born immigrant who was a free-lance journalist, wrote a response to *The Crisis* titled "Classic Music and Virtuous Ladies." After quoting from Dett's article four paragraphs that sarcastically describe the white American aboard their ship to Europe who wished to hear the choir sing a Negro ditty but was instead rendered classic selections, and that describe the prudent behavior of the Hampton choristers throughout the tour, Stolberg wrote:

> Lordy, what insufferable prigs this group of young men and women must be! Their dress so quiet! No bad language! Of course, never a drink! No cards! In other words, the sophisticated Dr. Dett accepts Octavus Roy Cohen's caricature of the American Negro and then denies it by turning his young people into sticks. All he forgot to mention is that the youngsters refrained from eating fried chicken and watermelons. Personally I think the good musical doctor maligns his Choir. . . .
>
> Just note this pseudo-subtle rebuke to what he considers white ignorance, which wants to hear "Ole Man River." The Hampton Choir, he'll have you know, sings "only classic music." And so he gives to a gay ship-board crowd a "Concert de Bienfaisance" of only highbrow stuff, to show that the Negro knows how. Now, no sensible person doubts that well trained musicians of *any* race can play and sing *any* kind of music. But what's wrong with the Spirituals? We have rediscovered them only three short years ago. Are the Messers Dett already ashamed of them? Why is it such a racial insult to believe, with common horse sense, that the Spirituals *are* "characteristic" of the American Negro. Are they characteristic of Roumanians? What perfect nonsense! The Negro is not a monstrosity who can feel other people's cultural

heritage better than his own. And whatever hick from the Dakotas may have asked . . . for "Ole Man River," in addition to Bach, merely showed his good sense. If the Hampton Choir cannot sing spirituals and even play jazz, the worse for its musicianship. It would be much better off without classical "religious" songs, anyway. What the American Negro needs least is "religion," especially the "liberal" religion which is sneaking in on all of us just when the old religion, thank goodness, is beginning to show the first signs of disintegration. Dr. Dett's whole attitude reeks with a "refined" inferiority feeling and all its correlatives of racial shame and racial prejudice.[17]

Stolberg did not take into consideration the fact that Dett was crafting a voice out of tight places; for whites were by no means sensible when it came to the issue of race and certainly were not inclined to believe that well-trained musicians of any race could perform any kind of music. Neither did Stolberg consider, more particularly, how tight those tight places were in the South during an age of Jim Crow. As regards the choir being well-dressed, for instance, the mandate for that came to Hampton Institute's white administrators well before the tour (at least in terms of their performance attire). Albert Morini, the Italian manager of the tour, made it clear that the men in the choir had to be dressed in tuxedoes and the ladies in white gowns.[18] The presumption would have been, if the mandate had not in fact been made by Hampton's white administrators, that a strict dress code was to be maintained throughout the tour. At least in terms of the behavior of the choristers, the principal of Hampton Institute, George Phenix, had emphasized the necessity of strict discipline and had put George Ketcham, rather than Dett, in charge of the Hampton entourage. Phenix also told Ketcham, one white man to another, that he wanted to receive weekly reports on the tour's progress.[19] Moreover, a strict code of conduct was part of the education experience of blacks at such white-run southern colleges. So as one writer to *The Crisis* said in response to Stolberg's article:

> When we think of the group of southern students who composed the Hampton choir, we must think of their environment, their training and their experience. How could anyone expect boys and girls bred in the backwoods of Virginia, the Carolinas, Georgia and other Southern states, amidst an environment of white domination and Nordic superiority, to be otherwise than the de-

scription Mr. Dett gives them? The musician from Hampton knew that if his group dressed as "flappers" and "sheiks" the message would be heralded to all of the white philanthropists who send their dollars to support his institution. He realized that if they tried to mingle freely with the "superior" white passengers on board, they would be classed as believers in "social equality." The only recourse left was to assume the demure, passive, thankful attitude and save the good name of Hampton or any other Negro school supported by Nordic dollars. So after all, Mr. Stolberg, it was a situation that had to carry a false reaction for the public's sake and a true reaction from the student's point of view.[20]

Thus, on the one hand we have Dett engaging behaviorally in the "mastery of form" (the tradition of Washington's Atlanta Exposition speech) and the respondent to Stolberg's article understanding the forces that required this kind of "mastery," while on the other hand we have Stolberg's preference for the "deformation of mastery" (an easy preference for a white man who did not have to fear being lynched).

By revealing to us these two "discursive strategies" used by black artists and intellectuals, Baker enables us to view the Renaissance as a broader, ongoing, and successful movement that commenced around the turn of the century, burgeoned in the 1920s, and that, he contends, has continued to the present day. He terms this broader period "renaissancism":

> By this term, I want to suggest a *spirit* of nationalistic engagement that begins with intellectuals, artists, and spokespersons at the turn of the century and receives extensive definition and expression during the 1920s. This spirit is one that prompts the black artist's awareness that his or her only possible foundation for authentic and modern expressivity resides in a discursive field marked by formal mastery and sounding deformation. Further, I want to suggest that "renaissancism" connotes something quite removed from a single, exotic set of "failed" highjinks confined to less than a decade. It signals in fact a resonantly and continuously productive set of tactics, strategies, and syllables that takes form at the turn of the century and extends to our own day.[21]

Locke said this very thing in an essay of 1938: that there was a new movement of self-conscious racialism that commenced in 1895 and laid the groundwork for the burgeoning of the Negro Renaissance in the 1920s. Not only did Locke mention the key figures and works on which Baker relies for his claim of renaissancism—Washington's Atlanta Exposition speech ("mastery of form") and Du Bois's *The Souls of Black Folk* ("deformation of mastery")—but Locke also mentioned, to the favor of my own argument, the musical contribution to this burgeoning epoch. In this passage in *The Crisis,* which must be heard in its entirety, Locke wrote:

> Anti-slavery controversy and the hope of freedom brought poetry and fire to the Negro tongue and pen; whereas the setbacks and strained ambitions of Reconstruction brought forth, in the main, leaden rhetoric and alloyed pedantry. Thus the 70's and the 80's were the awkward age in our artistic development. They were the period of prosaic self-justification and painful apprenticeship to formal culture. Yet these years saw the creditable beginnings of Negro historical and sociological scholarship, even at the expense of an endless elaboration of problem discussion themes, and saw also an adolescent attack on the more formal arts of the novel, the drama, formal music, painting and sculpture. Before this almost all of our artistic expression had flowed in the narrow channels of the sermon, the oration, the slave narrative and didactic poetry.
>
> But in spite of their talents and labors, authors like Highland Garnet, Alexander Crummell, George Williams, the historian, Martin Delaney, and even Frederick Douglass in these later days had a restricted audience, much narrower than the wide national and international stage of anti-slavery times. There was, instead of the glamor of the crusade against the slave power, the dull grind of the unexpected fight against reaction. The larger audience and a more positive mood were not recaptured until the mid-nineties, when strangely enough a clustered group of significant events came together, any one of which would have been notable. In 1895, Booker Washington caught national attention with his Atlanta Exposition speech; in 1896 Paul Laurence Dunbar rode into fame and popular favor; in the same year the first Negro musical comedy took Broadway; in '98 and '99, Chestnut, the novelist, came to the fore; in '95 Burleigh was helping Dvořák with the Negro folk themes of the "New World Symphony" and at the same time making his first entry to the New York concert world; in '98 Will Marion Cook launched serious syncopated music with "Clorindy;" '96 was the year of Tanner's first substantial Paris recognition; and in '98 Coleridge Taylor came to maturity and fame

in the first part of the Hiawatha Trilogy. The only other stellar artistic event of this period for which we have to wait is the appearance in 1903 of Dr. Du Bois's "Souls of Black Folk."

Quite obviously there was a sudden change of trend as this blaze of talent ushered in a new era of racial expression. It was more than a mere accession of new talent; it was the discovery of a new racial attitude. The leading motive of Reconstruction thought was assimilation and political equality; following the cry for physical freedom there had been the fight for the larger freedom of status and the right to be the same and equal. But the leading motive of the new era (1895–1910) seems to have been racialism and its new dynamic of self-help and self-assertion. Even the motivations of Du Bois's equal rights crusade were militantly self-conscious and racial; in fact, race consciousness was now definitely in the saddle striving to re-direct the stalled logic of the assimilation program and revive the balked hopes of the thwarted equal rights struggle. The formula of special gifts and particular paths had been discovered, and became the dominant rationalization of the period. The leading conception of freedom now was the right to be oneself and different. Thus the groundwork was laid for the cultural racialism of the "Negro Renaissance" movement which, however, was not to appear definitely till the mid-twenties and the next literary generation. In its first phase this racialism was naive, emotional and almost provincial; later under the influence of the World War principles of self-determination and the rise of other cultural nationalism, it was to become sophisticated and historically grounded in Africanism and the philosophy of cultural revivals.[22]

James Weldon Johnson's *Autobiography of an Ex-Colored Man* belongs prominently in this "new era." First of all, it was during the year 1899 that Johnson began thinking about the idea that would lay the groundwork for the cultural racialism of the burgeoned Renaissance of the 1920s. Of that year Johnson wrote, "I now began to grope toward a realization of the importance of the American Negro's cultural background and his creative folk-art, and to speculate on the superstructure of conscious art that might be reared upon them."[23] It was within the next three to six years that *The Autobiography* began to take shape.[24] Thus, the book belonged prominently in the new era that pushed toward a burgeoned Renaissance of the 1920s, even though Johnson did not seem to realize this prior to its re-publication in 1927. He said in 1924:

I published the book anonymously about fourteen years ago with a firm in Boston that went out of business during the war. I believe the book was published out of time. Fourteen years ago there was little or no interest in the Negro. In fact, we had reached the deepest depths of apathy regarding him so far as the general public is concerned.

I believe that if the book had been published ten years later it might have attracted some attention. I have sometimes thought that I might bring it down through the Great War and try for another publication of it. I am not sure that it would be worth while.[25]

Indeed, the book was "published out of time." It was prophetic, foreseeing of the Renaissance that would come to be recognized in the mid-1920s: All the major motifs important to an understanding of the Renaissance were present in this work of so-called fiction. Regarding this aspect of Johnson's novel, Carl Van Vechten said to the author: "I was particularly interested to discover that you were apparently the first to sense the musical possibilities of ragtime and to predict for it a future as an art-form."[26] Aaron Douglas, the Renaissance artist who designed the cover for the 1927 reprint of the book, said even more about the work's importance to the Renaissance:

I have just finished reading the book and I am carried away with amazement and admiration. Your depth of thought, breadth of vision, and subtlety and beauty of expression awakens in me the greatest admiration. I am amazed at the gigantic effort which must have been necessary for the writing and publishing of the book at such an early date. The post-war Negro, blinded by the glare and almost sudden bursting of a new day, finds much difficulty in realizing the immense power and effort, which the pre-war Negro has made to prepare the country for what we now feel to be the "Awakening."[27]

The work was therefore only "published out of time" to the degree that it was prophetic; for its prophecy was part of what Locke called a racialism comprised of a "new dynamic of self-help and self-assertion."

Booker T. Washington's placement at the beginning of this period of "renaissancism" that burgeoned in the 1920s, a placement that is permitted by our comprehension of the two "discursive strategies" that Baker says Renaissance Negroes utilized, is also suggested by the title of the edited book to which Washington contributed (and which prominently displays his name as though he were the author), *A New Negro for a New Century* (1900). This broader perspective on and time frame of the Renaissance as a much more protracted movement is further suggested in William Pickens's book, *The New Negro* (1916), in the opening essay titled "The Renaissance of the New Negro." Pickens wrote, "The history of the race has been distorted or buried in contempt. But along with the great advance which the Negro can be expected to make in the United States in the next fifty years, every few years should see a book up to date on the general subject of 'The Renaissance of the Negro Race' or 'The New Negro.'"[28] Locke's *The New Negro* (1925) and *The Negro and His Music* (1936) also fit into this lineage of books that update the Renaissance of the Negro, as does James Weldon Johnson's *Autobiography of an Ex-Colored Man* (1912), which was greatly influenced by Du Bois's *Souls of Black Folk.*[29] So, the books *A New Negro for a New Century* (1900), *The Souls of Black Folk* (1903), *The Autobiography of an Ex-Colored Man* (1912), and *The New Negro* (1916) were not foretelling of a Renaissance to come; they were part of a spirit of nationalistic engagement, expressed by way of Baker's two "discursive strategies," which commenced with artists and intellectuals around 1895 and burgeoned with extensive expression and broad recognition during the 1920s.

II

There is another avenue of argument to pursue in order to contest the notion that the Renaissance suffered a violent demise at the hands of the world market: that there was an institutionalization of the Renaissance in the black church. This institutionalization came in the form of the social gospel movement, a movement of social Christianity (as opposed to the individualistic evangelical Christianity) which commenced among white Protestants in the North around 1880 and spread to the black church around 1895, and which therefore can be understood as part of that "clustered group of significant events" that Locke said came together in the mid-1890s. Reverdy Ransom, a social gospeler himself, seemed to have understood this, as evidenced in his poem of 1923 titled "The New Negro." Slavery and oppression, wrote the black bishop, made the old Negro stronger, chiseled him to form, so that he could bear "rich gifts to science, religion, poetry and song."[30]

That the social gospel in the black church should be included in the "clustered group of significant events" that came together in the mid-1890s and burgeoned in the 1920s is further suggested by the Harmon awards, which were given not only to talented blacks in the arts, letters, and sciences, but also in religion. In 1928, the same year James Weldon Johnson won the Harmon award in literature and Dett and Still in music, two pastors won it in the area of religion—in recognition of their efforts to develop the church into an entity of social and community service.[31] Two years later, in 1930, the Harmon award was given to, among others, Lawrence Freeman, Harry T. Burleigh, and Carl Diton in music, Walter White in literature, Sargent Johnson in fine arts, and Adam Clayton Powell, Sr., for religious service.[32]

Had Harry V. Richardson, the black scholar who wrote on the black church, taken a cue from the Harmon awards or at least from Ransom's poem "The New Negro" (which he might have been familiar with), he might have brought more insight to his article of 1933 in *Opportunity*, "The New Negro and Religion." But Richardson failed to recognize that the New Negro (the Renaissance man and woman) had become institutionalized in the black church in the form of the social gospel ministry. Instead, Richardson sarcastically argued that most New Negroes were atheists devoid of spiritual interests, due in part to their belief that the church had failed to keep abreast of their intellectual development.[33]

There were such Renaissance artists and intellectuals who were or seemed to be professed atheists—novelist Nella Larsen, journalist J. A. Rogers, Alain Locke, Langston Hughes, Zora Neale Hurston, and James Weldon Johnson, to name a few. Larsen said outright that she did not believe in religion and churches.[34] Rogers probably sounded identical to Larsen in many respects when he said in a review of the black musical comedy *The Green Pastures*: "The story of Jehovah creating the earth and man we now realize belongs to the infancy of our civilization despite the rivers of blood that exploiting tyrants and their henchmen, the theologians, spilt for centuries in an effort to clamp down that doctrine on the human brain. We now know that it is on a level with the belief that babies are brought by storks."[35] Locke was so disdainful of Christianity in the West that he said, "When I think of the warped and narrow beliefs and teachings Christianity rammed down our Negro throats, I really feel like burning the churches."[36] Hughes seemed to reject Christianity in his dramatic monologue titled "Good-bye, Christ," a piece that caused Kelly Miller to suggest that Hughes was one of the radical Negroes who were atheists.[37] Hurston, in her autobiography, *Dust Tracks on a Road*, uttered words of seeming sacrilege about prayer:

As for me, I do not pretend to read God's mind. If He has a plan of the universe worked out to the smallest detail, it would be folly for me to presume to get down on my knees and attempt to revise it. That, to me, seems the highest form of sacrilege. So I do not pray. I accept the means at my disposal for working out my destiny. It seems to me that I have been given a mind and will-power for that very purpose. I do not expect God to single me out and grant me advantages over my fellow men. Prayer is for those who need it. Prayer seems to me a cry of weakness, and an attempt to avoid, by trickery, the rules of the game as laid down.[38]

Johnson, in *The Autobiography of an Ex-Colored Man,* portrayed a protagonist who was critical of the Bible from the time he began reading it at the young age of eleven. The protagonist said, "I became interested in the life of Christ, but became impatient and disappointed when I found that, notwithstanding the great power he possessed, he did not make use of them when, in my judgment, he most needed to do so. And so my first general impression of the Bible was what my later impression has been of a number of modern books, that the authors put their best work in the first part, and grew either exhausted or careless toward the end." The consequence of this impression of the Bible by Johnson's protagonist was his "permanent dislike for all kinds of theology."

Indeed, Johnson himself rejected the notion of a personal God, identifying himself as an agnostic as early as his college years at Atlanta University.[39] He also believed human beings were blind victims of institutional religion which was but a cruel mechanism of human manipulation.[40] Johnson was evidently one of the "younger men" spoken of in an article of 1930 which he clipped and pasted into his scrapbook:

> A large group of younger men, college men, authors, doctors, intellectuals, denounce the church as a foe to racial progress.
>
> They say that the pittances of the poor go into extravagantly expensive church buildings; that the ministers' energies are divided between exhorting their parishioners to help pay off the church debt, raking over the dry bones of dead theological controversy, and lulling the Negroes into indifference to their miserable economic situation by promises of eternal happiness to come. They say, these younger men, that the energy, time and money

which Negroes spend in their churches should be devoted to a constructive effort to meet the problems of this world.[41]

This article of 1930 was in fact the basis of the mood and language in Johnson's comments on the black church in his book of 1934, *Negro Americans, What Now?* Johnson wrote, "First of all, the church together with the race as a whole must do a certain amount of clearing away in the religious field. We must stamp out as far as we can the bootleggers of religion, those parasites who, whenever they can get together a sufficient number of poor, hard-working women, will . . . peddle a spurious brand of Christianity at a relatively exorbitant price."[42] Johnson continued, "The church must as nearly as it can abolish hypnotic religion, that religion which excites visions of the delights of life in the world to come, while it gives us no insight into the conditions we encounter in the world in which we now live. There is still to be found in the Negro church too much obsolete doctrine."[43]

But while such Renaissance artists and intellectuals as Larsen, Rogers, Locke, Hughes, Hurston, and Johnson may have convinced Richardson that the New Negro was largely atheistic, Richardson could not have accused all Renaissance Negroes of atheism. Once again, by putting music back into the center of discussion about the Negro Renaissance we see that Burleigh, a New Negro, remained a lifelong Episcopalian as well as a soloist in the choir of St. George Episcopal Church for fifty-two years. Dett was a long-time Presbyterian whose Hampton choir performed at black churches throughout the country, including Harlem's Metropolitan Baptist Church the evening before the Hampton entourage set sail for their European tour of 1930. Maynor was raised a member of her father's African Methodist Episcopal church in the Norfolk, Virginia, area, and she later married a minister, Shelby Rooks, who became the pastor of St. James Presbyterian Church in Harlem. After she retired from the concert stage in 1963, Maynor even became the choir director at St. James. William Grant Still, raised in the church by his mother, seemed to have been converted anew in 1930 while going through an emotionally turbulent time in his life—unemployed due to the Depression and his relationship with his first wife again deteriorating. Still also spoke at black churches on occasion, as did other Renaissance Negroes such as Locke, James Weldon Johnson, Carter G. Woodson, and Du Bois. At least once, Locke had been of service to the Lombard Street Central Presbyterian Church in Philadelphia under William Lloyd Imes, before Imes became the pastor of St. James Presbyterian Church in Harlem.[44] Johnson was one of the keynote speakers at the first annual conference on "Religion among Young People" at St. Philip's in

1928.[45] Woodson appeared at St. James on a Sunday afternoon in 1926 under the auspices of the organization he founded, the Association for the Study of Negro Life and History.[46] Du Bois gave a talk on the race problem on a Sunday at St. Mark's Methodist Episcopal Church in 1930.[47]

As is often the case with artists and intellectuals who appear to be (or even claim to be) atheists, many were not in reality. For instance, Hurston implied that it was prayer, not God, in which she lacked belief.[48] Hughes explained that he wrote "Good-bye Christ" simply to shock Christians, black and white, into recognizing the shortcomings of the church with regard to addressing the condition of the poor and oppressed of the world, particularly the poor and oppressed blacks of the American South.[49] Neither was James Weldon Johnson anti-Christianity, a rebel against his upbringing in the Methodist Episcopal Church or against his father who became a minister when he was young. At the request of Henry Smith Leiper, executive secretary of the American branch of the Universal Christian Council, William Lloyd Imes (pastor of St. James) implored Johnson to accept the invitation to be a member of the American Advisory Committee of the Universal Christian Council, an organization that was part of the Federal Council of the Church of Christ in America.[50] Johnson accepted the offer to represent the black community on this committee whose task was to examine the relationship between church, state, and society,[51] and thus in 1936 he served on this committee of Christians alongside such distinguished churchmen as Henry Sloane Coffin and Harry Emerson Fosdick. The following year he accepted the invitation of Howard Thurman, the distinguished dean of Howard University's chapel, to speak at a vesper service.[52]

As for Johnson's rejection of a personal God and claim that he had lived forty years outside the atmosphere of religion, Wilber Thirkield denied any suggestion that Johnson was Godless. He said to Johnson, "Would not music also have died in you if you had not kept your heart and mind attuned to noble strains of music?"—by which he meant the noble strains of divine music.[53] Thirkield was correct: It was by no means the case that Johnson was an atheist—not when his hymn "Lift Every Voice and Sing" and the poems comprising *God's Trombones* reveal his heart and mind to be so attuned with the spiritual. Indeed, Johnson was not anti-Christianity or anti-church; and he certainly was not anti-black church, for his respect for the institution ran deep like his respect for black folk song. Just as he felt that black folk song could be the basis of higher forms of art more befitting of the need of blacks to acquire culture citizenship, so did he feel the black church could be the most effective medium for the pursuit of equal rights for blacks.[54] Thus, Johnson petitioned the black church to nurture the growth of an educated black ministry that would engage in an "applied Christianity."[55]

Locke was not anti-Christianity either, but like Johnson felt the institution was corrupt. He felt that the church was really at its best in the East but that it began to decline as soon as it was transplanted to the West.[56] In particular, Locke, like Johnson, was opposed to religion being an "opiate" that retards the human quest for social justice. "The salvation we have sought after as individuals in an after-life and another sphere must be striven for as the practical peace and unity of the human family here in this," wrote Locke in an unpublished piece that may have been the talk he delivered at some of his church engagements. "In some very vital respects God will be rediscovered to our age if we succeed in discovering the common denominator of humanity and living in terms of it and valuing all things in accordance with it." Locke went on to say that reconciliation between the world's racial and national factions could not occur without a revolution within the human soul: "If the world had believingly understood the full significance of Him who taught it to pray and hope 'Thy Kingdom come on earth as it is in Heaven,' who also said 'In my Father's house are many mansions,' already we should be further toward the realization of this great millennial vision. The word of God is still insistent, and more emphatic as the human redemption delays and becomes more crucial."[57]

The latter passage reads as though Locke were drawing directly from "The Social Meaning of the Lord's Prayer," the introduction to Walter Rauschenbusch's *For God and the People: Prayers of the Social Gospel* (1910). Locke owned a copy of the famous little book by the theological father of the social gospel, for in April 1928 he was given one by Rauschenbusch's widow, Pauline Rauschenbusch, who inscribed the words: "To Dr. Alain Locke in Remembrance of the author and their common task." Like Walter Rauschenbusch, Locke believed the words and teachings of Christ had been falsified and misused, so that Christians at best only knew some of the words Christ is reported to have said.[58] Like such black churchmen as Reverdy Ransom who had adapted the social gospel theology to the needs of the black church, Locke viewed "Social Christianity," as he termed it, as a possible rubric under which a new and more just social order could be worked out to benefit blacks, the poor, and women.[59] Locke also sounded like the theologians of the social gospel, with their anthropological theology, when, upon a ship tour of 1934 that took him through southern Europe, the Middle East, northern Africa (Egypt), and Russia, he saw in Istanbul (historic Constantinople) a recent discovery of original

Christian frescoes and mosaics. He said the best fresco of Mary and Jesus was but a human idealization of mother and son.[60]

So, the connection between the Negro Renaissance and the church was not dependent upon the religious faith of particular Renaissance artists and intellectuals. Therefore it does not matter that Claude McKay considered himself to be a "pagan" whose work he himself felt was absent of expressions of Christian morality.[61] Neither does the connection between the Renaissance and the church need to be argued on the basis that particular Renaissance artists and intellectuals sometimes attended or performed and lectured in black churches. The point is that the black churches that practiced the social gospel themselves comprised a component of the Renaissance, a component containing its own corpus of intellectuals—namely, an educated and sophisticated black clergy. Thus, it is no coincidence that James Weldon Johnson sent a complimentary copy of *God's Trombones* to social gospel ministers Reverdy Ransom and Adam Clayton Powell, Sr.[62]

Among the oldest and most prominent of the Harlem churches that practiced the social gospel under the leadership of educated and progressive pastors were Abyssinian Baptist Church, St. Philip's Protestant Episcopal Church, and St. James Presbyterian Church. St. James, founded in 1895, was considered the largest Presbyterian church comprised of a black membership and headed by a black minister. In 1943, Dorothy Maynor's husband, Shelby Rooks, took over the pastorate of the church, replacing William Lloyd Imes. St. Philip's, under the pastorate of Rev. Hutchins C. Bishop, became the largest black congregation in the Protestant Episcopal denomination and the wealthiest of all black churches in the country. The church owned a substantial amount of property in Harlem, including apartment buildings extending a full block on 135th Street. Its financial capacity was due to the fact that more New Negroes of educational attainment and financial means were members there than at any other black church in the city. Prior to its move to Harlem from another part of larger Manhattan in 1910, Burleigh sang in its choir to make some extra money during his four years of study (beginning in 1892) at the National Conservatory of Music.

Of the distinguished black churches to relocate to Harlem from another location in Manhattan, the first was Abyssinian Baptist Church, touted as the largest and wealthiest of black Baptist churches in the country. It moved to Harlem in 1908 under Adam Clayton Powell, Sr., who had assumed the pastorate that year. Powell soon began to establish himself as a practitioner of the social gospel. His church maintained a home for the elderly and a social center called the Community House. During the summers the Community House, which housed evening training schools for religious teachers and Red Cross nurses, also hosted the largest youth Vacation Bible School in the city.[63] Although Rev. W. W. Brown, pastor of the Metropolitan Baptist Church, was not as well known as Powell, he was known for his involvement in Harlem's economic concerns. Brown repeatedly made "Buy property" the theme of his sermons, to the extent that buying property became a fever among blacks that climaxed around 1921.[64]

The church music that seemed to go hand in hand with the progressive Protestantism of the black social gospel movement were not the traditional hymns of evangelical Christianity or even the new hymns of social Christianity written by the new corpus of white social gospel hymnists, but the arranged spirituals of such Renaissance composers as Dett. That the arranged spirituals were a principal musical corpus for the educated and sophisticated ministry of the black social gospel was evidenced at the Atlanta church of the well-respected social gospeler Henry Hugh Proctor. As part of the social ministry of his First Congregational Church, Proctor founded the Atlanta Colored Music Festival Association in 1910 (after 1915, the Georgia Music Festival Association), which annually brought to Atlanta such well-known black performers as Burleigh, Hayes, John W. Work, Clarence Cameron White, Carl Diton, and the Fisk Jubilee Singers. Thus, it is no surprise that it was at Metropolitan that the Hampton Institute choir performed the night before they sailed for Europe.[65] To a full house, the choir sang several of Dett's arrangements of spirituals, including "Listen to the Lambs," "No More Auction Block For Me," and "Don't Weep No More, Mary." Among the listeners sharing in the applause at Metropolitan Baptist Church that night was Burleigh, who appeared to be impressed by the quality of Dett's work.[66]

When the Great Depression hit in 1929, the arranged spirituals were still being sung in the progressive black churches, as evidenced by the Hampton choir's concert at Metropolitan Baptist Church when on their way to Europe in 1930. But more importantly, all of those arranged spirituals with social meanings paid off when the Renaissance men of the social gospel positioned their churches to help Harlem's residents contend with the economic crisis when it came crashing down. In September 1930, St. Mark's Methodist Episcopal Church hosted a mass meeting in order to determine ways of creating jobs, and within a couple of months a centralized movement had been organized, the Harlem Co-operating Committee on Relief and Employment, directed by Rev. Shelton Hale Bishop.[67] Bishop, the assistant pastor of St. Philip's Church, was the son of the pastor. Under his youthful leadership the Committee solicited clothing, food supplies, and monetary contributions from Harlem's churches for immediate relief of families in the community. Abyssinian Baptist Church, given its size and prominence, ran its own relief bureau, headed by the pastor's son, Adam Clayton Powell, Jr., who coordinated the church's work with that of the larger committee under Bishop.

So, there is another avenue of argument to pursue in order to contest the notion that the Renaissance suffered a violent demise at the hands of the world market—that there was an institutionalization of the Renaissance in the black church in the form of the social gospel, whose musical correlate was the arranged spirituals of Burleigh, Dett, and the others of their ilk.

III

In September 1930, the Harlem churches that practiced the social gospel formed the Harlem Co-operating Committee on Relief and Employment, which helped navigate the black community through the Depression. A few months earlier, on April 22, the Hampton choir performed its Renaissance repertoire in Harlem's Metropolitan Baptist Church, and the next day headed abroad for a successful tour of Europe. Three years later, in 1933, black composer Shirley Graham wrote an article on Negro music for *The Crisis,* in which she spoke as though the Renaissance was still underway: "The Fisk Jubilee Singers blazed a path; they marched around the walls of Jericho and 'da walls came a-tumblin' down.' . . . Now the challenge comes to us, the New Negro."[68] One year later, in 1934, William Dawson's *Negro Folk Symphony* was premièred on November 14, 15, and 17 by the Philadelphia Orchestra under Leopold Stokowski at the Philadelphia Academy of Music, and then on November 20 at Carnegie Hall, a great success and an important landmark in black cultural progress. Without considering the world of literature, then, the Negro Renaissance was evidently still in progress. But as I said earlier, this suggests that we should take a sidewards look at the world of literature and not presume that it had met its demise because of the Depression. According to Locke, the literary world of the Renaissance was not brought to a halt by the Depression either. "Things seem to be at an awful ebb," he wrote to Mason in late 1932, "but of course we drained our own pond long before the great ebb came. In fact it is rather a pity we have the general depression as an alibi. I am challenged with that whenever I criticize the young Negroes who certainly had their chance."[69]

It is with regard to Locke's "mastery of form" in dealing with Mason, which I discussed in chapter 1, that we are to understand not only the latter remark but Locke's comment to Mason a month later, a comment that historian David Levering Lewis erroneously cites as evidence that Locke viewed the Renaissance as a failure: "I'll someday have to write out for my own satisfaction, and absolution, the inside story of 'the Negro renaissance' and how it was scuttled from within."[70] The fact is, Locke never did write that "inside story." Even if he had written it, it would have been so inside as to have been for Mason's satisfaction only—appeasement to Mason for the fact that the Renaissance artists had neglected to adopt her philosophy of primitivism. Whatever the "inside story" between Locke and Mason, the outside story that Locke wrote in 1933 was that that year of economic depression had not adversely affected Negro literature, except for the fact that many manuscripts probably had gone unpublished.[71] Years later, Locke was still appeasing Mason by saying the Renaissance had failed, but he had not and would not commit the notion to writing. *Her* Renaissance had failed, he seemed to be thinking, but *the* Renaissance had not.

At the beginning of 1935, for instance, Locke reported to Mason that he had given a lecture on "The Negro Contribution to American Culture" at Bennett College, the black women's college in Greensboro, North Carolina, in which he said he hinted that the Renaissance had failed. "The talk was sound, I think," he wrote to Mason, "especially since it admitted what we haven't done—and that statement seems to have [pre]pared the way for me to speak out in an article on 'Why the Negro Renaissance Failed.'" Locke went on to say to Mason that the failure of several of the artists who had betrayed her, including Langston Hughes, could make up the text of the article and that he was wondering if she would care to see such an article published. But having worn this mask of accommodation ever so adroitly, Locke withdrew the idea as quickly and shrewdly as he posited it. "However, it does not seem the right moment for this, even if there were the right medium," his letter continued. "However, it is impossible to keep completely silent, having been so intimately involved."[72]

Actually, in the notes that Locke used for that lecture at Bennett College there is nothing to suggest that he said anything about the Renaissance failing.[73] In fact, the notes suggest just the opposite: that Locke had portrayed the Renaissance as a success and the New Negro as still making an important contribution to American culture. Furthermore, if the Bennett lecture at all resembled Locke's article of a similar title published four years later, "The Negro's Cultural Contribution to American Culture," then we can reasonably surmise that Locke was telling Mason one thing about the Renaissance failing while saying quite the opposite in his articles and lectures. In this article of 1939, Locke not only spoke positively of the Negro

Renaissance but positively of those who had allegedly betrayed Mason, indeed those whom together he and Mason had belittled in their private conversations.[74] Similarly, James Weldon Johnson, as early as 1926 and up to the year of his accidental death in 1938, had been lecturing at universities, churches, and other institutions, white and black, on the subject of "The Negro's Cultural Contribution to American Civilization" or "The Negro's Contribution to American Culture."

So Locke was not about to concede the end of the Negro Renaissance, no matter what he said to Mason in private. Instead, in 1934 he was busy lauding Sterling Brown as the New Negro who superseded even Hughes in an intimate knowledge of folk life, which he skillfully encased in classic poetic form.[75] It was just a matter of good fortune that Brown was someone Mason approved of, so that Locke would not have to maneuver around her views as he had to with respect to Robeson, Hayes, and Hughes. "It was joyous news that you liked Sterling Brown's book," he wrote to Mason with a portion of relief and a plethora of appeasement. "I was hoping you would—but scarcely dared hope—for there have been so many disappointments—and so much has turned out to be tinsel under your revealing light."[76] So Locke was not about to concede the end of the Negro Renaissance. If he felt that anything about the Renaissance had been "scuttled from within," he certainly saw it to be that facet of the movement caused by the white Negrophiles who were its benefactors (including Mason herself).

In fact, as early as 1928, Locke had foretold the passing of the "vogue" of the Negro and the emergence of a more mature phase of the Renaissance, of which he evidently viewed Sterling Brown as exemplary. Writing at the end of that year, the year he called "the floodtide of the present Negrophile movement," Locke said:

> In this, as with many another boom, the water will need to be squeezed out of much inflated stock and many bubbles must burst. However, those who are interested in the real Negro movement which can be discerned behind the fad, will be glad to see the fad subside. Only then will the truest critical appraisal be possible, as the opportunity comes to discriminate between shoddy and wool, fair-weather friends and true supporters, the stock-brokers and the real productive talents. The real significance and potential power of the Negro renaissance may not reveal itself until after this reaction, and the entire top-soil of contemporary Negro expression

may need to be ploughed completely under for a second hardier and richer crop.

To my mind the movement for the vital expression of Negro life can only truly begin as the fad breaks off. There is inevitable distortion under the hectic interest and forcing of the present vogue for Negro idioms. An introspective calm, a spiritually poised approach, a deeply matured understanding are finally necessary. These may not, need not come entirely from the Negro artist; but no true and lasting expression of Negro life can come except from these more firmly established points of view.[77]

This idea that the real significance and potential power of the Renaissance was yet to reveal itself following the flood tide of the Negrophile fad was no mere passing thought; for two years later, at the beginning of 1931, Locke repeated the point in no uncertain terms:

The much exploited Negro renaissance was after all a product of the expansive period we are now willing to call the period of inflation and overproduction; perhaps there was much in it that was unsound, and perhaps our aesthetic gods are turning their backs only a little more gracefully than the gods of the market-place. Are we then, in a period of cultural depression, verging on spiritual bankruptcy? Has the afflatus of Negro self-expression died down? Are we outliving the Negro fad? Has the Negro creative artist wandered into the ambush of the professional exploiters? By some signs and symptoms. Yes. But to anticipate my conclusion,—"Let us rejoice and be exceedingly glad." The second and truly sound phase of the cultural development of the Negro in American literature and art cannot begin without a collapse of the boom, a change to more responsible and devoted leadership, a revision of basic values, and along with a penitential purgation of spirit, a wholesale expulsion of the money-changers from the temple of art.[78]

Again, three years after that, at the beginning of 1934, in his retrospective review of black literature of 1933, Locke re-emphasized his belief that a second and truly sound phase of black cultural development in the arts and letters was taking root:

As year by year the literature by and about the Negro not only maintains its volume, but deepens and clarifies in quality, there can be no doubt that the Negro theme has become a prominent and permanent strain in contemporary American literature. No mere fad or fashion could have sustained itself for ten or more years with increasing momentum and undiminished appeal and effect. In fact, as the fad subsides, a sounder, more artistic expression of Negro life and character takes its place. What was once prevalent enough almost to be the rule has now become quite the exception; the typical Negro author is no longer propagandist on the one hand or exhibitionist on the other; the average white author is now neither a hectic faddist nor a superficial or commercialized exploiter in his attitude toward Negro subject matter;— and as a result the unexpected has happened, sobriety, poise and dignity are becoming the dominant keynotes of the developing Negro theme.[79]

Carl Van Vechten might have read the above assessment, which came out in the January 1934 issue of *Opportunity*, for a month later he made a similar comment to James Weldon Johnson. He said that considering such works as Johnson's *Along This Way*, Hughes's *The Ways of White Folks*, and Hurston's *Jonah's Gourd Vine*, there was much more solid evidence of a Negro Renaissance then, in 1934, than around 1926 and 1927.[80] Johnson himself viewed such works as fulfilling the mandate of the Renaissance to challenge white stereotypes of blacks by capturing the life, ambitions, struggles, and passions of the Negro race within the "higher" classical forms. "Some" of this work had already been done, he wrote in 1934 in *Negro Americans, What Now?* To this he added, "but the greater portion remains to be done—and by Negro writers and artists."[81] Three years later, Johnson had not changed his opinion about this and Van Vechten had not changed his mind about the Renaissance being stronger than in the mid-1920s. He said to Johnson with regard to the forthcoming new edition of *The Autobiography of an Ex-Colored Man*: "I would suggest . . . that you yourself add a further Introduction (or appendix) to this new edition, a chapter in which you can relate how much further the Negro has progressed, how his presence at the opera, concert, and art gallery is now very generally expected."[82]

About seven months later, at the beginning of 1938, in his retrospective review of Negro literature for 1937, Locke identified the years 1917 to 1934 as comprising the first generation of Renaissance artists. As though he were anticipating the criticism of someone like Harold Cruse,[83] he said the first generation was "choked in shallow cultural soil by the cheap weeds of group flattery, vainglory and escapist emotionalism," which resulted in the movement being tainted by exhibitionism and demagoguery. But the demise of this phase was but the beginning of a "second generation" of writers and artists, he said, which included Langston Hughes, Zora Neale Hurston, Arna Bontemps, and Sterling Brown. Of these artists Locke wrote, "Their more penetrating, evenhanded and less-illusioned portrayal of Negro life is realizing more deeply the original aims of what was too poetically and glibly styled 'The Negro Renaissance?'"[84] From Locke's perspective, then, what "failed" with regard to the Negro Renaissance was but its early phase, an early phase that gave way to "a sounder, more artistic expression of Negro life and character." Understanding this not only gives further connotation to Locke's comment to Mason that the Renaissance was "scuttled from within," but also to Claude McKay's comment that the Renaissance seemed like a "hopeless mess,"[85] and to Langston Hughes's comment that the Renaissance was but short-lived fun.[86]

In his retrospective review of black literature for 1938, Locke explained the "hopeless mess" of the Negro Renaissance. Addressing the question of whether the present artistic movement was a matured phase of the Renaissance or a countermovement (as some black artists of the younger generation were arguing), Locke said it was his conviction that the former was true and that the Renaissance was just coming into its own after a "frothy adolescence," just as he had predicted.[87] Almost two years later, in 1940, Locke was still excited about the burgeoning of the Renaissance—a Renaissance where sobriety, poise, and dignity were the dominant keynotes in addressing black subject matter. In addition to his excitement over a few visual artists, he was exuberant about William Grant Still's completion of *And They Lynched Him on a Tree*, about Dorothy Maynor's concert career, and about Ulysses Kay (one of Still's protégés who Locke called "another straightforward, sincere genius"). He assertively told this to Mason, of all people, but not (as we would suspect) without the requisite appeasement. "You know real Negro genius has been spurting up lately like an oil-well freshly drilled," he said. "And just at this moment of the almost complete downfall of white civilization. It has great significance to those who understand—or rather I should say—to those whose eyes have been opened by you."[88] Even Hughes, who had characterized the Renaissance as a fad that was fun while it lasted, came around to the point where Locke had been all along. While visiting Los Angeles in 1946, Hughes publicized his opinion that there had been a reawakening of interest in blacks, particularly with regard to the arts. "We are going through a second Negro renaissance in the arts," declared Hughes.[89]

IV

Even when, at the end of 1949, the National Urban League suspended its publication of *Opportunity*, a magazine that had been an important source of artistic and intellectual expression for the Renaissance Negro, Locke still considered the movement to be progressing. The fortieth anniversary of *The Pittsburgh Courier* in 1950 must have confirmed this for him and many others by having foremost authoritative writers review black progress along every important front.[90] A total of twenty-one articles (rather than the planned twenty-six), published approximately every other week for the entire year, celebrated the advancement of the New Negro (the Renaissance man and woman) in literature, music, theater, art, religion, civil and human rights, public and higher education, journalism, the professions, human welfare, and so on. This theme of progress, by the way, is a prominent one in *The Autobiography of an Ex-Colored Man*. "In spite of all that is written, said, and done," said the Negro man met aboard ship by the protagonist as he was leaving Europe, "this great, big, incontrovertible fact stands out—the Negro is progressing, and that disproves all the arguments in the world that he is incapable of progress."

The first article in *The Pittsburgh Courier* series, published the second week in January, was a general overview of race progress by Du Bois. In this article illustrated by photographs of such black artists as James Weldon Johnson and Harry T. Burleigh, Du Bois asked: "What have we gained and accomplished?" He answered, "The advance has not been equal on all fronts, nor complete on any. . . . But we have advanced. Of that there can be no atom of doubt."[91] Did Du Bois also agree with Locke that there had been advances made in black literature? Like Locke, Du Bois criticized black literature that was not authentically about black people, literature that was about those things whites liked to hear about blacks; but he also concluded that there was an increasing number of excellent black writers.[92] With regard to the other arts, Du Bois said: "We have done something in sculpture and painting, but in drama and music we have markedly advanced. All the world listens to our singers, sings our music and dances to our rhythms."[93]

"Fifty Years of Progress in Literature" was written by James W. Ivy, who had taught black literature for five years on the faculty at Hampton Institute before becoming the acting editor of *The Crisis*. In this article, illustrated by photographs of such writers as James Weldon Johnson, Langston Hughes, Countee Cullen, Jessie Fauset, Sterling Brown, Locke, and Du Bois, Ivy said the common task of Negro writers during the first quarter of the century was to rid their art of the plantation perspective on Negro life represented by Paul Laurence Dunbar's dialect verse. On the other hand, wrote Ivy in agreement with Locke, Charles Chesnutt foreshadowed the spirit of the rebellious 1920s.[94] "What then has been the Negro's contribution to the last fifty years of American literature?" Ivy asked. "We have brought a new sensitivity and a new point of view into American letters," he answered. "We have contributed a creditable body of work in every literary form and we have produced writers of real achievement who are appraised as American and not just 'Negro' writers. And we have all but abandoned the old crippling concern with the gap between the Negro and the white audience." Ivy concluded with words that coincided with Locke's views: "We can look forward to every new generation of Negro writers adding a new chapter and a new verse to the book of American literary achievement."[95]

Alongside the development of black literature was that of black art, as James A. Porter reported in his article titled "Progress of the Negro in Art During the Past Fifty Years." Porter, a professor of art at Howard University, credited the Renaissance for the advances made in this field. He said that artists such as Aaron Douglas, Richmond Barthe, Sargent Johnson, Jacob Lawrence, Augusta Savage, and Selma Burke were to be credited for doing the actual creative work, while writers such as Locke and Benjamin Brawley were to be credited for broadening the perspective of Negroes on the history of Negro art.[96] He was evidently referring to Locke's book titled *Negro Art: Past and Present* (1936) and Brawley's *The Negro Genius* (1937).

In "Fifty Years of Progress in the Professions," Ira Reid, a black professor of sociology at Haverford College, formerly at Atlanta University, covered such areas as teaching, medicine, dentistry, law, technology, religion, and the "cultural professions." With regard to the cultural professions, he said that today's Negro musicians—singers, arrangers, composers, and conductors—have made great strides. The Negro singer, for instance, is not only a respected interpreter of Negro spirituals, he wrote, but a foremost interpreter of Bach.[97]

William Grant Still elaborated on this point in his essay for the series, "Fifty Years of Progress in Music." Supported by photographs of Burleigh, Hayes, Dett, and Clarence Cameron White, Still listed all the evidence of black progress in the choral and instrumental fields of music (namely, the historic "firsts" and subsequent achievements that I discussed in chapters 2 and 3). He concluded the article saying, "we can indeed look back over the last half century with pride and forward to the next with keen anticipation. We can be proud, yes—but not complacent. The time for fighting has just begun!"[98] This certainly is not representative of a pessimistic attitude with respect to the Renaissance, but rather of an optimistic one based on the presumption that there was steady progress.

This progress was not only evident in the "cultural professions" in general and music in particular, but also in the black church, as documented in "Fifty Years of Progress in the Negro Church" by Morehouse College president Benjamin Mays. Mays's essay is on the black social gospel, as we would anticipate in the age of the New Negro, for he cites evidence of progress in those churches that supplemented their spiritual ministry with a social ministry concerned with such aspects of secular life as education, recreation, business, and politics.[99] This was the kind of expression of Christianity, as I pointed out earlier, that Locke and Johnson approved of.

The aforementioned advances in the arts, letters, professions, and religion, all carried out during the Negro Renaissance by the New Negro, were accompanied by advances in those areas that were perhaps most important to the masses of blacks—their acquisition of civil and human rights. Walter White, secretary for the NAACP, said in "Civil Rights: Fifty Years of Fighting" that the Negro civil rights organizations founded in the early part of the century joined forces with the Negro newspapers in calling for the civil rights of Negroes.[100] White continued, "the first half of the Twentieth Century has been devoted to a struggle to move the ball from the shadow of one's own goal posts up to the center of the field. The advocates of civil rights have certainly moved the ball at least to the fifty-yard line." He concluded, "I might be even more optimistic and say that it has been rushed even further into the enemy's territory. The fight during the second half of the century will be that of carrying further down the field and across the goal line of the enemy."[101] Following these words are a list of twenty-four cases that the NAACP won before the United States Supreme Court.

Finally, in the piece titled "Fifty Years of Progress in Human Relations," all of the areas of black progress were tied together by Edwin R. Embree, who with Walter White was the moving force behind the founding of the American Council of Race Relations. Above photographs of such diverse scholars, leaders, and artists as Du Bois, Duke Ellington, Marian Anderson, and Ralph Bunche, Embree discussed the contribution of the Negro Renaissance alongside economic advance. He viewed all of this as distinct progress over the previous fifty years when the social and economic position of blacks permitted whites to go unchallenged in their belief in white supremacy. He wrote, "There was nothing like the present Harlem or South Chicago or the dozen other flourishing centers where Negroes today form their own societies, publish their own newspapers, develop their own businesses, and foster their own arts."[102] In terms of my argument that the Renaissance worked to help blacks transgress the essentialist color line, Embree said that in 1900, white supremacy was accepted throughout America and the world as the law of nature, but that in 1950, white supremacy was finished, even if vestigial traces remained: "While glaring discriminations persist, they, too, are but remnants of an outgrown order. No intelligent man today claims the biological superiority of one race over another. . . . The triumph of the first half of the Twentieth Century is not yet seen in democratic practices, but it is a triumph nonetheless, a transformation in the minds of men."[103] What sweet vindication, Locke must have been thinking.

V

So, first of all, the artistic productivity of the Renaissance continued. The "hopeless mess" that Claude McKay said characterized the Renaissance in 1930 was but the passing of a faddish phase that made way for "a sounder, more artistic expression of Negro life"; and the decreasing quantity of published output caused by the Depression was compensated for by a rise in the quality of the art. Secondly, the strategy that undergirded the Renaissance increasingly became a very good answer to the old problem of racism; for as Edwin Embree commented in "Fifty Years of Progress in Human Relations," the triumph of the first half of the century involved the transformation of the minds of whites to the point where no intelligent white person could believe any longer that blacks were their biological inferiors. Locke concluded that this re-imaging of the Negro, the prerequisite to "culture citizenship," resulted in the freeing of all Negro artists:

Not that all contemporary Negro artists are conscious racialists— far from it. But they all benefit, whether they choose to be racially expressive or not, from the new freedom and dignity that Negro life and materials have attained in the world of contemporary art. And, as might be expected, with the removal of the cultural stigma and burdensome artistic onus of the past, Negro artists are showing an increasing tendency toward their own racial milieu as a special province and in their general work are reflecting more racially distinctive notes and overtones.[104]

Indeed, not all contemporary artists were conscious racialists—far from it, as Jean Toomer proved. But all artists, whether they chose to be racially expressive or not, benefited by the new freedom and dignity that Renaissance art had attained. This was a concept that Toomer failed to grasp. He said he recognized that the Renaissance movement had "some valuable results," but only for those who had and would benefit by it, which did not include him, he said.[105]

Thus, when Nathan Huggins measures the Negro Renaissance artists against artists of the late 1960s and early 1970s and says the latter writers exploded into the American mind in a way that the Renaissance literati would not have dared to do,[106] he is disregarding the sacrifice of their predecessors who removed "the cultural stigma and burdensome artistic onus of the past." He is disregarding those whose "mastery of form" (Baker) and particularized expression of this "mastery" in the two-tiered "mastery of form and technique" and "mastery of mood and spirit" (Locke) enabled the next generation of black artists to show "an increasing tendency toward their own racial milieu."

I believe it was due to the accomplishments resulting from the "mastery of form" by the Renaissance Negroes (Baker) that the door was opened for the "deformation of mastery" to become the dominant strategy, as well as a luxury, beginning in the early 1960s. However, the radical black youths of the late 1960s and the 1970s failed to understand their indebtedness. For instance, Still was attacked in the same way the Renaissance literati of the 1920s were attacked by Huggins around the same time and with the same mindset—indeed, in the same way that Benjamin Stolberg attacked Dett in *The Crisis* for the way he handled the European tour of the Hampton choir in 1930. Still recalled the incident as having occurred when he was teaching a college music class during a visiting lecture. Two militant black students rudely challenged him, he said:

> Basically, they told me my music was not Negro music which, in their opinion, was the jungle-type sounds heard over a particular radio station in that city. All else was what they termed "Eur"-American music, rather than Afro-American. They also seemed disturbed because the clarinetists in the orchestras that played my music (one of them was the Royal Philharmonic of London) didn't play like Duke Ellington's clarinetist. Indeed, they seemed aston-

ished that my compositions didn't sound like the Duke's! They were even a little sad when I told them they were not intended to sound that way. One of them prattled about the bourgeois and White man's music, while the other made it a point to let me know that he did not "identify" with my music, no doubt expecting me to be crushed by this verdict.[107]

These militants who challenged Still were of a new generation, a generation that had unacknowledgably benefited from the strategy of the "mastery of form," which had opened the doors for that generation to be able to appreciate the spirituals and blues without needing to fear the image of inferiority once associated with these forms of folk music. Still also touched on this idea about the Renaissance Negro ushering in an atmosphere of artistic freedom via their removal of the cultural stigma and the burdensome artistic onus of the past. He said there were as many different kinds of Negro music as there were different types of Negroes, and that if the film industry would depart from their stereotypes of Negroes long enough to show the public a "finer type of Negro and more sophisticated Negro music," then even Negroes themselves would be able to enjoy the "cruder aspects of Negro life" because they would know that the public, at home and abroad, would no longer have a one-sided view of their race.[108] With regard to the militants who challenged Still, the point is that history has repeatedly borne out the fact that it is from within the interstices of "form" that has been mastered that blacks have gleaned the ability to debunk that "form" most effectively. In other words, people brought up in an age of Jim Crow could and did move most capably and confidently from the "mastery of form" to stripping themselves of these formulary limitations that were requisite if they were to forge out a voice in tight places.

Mastery of "form" has long functioned strategically in the black community as a means of holding the oppressor at bay long enough to permit the fashioning of "deformative creativity" as a strategy. This is exactly what occurred in the years following the 1920s. The "deformation of mastery," which was a subdued or masked characteristic in the "mastery of form" during the 1920s and early 1930s, began to "strip" and run parallel to its incubator around 1934 and during the 1940s and 1950s when the maturer phase of the Renaissance evolved. The transition that led to the strategy of "creative deformation" emerging to the forefront of the discourse of self-conscious racialism had begun around 1934 and was well in place by the late 1940s, if we accept Locke's view of the Negro Renaissance. In his retrospective review of black literature for 1947, Locke said: "There can be little doubt that we have entered an era of crisis literature and crisis art, when even our fiction reflects, like a sorcerer's mirror, instead of the face of society, the crucial inner conflict and anxiety of society itself. Our artists increasingly become social critics and reformers as our novelists are fast becoming strident sociologists and castigating prophets."[109] Among the crisis literature was not only the fiction of Richard Wright, Chester B. Himes, Ralph Ellison, and James Baldwin, but also the nonfiction of James Weldon Johnson—namely, Johnson's powerful little book, *Negro Americans, What Now?* (1934). Among the crisis art was William Grant Still's *And They Lynched Him on a Tree* (1940).

So, the Negro Renaissance had its roots in the end of the nineteenth century, about 1895, and began to develop in 1917, burgeoning in the mid-1920s and tapering off over a six-year anti-climax that the Great Depression helped bring on in 1929—thus Locke's designation of the years 1917 to 1934 as comprising the first generation of the Negro Renaissance. The year 1934 also commenced the second generation of the Renaissance and the emergence of protest literature. It was a transitional period, lasting about three decades, during which "creative deformation" began to run parallel with and eventually surpassed "creative mastery." By 1964, the Negro Renaissance, what Baker terms "renaissancism," was something else, not because it "died" but because it was irrevocably modified: The strategy of "creative mastery" became tradition, and the tradition of "creative deformation" became the strategy.

Notes

Prologue

1. Throughout this book my citations are from James Weldon Johnson, *The Autobiography of an Ex-Colored Man,* in *Three Negro Classics* (1912; rpt. New York: Avon, 1965).

Introduction

1. James Weldon Johnson to Sherman, French and Company, 17 Feb. 1912, James Weldon Johnson Collection, Beinecke Rare Book and Manuscript Library, Yale Univ., New Haven, Conn., hereafter cited as Johnson Collection.
2. Carl Van Vechten, introduction to *The Autobiography of an Ex-Coloured Man,* by James Weldon Johnson (New York: Alfred A. Knopf, 1927), vi.
3. Johnson to Sherman, French and Company, 17 Feb. 1912, Johnson Collection.
4. Charles S. Johnson, introduction to *The Autobiography of an Ex-Colored Man,* by James Weldon Johnson (New York: Pelican Mentor, 1948), ii–iii.
5. Carl Diton to Alain Locke, 26 Dec. 1910, Alain Locke Papers, Manuscripts Division, Moorland-Spingarn Research Center, Howard Univ., Washington, D.C., hereafter cited as Locke Papers.
6. Diton to Locke, 26 Dec. 1910, Locke Papers.
7. Alain Locke to Charlotte Mason, 10 Sept. 1934, Locke Papers.
8. Roland Hayes to Locke, 31 Mar. 1937, Locke Papers.
9. Kemper Harreld to Locke, 25 Aug. 1941, Locke Papers.
10. William Grant Still to Locke, 22 Mar. 1937, Locke Papers.
11. Paul Burgett, "Vindication as a Thematic Principle in the Writings of Alain

Locke on the Music of Black Americans," in *Black Music in the Harlem Renaissance,* ed. Samuel A. Floyd, Jr., (1990; Knoxville: Univ. of Tennessee Press, 1993), 37–38, 39.

12. Carl Diton to Locke, 26 Dec. 1910, Locke Papers.

13. Georgia A. Ryder, "Harlem Renaissance Ideals in the Music of Robert Nathaniel Dett," in *Black Music in the Harlem Renaissance,* ed. Floyd, 55.

14. Rae Linda Brown, "William Grant Still, Florence Price, and William Dawson: Echoes of the Harlem Renaissance," in *Black Music in the Harlem Renaissance,* ed. Floyd, 75.

15. Locke to William Grant Still, 14 Mar. 1937, William Grant Still and Verna Arvey Papers, Special Collections, Univ. of Arkansas, Fayetteville.

16. Samuel A. Floyd, Jr., "Music in the Harlem Renaissance: An Overview," in *Black Music in the Harlem Renaissance,* ed. Floyd, 3.

17. Floyd, "Music in the Harlem Renaissance," 5.

18. Floyd, "Music in the Harlem Renaissance," 14.

19. Martin Blum, "Black Music: Pathmaker of the Harlem Renaissance," *Missouri Journal of Research in Music Education* 3, no. 3 (1974): 75.

20. Willis Richardson, "The Hope of a Negro Drama," *The Crisis* 19, no. 1 (Nov. 1919): 338.

21. James Weldon Johnson, ed., *The Second Book of the Negro Spirituals* (New York: Viking, 1926), 19.

22. Alfred A. Knopf, Inc., to "Dear Sir," form letter, 19 Nov. 1927, Johnson Collection.

23. Johnson to William C. Graves, 24 May 1919, Johnson Collection.

24. Alain L. Locke, "The Negro Spirituals," in *The New Negro,* ed. Alain L. Locke (1925; rpt. New York: Atheneum, 1980), 200.

Chapter 1. A Power That Will Some Day Be Applied to Higher Forms

1. Alain L. Locke, "The New Negro," in *The New Negro,* ed. Locke, 3.

2. Charles S. Johnson, "Public Opinion and the Negro," *Opportunity* 1, no. 7 (July 1923): 202.

3. Johnson, "Public Opinion and the Negro," 206.

4. James Weldon Johnson, "The Larger Success," *The Southern Workman* 52, no. 9 (Sept. 1923): 429–30.

5. Charles S. Johnson, editorial, "Blackness and Whiteness," *Opportunity* 6, no. 4 (Apr. 1928): 100.

6. Charles S. Johnson, editorial, "Welcoming the New Negro," *Opportunity* 4, no. 4 (Apr. 1926): 113.

7. James Weldon Johnson to Elisabeth Gilman, 23 Feb. 1935, Johnson Collection.

8. Alain L. Locke, *Race Contacts and Interracial Relations: Lectures on the*

Theory and Practice of Race, ed. Jeffrey C. Stewart (Washington, D.C.: Howard Univ. Press, 1992), 2–3.

9. Locke, "The New Negro," 3.

10. Carl Van Vechten, "Religious Folk Songs of the American Negro—A Review," *Opportunity* 3 (Nov. 1925): 331.

11. Hubert H. Harrison, "Homo Africanus Harlemi," *New York Amsterdam News,* 1 Sept. 1926, 20.

12. Charlotte Mason, notebook, "Memos. Negro Art," 19 Apr. 1927, Locke Papers.

13. James Weldon Johnson, *God's Trombones: Seven Negro Sermons in Verse* (New York: Viking, 1927), 7.

14. James Weldon Johnson, ed., *The Book of American Negro Poetry* (1922; rpt. rev. ed., New York: Harcourt, Brace and World, 1959), 41.

15. Johnson to Flora M. Todd, 8 Mar. 1938, Johnson Collection.

16. Kelly Miller, "Perfect Picture of Harlem," *New York Amsterdam News,* 30 July 1930, 20.

17. Harold Preece, "The Negro Folk Cult," *The Crisis* 43, no. 12 (Dec. 1936): 364.

18. Nathan Irvin Huggins, *Harlem Renaissance* (New York: Oxford Univ. Press, 1971), 65.

19. Huggins, *Harlem Renaissance,* 306.

20. Anne Key Simpson, *Hard Trials: The Life and Music of Harry T. Burleigh* (Metuchen, N.J.: Scarecrow, 1990), 107.

21. Zora Neale Hurston to Charlotte Mason, 15 Oct. 1931, Locke Papers.

22. Simpson, *Hard Trials,* 28.

23. Simpson, *Hard Trials,* 98.

24. Simpson, *Hard Trials,* 77.

25. Cited in Simpson, *Hard Trials,* 201.

26. Jean Toomer to Johnson, 11 July 1930, Johnson Collection.

27. Cited in John M. Burgess, "Opening Presentation (Convocation of Black Theologians, Apr. 1978)," *Saint Luke's Journal of Theology* 22, no. 4 (Sept. 1979): 245.

28. Zora Neale Hurston to Johnson, 16 Apr. 1934, Johnson Collection.

29. "Rector Hides Behind 'Smoke Screen' in Raising 'Jim Crow,'" *New York Amsterdam News,* 18 Sept. 1929, 1.

30. Delores Calvin to Verna Arvey, 3 Apr. 1944, William Grant Still and Verna Arvey Papers, Special Collections, Univ. of Arkansas, Fayetteville, Arkansas.

31. Huggins, *Harlem Renaissance,* 306.

32. MacKinley Helm, *Angel Mo' and Her Son, Roland Hayes* (Boston: Little Brown, 1942), 106–7.

33. Helm, *Angel Mo' and Her Son, Roland Hayes,* 283–84.

34. J. A. Rogers, "Roland Hayes in Paris," *New York Amsterdam News,* 11 Jan. 1928, 8.

35. W. E. B. Du Bois, "Criteria of Negro Art," *The Crisis* 36, no. 6 (Oct. 1926): 294.

36. Du Bois, "Criteria of Negro Art," 296.

37. "Burleigh," *The Crisis* 28, no. 1 (May 1924): 12.

38. Elmer Anderson Carter, editorial, "Harry Thacker Burleigh," *Opportunity* 16, no. 5 (May 1938): 132.

39. Allen Woll, *Black Musical Theatre: From Coontown to Dreamgirls* (Baton Rouge: Louisiana State Univ. Press, 1989), 137.

40. "Hayes," *The Crisis* 33, no. 3 (Jan. 1927): 129.

41. William Pickens, "The Negro's Religion and Music," *New York Amsterdam News,* 15 June 1932, 8.

42. Johnson, "The Larger Success," 434.

43. Houston A. Baker, Jr., *Modernism and the Harlem Renaissance* (Chicago: Univ. of Chicago Press, 1987), 17, 24, 27, 30.

44. Baker, *Modernism and the Harlem Renaissance,* 32.

45. Baker, *Modernism and the Harlem Renaissance,* 33.

46. James Weldon Johnson, *Negro Americans, What Now?* (New York: Viking, 1934), 81.

47. Johnson to Frank G. Yerby, 4 Nov. 1933, Johnson Collection.

48. Charlotte Mason, notebooks, 10 and 17 Mar. 1927, Locke Papers.

49. Langston Hughes to Alain Locke, n.d., 1928, Locke Papers.

50. Mason to Locke, 4 Mar. 1928, Locke Papers.

51. Mason to Locke, 20 Apr. 1929, Locke Papers.

52. Mason to Locke, 12 July 1929; Mason to Locke, 8 May 1930, Locke Papers.

53. Mason to Locke, 23 Apr. 1930, Locke Papers.

54. *News* (Chicago), 29 Sept. 1926. Cited in Martin Bauml Duberman, *Paul Robeson* (New York: Alfred A. Knopf, 1988), 81.

55. Arthur Ruhl, "Second Nights," *New York Herald Tribune,* 17 Jan. 1932.

56. Langston Hughes, *The Big Sea* (New York: Alfred A. Knopf, 1940), 325.

57. Mason, notebook, 20 Feb. 1927, Locke Papers.

58. Mason, notebooks, 20 and 21 Feb. 1927, Locke Papers.

59. Mason, notebooks, 19 and 24 Apr. 1927, Locke Papers.

60. Natalie Curtis, ed., *The Indians' Book* (New York: Harper and Brothers, 1907), xxi, xxiii.

61. Locke to Mason, 28 Feb. 1935; Mason to Locke, 2 Mar. 1935; Locke to Mason, 4 Oct. 1940, Locke Papers.

62. Curtis, ed., *The Indians' Book,* xxx.

63. Albert C. Barnes, "Negro Art and America," in *The New Negro,* ed. Locke,19, 20, 23, 24, 25.

64. Hurston to Mason, 28 Sept. 1932, Locke Papers.

65. Hurston to Mason, 15 Oct. 1931; Hurston to Mason, 10 Mar. 1931, Locke Papers.

66. Hurston to Mason, 4 Apr. 1932, Locke Papers.

67. Hurston to Mason, 27 Apr. 1932, Locke Papers.

68. Hurston to Mason, 23 July 1931, Locke Papers.

69. Hurston to Mason, 23 July 1931, Locke Papers.
70. Hurston to Mason, 26 Oct. 1931, Locke Papers.
71. Locke to Mason, 20 May 1933, Locke Papers.
72. Locke to Mason, 21 Dec. 1933, Locke Papers.
73. Locke to Mason, 6 July 1939, Locke Papers.
74. Locke to Mason, 7 Dec. 1937, Locke Papers.
75. Alain L. Locke, "Youth Speaks," in *The Critical Temper of Alain Locke: A Selection of His Essays on Art and Culture,* ed. Jeffrey C. Stewart (New York: Garland, 1983), 13. Originally published in *Survey Graphic* 53, no. 11 (Mar. 1, 1925).
76. Alain L. Locke, "Toward a Critique of Negro Music," in *The Critical Temper of Alain Locke,* ed. Stewart, 115. Originally published in *Opportunity* 12, nos. 11–12 (Nov. and Dec. 1934).
77. William Grant Still, "A Symphony of Dark Voices," in *The William Grant Still Reader: Essays on American Music,* ed. Jon Michael Spencer, a special issue of *Black Sacred Music: A Journal of Theomusicology* 6, no. 2 (Fall 1992): 137. Originally published in *Opera, Concert and Symphony,* May 1947.
78. William Grant Still, "The Music of My Race," in *The William Grant Still Reader,* ed. Spencer, 102. Originally published in *Musica* 1, no. 5 (Aug. 1941).
79. Alain L. Locke, *The Negro and His Music* (Washington, D.C.: Associates in Negro Folk Education, 1936), 139–40.
80. Alain L. Locke, "The American Negro as Artist," in *The Critical Temper of Alain Locke,* ed. Stewart, 171. Originally published in *American Magazine of Art* 23 (Sept. 1931).
81. William Grant Still, "The Negro Musician in America," in *The William Grant Still Reader,* ed. Spencer, 207–8. Originally published in *Music Educators Journal* 56 (Jan. 1970).
82. R. Nathaniel Dett, "Negro Music," in *The R. Nathaniel Dett Reader: Essays on Black Sacred Music,* ed. Jon Michael Spencer, a special issue of *Black Sacred Music: A Journal of Theomusicology* 5, no. 2 (Fall 1991): 127. Originally published in *The International Cyclopedia of Music and Musicians,* ed. Oscar Thompson (New York: Dodd, Mead, 1938).
83. Samuel A. Floyd, Jr., "Music of the Harlem Renaissance: An Overview," in *Black Music in the Harlem Renaissance,* ed. Floyd, 3.
84. Cited in Carl R. Diton to Locke, 26 Dec. 1910, Locke Papers.
85. William Grant Still, "The Structure of Music," in *The William Grant Still Reader,* ed. Spencer, 174. Originally published in *Etude* 68 (Mar. 1950).
86. Helm, *Angel Mo' and Her Son, Roland Hayes,* 188–89.
87. Wilber P. Thirkield to Johnson, 4 Dec. 1931, Johnson Collection.
88. Dett, "Negro Music," 128.
89. George Foster Peabody to Locke, 13 Feb. 1926, Locke Papers; and George Foster Peabody Papers, Hampton Univ. Archives, Hampton, Va.
90. Peabody to Anne Wolter, 11 Feb. 1924, Peabody Papers.
91. Peabody to Robert Norwood, 5 Mar. 1931, Peabody Papers.

92. Peabody to George F. Ketcham, 18 July 1929, Music Collection, Hampton Univ. Archives, Hampton, Va.
93. Sterling A. Brown to Johnson, 17 Feb. 1932, Johnson Collection.
94. Johnson to Sterling A. Brown, 22 Feb. 1932, Johnson Collection.
95. John Hurst to Johnson, 14 June 1927, Johnson Collection.
96. Thirkield to Johnson, 6 June 1927, Johnson Collection.
97. Zora Neale Hurston to Thomas E. Jones, president of Fisk Univ., 12 Oct. 1934, Johnson Collection.
98. Hurston to Jones, 12 Oct. 1934, Johnson Collection.
99. Hurston to Johnson, 8 May 1934, Johnson Collection.
100. Johnson to Hurston, 20 Apr. 1934, Johnson Collection.
101. "Harmon Foundation Director Explains Work," *New York Amsterdam News,* 18 July 1928, 16.
102. Kelly Miller, "Why So Much about Harlem?" *New York Amsterdam News,* 26 Mar. 1930, 20.
103. Hubert J. Cox, "Disagrees," *New York Amsterdam News,* 7 May 1930, 14.
104. Reverdy C. Ransom, "The New Negro," *New York Amsterdam News,* 3 Jan. 1923, 12.
105. Huggins, *Harlem Renaissance,* 64.
106. Locke, *The Negro and His Music,* 4.
107. James W. Brown to Johnson, 31 May 1927, Johnson Collection.
108. Huggins, *Harlem Renaissance,* 65.
109. William Pickens, *The New Negro: His Political, Civil and Mental Status and Related Essays* (New York: Neale Publishing Company, 1916), 224.
110. Pickens, *The New Negro,* 225.
111. Huggins, *Harlem Renaissance,* 64.
112. Locke, *Race Contacts and Interracial Relations,* 90.
113. Locke, *Race Contacts and Interracial Relations,* 99.
114. Alain L. Locke, "The Ethics of Culture," in *The Critical Temper of Alain Locke,* ed. Stewart, 421. Originally published in *Howard University Record* 17 (Jan. 1923).
115. Johnson, "The Larger Success," 432.
116. Johnson, "The Larger Success," 433–34.
117. Johnson, "The Larger Success," 434.
118. Johnson, *Negro Americans, What Now?* 52.
119. Johnson, *Negro Americans, What Now?* 92–93.
120. Toomer to Johnson, 11 July 1930, Johnson Collection.
121. Johnson to Toomer, 26 July 1930, Johnson Collection.
122. Huggins, *Harlem Renaissance,* 306.
123. R. Nathaniel Dett, program notes, concert by the Hampton Institute Choir, Carnegie Hall, New York, 16 Apr. 1928, in *The R. Nathaniel Dett Reader,* ed. Spencer, 94.
124. Locke, "Youth Speaks," 13.
125. William Grant Still and Verna Arvey, "Our American Musical Resources," in *The William Grant Still Reader,* ed. Spencer, 196–97. Originally published in *Music Clubs Magazine,* Fall 1961.
126. William Grant Still, "An Afro-American Composer's Viewpoint," in *The*

William Grant Still Reader, ed. Spencer, 232. Originally published in William Grant Still and the Fusion of Cultures in American Music, ed. Robert Bartlett Haas (Los Angeles: Black Sparrow, 1975).

127. Locke, "Youth Speaks," 14.

128. R. Nathaniel Dett, "From Bell Stand to Throne Room," in The R. Nathaniel Dett Reader, ed. Spencer, 97. Originally published in Etude 52 (Feb. 1934).

129. William Grant Still, "My Arkansas Boyhood," in The William Grant Still Reader, ed. Spencer, 248. Originally published in William Grant Still and the Fusion of Cultures in American Music, ed. Haas.

130. Cited in Anne Key Simpson, Follow Me: The Life and Music of R. Nathaniel Dett (Metuchen, N.J.: Scarecrow, 1993), 333.

131. Locke to Mason, 12 Mar. 1936, Locke Papers.

132. Huggins, Harlem Renaissance, 65.

133. Locke, "The New Negro," 8.

134. Locke, "The New Negro," 10.

135. Dett, "Negro Music," 123.

136. Still, "A Composer's Viewpoint," in The William Grant Still Reader, ed. Spencer, 217. Originally published in William Grant Still and the Fusion of Cultures in American Music, ed. Haas.

137. Locke, Race Contacts and Interracial Relations, 1.

138. Locke, Race Contacts and Interracial Relations, 84–85.

139. "Paul Robeson," New York Amsterdam News, 8 Jan. 1930, 9. Originally published in Cornell Sun.

140. Johnson to Roberta Bosley, 5 Apr. 1932, Johnson Collection.

141. Johnson to (Mrs.) C. H. Trowbridge, 27 Mar. 1936, Johnson Collection.

142. James Weldon Johnson, ed., The Book of American Negro Spirituals (New York: Viking, 1925), 12.

143. "Collapsible Color Line," Boston Globe, 11 Mar. 1929.

144. Helm, Angel Mo' and Her Son, Roland Hayes, 192–93.

145. Sterling Brown, "Roland Hayes," Opportunity 3, no. 6 (June 1925): 173.

146. Brown, "Roland Hayes," 174.

Chapter 2. Wild Dreams of Bringing Glory and Honor to the Negro Race

1. R. Nathaniel Dett, "Religious Folk-Songs of the Negro," in The R. Nathaniel Dett Reader: Essays on Black Sacred Music, a special issue of Black Sacred Music: A Journal of Theomusicology 5, no. 2 (Fall 1991): 59. Originally published as introduction to Religious Folk-Songs of the Negro: As Sung at Hampton Institute (Hampton, Va.: Hampton Institute Press, 1927).

2. R. Nathaniel Dett, "Negro Music," in The R. Nathaniel Dett Reader, ed. Spencer, 123. Originally published in The International Cyclopedia of Music and Musicians.

3. R. Nathaniel Dett, review of Negro Workaday Songs, by Howard W.

Odum and Guy B. Johnson, in *The R. Nathaniel Dett Reader,* ed. Spencer, 52. Originally published in *Southern Workman* 56 (1927).

4. R. Nathaniel Dett, "Understanding the Negro Spiritual," in *The R. Nathaniel Dett Reader,* ed. Spencer, 104. Originally published in *The Dett Collection of Negro Spirituals,* 2nd group (Minneapolis: Hall and McCreary, 1936).

5. R. Nathaniel Dett, "The Development of Negro Religious Music," in *Negro Music,* Bowdoin Literary Prize Thesis, Harvard Univ., 1920, in *The R. Nathaniel Dett Reader,* ed. Spencer, 38.

6. Dett, "The Development of Negro Religious Music," 38.

7. Dett, "Religious Folk-Songs of the Negro," 59.

8. Dett, "The Development of Negro Religious Music," 38.

9. Dett, "The Development of Negro Religious Music," 39.

10. Dett, "The Development of Negro Religious Music," 39–40.

11. Olin Downes, "Hampton Institute Choir," *New York Times,* 18 Apr. 1928.

12. Downes, "Hampton Institute Choir."

13. Olin Downes, "Cincinnati Hears Music by Burlioz; Dett Piece also is Heard," *New York Times,* 8 May 1937, 22.

14. Downes, "Cincinnati Hears Music by Berlioz; Dett Piece also is Heard," 22.

15. Charlotte Mason to Alain Locke, 6 Aug. 1929, Locke Papers.

16. Mason to Locke, 1 Dec. 1928, Locke Papers.

17. Mason to Locke, 26 Aug. 1929, Locke Papers.

18. Mason to Locke, 26 Aug. 1929, Locke Papers.

19. George Foster Peabody to Arthur Howe, 16 Feb. 1932, Arthur Howe Papers, Hampton Univ. Archives, Hampton, Va.

20. Peabody to Robert Ogden Purves, 11 Sept. 1929, Music Collection, Hampton Univ. Archives, Hampton, Va.

21. Dett, "The Development of Negro Religious Music," 36.

22. *Boston Globe,* 11 Mar. 1929. Cited in Anne Key Simpson, *Follow Me,* 154.

23. *Boston Globe,* 11 Mar. 1929. Cited in Simpson, *Follow Me,* 156.

24. Peabody to Dett, 7 June [1920], George Foster Peabody Papers, Hampton Univ. Archives, Hampton, Va.

25. Johnson, "The Larger Success," 432.

26. Peabody to Purves, 18 July 1929, Music Collection.

27. Peabody to George F. Ketcham, 13 July 1929, Music Collection.

28. Cited in Peabody to Robert Russa Moton, 29 Aug. 1929, Music Collection.

29. Mason to Locke, 6 Aug. 1929, Locke Papers.

30. Peabody to Ketcham, 18 July 1929, Music Collection.

31. Peabody to Dett, 2 Dec. 1929, Music Collection.

32. Peabody to George P. Phenix, 2 Dec. 1929, Music Collection.

33. Peabody to Howe, 5 Aug. 1931, Howe Papers; Peabody to John H. Finley, 12 May 1930, Music Collection.

34. Peabody to Moton, 5 Nov. 1929; Peabody to (Miss) G. A. Gollock, 26 Aug. 1929, Music Collection.

35. Solomon Phillips, Jr., diary, 6 May 1930, Phillips Collection, Hampton Univ. Archives, Hampton, Va.

36. Ketcham to Phenix, 11 May 1930, Music Collection. Also see R. Nathaniel

Dett, "A Musical Invasion of Europe," in *The R. Nathaniel Dett Reader,* ed. Spencer, 88. Originally published in *The Crisis* 37 (1930).

37. "The Administrative Board, at a Meeting Held on October 23, 1929," manuscript, Hampton Institute European Tour Collection, Hampton Univ. Archives, Hampton, Va.

38. Second Vice President, Hampton Board of Trustees to Albert Morini, 6 Jan. 1930, Music Collection.

39. Purves to Peabody, 11 Jan. 1930, Music Collection.

40. Purves to Peabody, 11 Jan. 1930, Music Collection.

41. Arthur W. Packard, representative of Mr. and Mrs. John D. Rockefeller, Jr., to Moton, 2 Dec. 1929, Music Collection.

42. Peabody to Purves, 11 Sept. 1929, Music Collection.

43. Dett to Phenix, 7 Apr. 1930, Music Collection.

44. Phenix to Ketcham, 21 Apr. 1930, Music Collection.

45. Ketcham to Phenix, 25 Apr. 1930, Music Collection.

46. Dett, "Negro Music," 126–27.

47. Dett, "Understanding the Negro Spiritual," 106.

48. Dett, "Religious Folk-Songs of the Negro," 65.

49. Dett, "Religious Folk-Songs of the Negro," 64.

50. Charles W. Dabney to Peabody, 8 May 1937, Peabody Papers.

51. Dett, review of *Negro Workaday Songs,* 46.

52. R. Nathaniel Dett, "The Development of Negro Secular Music," in *Negro Music,* 6.

53. R. Nathaniel Dett, "The Authenticity of the Spiritual," in *The R. Nathaniel Dett Reader,* ed. Spencer, 108. Originally published in *The Dett Collection of Negro Spirituals,* 3rd group (Minneapolis: Hall and McCreary, 1936).

54. Dett, "Negro Music," 127.

55. R. Nathaniel Dett, program notes, concert by the Hampton Institute Choir, Carnegie Hall, New York, 16 Apr. 1928, in *The R. Nathaniel Dett Reader,* 73.

56. *Boston Evening Transcript,* 11 Mar. 1929.

57. Allen B. Doggett, Jr., "Artistic Achievement," *Christian Advocate,* 20 Jan. 1927.

58. C. G. Jung, "Your Negroid and Indian Behavior," *The Forum,* Apr. 1930, 193, 194, 195.

59. Jung, "Your Negroid and Indian Behavior," 196.

60. See James Oppenheim, *American Types: A Preface to Analytic Psychology* (New York: Alfred A. Knopf, 1931).

61. James Oppenheim to James Weldon Johnson, 18 Dec. 1930, Johnson Collection.

62. Phenix to Dett, 21 Apr. 1930, Dett Collection, Hampton Univ. Archives, Hampton, Va.

63. Dett, "A Musical Invasion of Europe," 84–85.

64. Dett, "A Musical Invasion of Europe," 85.

65. Ketcham to Phenix, 2 May 1930, Music Collection.

66. Peabody to Purves, 3 Apr. 1930, Music Collection.

67. Ketcham to Phenix, 25 Apr. 1930, Music Collection.

68. "Descendants of Slaves Honored Africa's Friend," *Colonist* (Victoria, British Columbia), 14 June 1930.

69. "Cabin and Cloister," *Christian Science Monthly,* 10 May 1930.

70. "Deserving," *Musical Courier,* 24 May 1930.

71. "Deserving," *Musical Courier,* 24 May 1930.

72. Harold Butcher, "The Dawson Folk Symphony," *The Crisis* 42, no. 2 (Feb. 1935): 52.

73. Ketcham to Phenix, 4 May 1930, Music Collection.

74. Ketcham to Phenix, 2 May 1930, Music Collection.

75. Ketcham to Phenix, 4 May 1930, Music Collection.

76. Ketcham to Phenix, 4 May 1930, Music Collection.

77. Ketcham to Phenix, 17 May 1930, Music Collection.

78. "European Papers on Negro Artists," *New York Amsterdam News,* 21 May 1930, 8.

79. Phillips diary, 9 May 1930, Phillips Collection.

80. Cited in "Hampton Choir Sings Here Monday Night," *Chicago Defender,* 14 Mar. 1931, 3.

81. Ketcham to Phenix, 11 May 1930, Music Collection.

82. Cited in "Hampton Choir Sings Here Monday Night."

83. Phillips diary, 20 May 1930, Phillips Collection.

84. Cited in "Hampton Choir Sings Here Monday Night."

85. Ketcham to Phenix, 17 May 1930, Music Collection.

86. Ketcham to Phenix, 25 Apr. 1930, Music Collection.

87. Cited in "Hampton Choir Sings Here Monday Night."

88. Phillips diary, 14 May 1930, Phillips Collection.

89. Lewis D. Crenshaw to the President of Hampton Institute [George P. Phenix], 15 May 1930, Hampton Institute European Tour Collection.

90. Phenix to Lewis D. Crenshaw, 3 June 1930, Music Collection.

91. Phillips diary, 31 May 1930, Phillips Collection.

92. Cited in "Hampton Choir Sings Here Monday Night."

93. Phillips diary, 23 May 1930, Phillips Collection.

94. Cited in "Hampton Choir Sings Here Monday Night."

95. Peabody to Robert Norwood, 5 Mar. 1931, Peabody Papers.

96. R. Nathaniel Dett, "The Emancipation of Negro Music," in *The R. Nathaniel Dett Reader,* ed. Spencer, 28. Originally published in *Negro Music.*

97. Phillips diary, 1 May 1930, Phillips Collection.

98. Peabody to Dett, 2 Aug. 1931, Peabody Papers.

99. Peabody to Dett, 2 Aug. 1931, Peabody Papers.

100. *Norfolk Journal and Guide,* 12 Oct. 1931. Cited in Vivian Flagg McBrier, *R. Nathaniel Dett: His Life and Works (1882–1943)* (Washington: Associated Publishers, 1977), 68–69.

101. Morini to Purves, 4 June 1930, Music Collection.

102. Purves to Morini, 19 June 1930, Music Collection.

103. Morini to Purves, 2 July 1930, Music Collection.

104. Purves to Morini, 16 July 1930, Music Collection.

105. Morini to Ketcham, 7 Sept. 1930, Music Collection.

106. Ketcham to Morini, 20 Sept. 1930, Music Collection.

107. Dett to Phenix, 7 Apr. 1930, Music Collection.

108. Dett to Howe, 5 Feb. 1931, Music Collection.

109. Dett to Howe, 5 Feb. 1931, Music Collection.

110. William Pickens, "The Missionary—John Work," *New York Amsterdam News,* 23 Sept. 1925, 16.

111. Peabody to Howe, 27 Nov. 1931, Howe Papers.

112. Cited in Simpson, *Follow Me,* 333.

113. Elmer Anderson Carter, editorial, "Marian Anderson," *Opportunity* 14, no. 1 (Jan. 1936): 5.

114. Johnson, "Public Opinion and the Negro," 202, 204.

115. "New Singer Interviewed," *New York Times,* 13 Aug. 1939.

116. Cited in William F. Rogers, Jr., *Dorothy Maynor and the Harlem School of the Arts: The Diva and the Dream* (Lewiston, N.Y.: Edwin Mellen, 1993), 85.

117. "Dorothy Maynor Dedicates Her Talent to Advancing Culture," *California Eagle* (Los Angeles), 30 Nov. 1950, 7.

118. Locke, *The Negro and His Music,* 123.

119. Alain L. Locke, "Roland Hayes: An Appreciation," in *The Critical Temper of Alain Locke,* ed. Stewart, 105.

120. G. James Fleming, "Hundreds Turned Away as Dorothy Maynor Sings," *Norfolk Journal and Guide,* 25 Nov. 1939.

121. Elmer Anderson Carter, editorial, "Dorothy Maynor," *Opportunity* 18, no. 2 (Feb. 1940): 34.

122. *Norfolk Journal and Guide,* 18 Jan. 1947.

123. Olin Downes, "Dorothy Maynor in Debut Recital," *New York Times,* 21 Nov. 1939.

124. Olin Downes, "Dorothy Maynor Heard in Recital," *New York Times,* 27 Oct. 1940.

125. Michael Mok, "The World Must Hear Her," *New York Post,* 22 Nov. 1939.

126. Mok, "The World Must Hear Her."

127. "A Negro Singer from Virginia Makes Exciting Concert Debut," *Life,* 11 Dec. 1939, 42.

128. "A Negro Singer from Virginia Makes Exciting Concert Debut," 41.

129. See Mok "The World Must Hear Her"; and Mok, "A Native Flagstad," *Newsweek,* 21 Aug. 1939.

130. "Dorothy Maynor's Debut," *Boston Herald,* Nov. 1939.

131. Phillips diary, 21 Apr. 1930, Phillips Collection.

Chapter 3. The Terrible Handicap of Working as a Negro Composer

1. William Grant Still, "Serious Music: New Field for the Negro," in *The William Grant Still Reader,* ed. Spencer, 192. Originally published in *Variety,* 5 Jan. 1955.

2. William Grant Still, "The Composer Needs Determination and Faith," in *The William Grant Still Reader,* ed. Spencer, 166. Originally published in *Etude* 67 (Jan. 1949).
3. Still, "Serious Music," 192.
4. Still, "The Composer Needs Determination and Faith," 164.
5. R. Nathaniel Dett, "From Bell Stand to Throne Room," in *The R. Nathaniel Dett Reader,* ed. Spencer, 94. Originally published in *Etude* 52 (Feb. 1934).
6. Still, "The Composer Needs Determination and Faith," 164.
7. William Grant Still, "My Arkansas Boyhood," in *The William Grant Still Reader,* ed. Spencer, 251. Originally published in *William Grant Still and the Fusion of Cultures in American Music,* ed. Haas.
8. William Grant Still, "A Composer's Viewpoint," *The William Grant Still Reader,* ed. Spencer, 130. Originally published in *William Grant Still and the Fusion of Cultures in American Music,* ed. Haas.
9. Still, "Serious Music," 192.
10. William Grant Still to Karl Wecker, Hollywood Bowl Association, 27 Apr. 1946, William Grant Still and Verna Arvey Papers, Special Collections, Univ. of Arkansas, Fayetteville.
11. William Grant Still, "Still Calls Nathaniel Dett One of Our 'Cultural Pioneers,'" *Los Angeles Tribune,* 8 Nov. 1943.
12. Hale Smith, "An Experience in Jazz History," in *Black Music in Our Culture,* ed. Dominique Rene de Lerma (Kent, Ohio: Kent State Univ. Press, 1970), 18.
13. Hale Smith to Still, 17 June 1964, Still-Arvey Papers.
14. Still to Hale Smith, 24 June 1964, Still-Arvey Papers.
15. William Grant Still, "For Finer Negro Music," *The William Grant Still Reader,* ed. Spencer, 95. Originally published in *Opportunity,* May 1939.
16. Mabel D. Brown, secretary, Oberlin Conservatory of Music, to Verna Arvey, 10 Apr. 1936, Still-Arvey Papers.
17. Eubie Blake to Arvey, 6 Dec. 1978, Still-Arvey Papers.
18. Carl Johnson to Arvey, 14 Mar. 1977, Still-Arvey Papers.
19. Arvey to Carl Johnson, assistant curator of the Whiteman Collection at Williams College in Massachusetts, 10 Mar. 1977, Still-Arvey Papers.
20. William Grant Still, "The Negro Musician in America," *The William Grant Still Reader,* ed. Spencer, 212. Originally published in *Music Educators Journal* 56 (Jan. 1970).
21. Alain L. Locke, introduction to *Plays of Negro Life: A Source-Book of Native American Drama,* ed. Alain L. Locke and Montgomery Gregory (New York: Harper and Brothers, 1927), iii.
22. Gwendolyn B. Bennett, "Edmund T. Jenkins: Musician," *Opportunity* 3 (Nov. 1925): 339.
23. Ignatz Waghalter to Johnson, 2 Feb. 1937 [1938], Johnson Collection.
24. Johnson to Waghalter, 17 Feb. 1938, Johnson Collection.
25. Walter White to Johnson, 26 Mar. 1938, Johnson Collection.
26. Johnson to White, 29 Mar. 1938, Johnson Collection.
27. White to Johnson, 1 Apr. 1938, Johnson Collection.

28. William Grant Still, "A Negro Symphony Orchestra," in *The William Grant Still Reader,* ed. Spencer, 97. Originally published in *Opportunity,* Sept. 1939.

29. Still, "A Negro Symphony Orchestra," 97.

30. Still, "A Negro Symphony Orchestra," 98.

31. Alain L. Locke, "Negro Music Goes to Par," in *The Critical Temper of Alain Locke,* ed. Stewart, 120. Originally published in *Opportunity* 17, no. 7 (July 1939).

32. Sigurd M. Rascher to Still, 20 Jan. 1951, Still-Arvey Papers.

33. Still, "A Symphony of Dark Voices," in *The William Grant Still Reader,* ed. Spencer, 140. Originally published in *Opera, Concert and Symphony,* May 1947.

34. Still to Leopold Stokowski, 27 Nov. 1948, Still-Arvey Papers.

35. Olin Downes, "More of the Ultra-Modern," *New York Times,* 29 Nov. 1926, 16.

36. Locke, "Negro Music Goes to Par," 120.

37. Still, "My Arkansas Boyhood," 251.

38. Still, "A Composer's Viewpoint," 225–26.

39. Locke to Carl Van Vechten, 16 Mar. 1942, Still-Arvey Papers.

40. Locke to Charlotte Mason, 24 May 1931, Locke Papers.

41. Locke to Van Vechten, 16 Mar. 1942, Still-Arvey Papers.

42. Locke to Mason, 24 May 1931, Locke Papers.

43. Olin Downes, "Ballet Presented at Rochester Fete," *New York Times,* 24 May 1931.

44. Locke to Mason, 22 May 1931, Locke Papers.

45. Locke to Mason, 24 May 1931, Locke Papers.

46. Alain Locke, "Toward a Critique of Negro Music," in *The Critical Temper of Alain Locke,* ed. Stewart, 113. Originally published in *Opportunity* 12, nos. 11–12 (Nov. and Dec. 1934).

47. Mason to Locke, 1 Feb. 1932, Locke Papers.

48. Locke to Mason, 24 July 1931, Locke Papers.

49. Locke to Still, [1942?], Still-Arvey Papers.

50. Locke to Still and Arvey, 2 July 1940, Still-Arvey Papers.

51. Eubie Blake to Still, 5 Sept. 1955, Still-Arvey Papers.

52. William Grant Still, "What a Composer Is," in *The William Grant Still Reader,* ed. Spencer, 260. Originally published in *William Grant Still and the Fusion of Cultures in American Music,* ed. Haas.

53. William Grant Still and Verna Arvey, "Negro Music in the Americas," in *The William Grant Still Reader,* ed. Spencer, 92. *Revue Internationale de Musique,* May–June 1938.

54. William Grant Still, "Spirituals, Blues Important Section of American Music," in *The William Grant Still Reader,* 100. Originally published in *New York Amsterdam News,* 29 June 1940.

55. Still to Rudolph Dunbar, 5 Apr. 1946, Still-Arvey Papers.

56. Still to P. L. Prattis, 20 Jan. 1946, Still-Arvey Papers.

57. Clarence Cameron White to James Weldon Johnson, 31 Dec. 1934, Johnson Collection.

58. William Grant Still, "Can Music Make a Career?" in *The William Grant Still Reader*, ed. Spencer, 157. Originally published in *Negro Digest*, Dec. 1948.

59. Still, "A Symphony of Dark Voices," 140.

60. William Grant Still, "The Men Behind American Music," in *The William Grant Still Reader*, ed. Spencer, 118. Originally published in *Crisis*, Jan. 1944.

61. William Grant Still, "How Do We Stand in Hollywood?" in *The William Grant Still Reader*, ed. Spencer, 124–25. Originally published in *Opportunity*, Spring 1945.

62. Still, "How Do We Stand in Hollywood?" 125.

63. Leopold Stokowski to Still, 20 Nov. 1937, Still-Arvey Papers.

64. Stokowski to Still, 27 May 1944, Still-Arvey Papers.

65. Delores Calvin to Arvey, 24 Mar. 1944, Still-Arvey Papers.

66. San Diego *Tribune*, 2 Aug. 1939.

67. Still to Arna Bontemps, 3 Oct. 1946, Still-Arvey Papers.

68. Verna Arvey, *In One Lifetime* (Fayetteville: Univ. of Arkansas Press, 1984), 126.

69. Verna Arvey, "Symphonies in Black," *Musical Journal* 32 (Apr. 1974): 35. Emphasis added.

70. Still and Arvey, "Negro Music in the Americas," 93. Emphasis added.

71. Alain Locke, "Youth Speaks," in *The Critical Temper of Alain Locke*, ed. Stewart, 13. Emphasis added. Originally published in *Survey Graphic* 53, no. 11 (Mar. 1, 1925).

72. William Grant Still, "The Negro and His Music," in *The William Grant Still Reader*, ed. Spencer, 107–8. Originally published in *War Worker*, Oct. 1943.

73. Still, "The Men Behind American Music," 114.

74. Still, "Spirituals, Blues Important Section of American Music," 100.

75. Still to Rudolph Dunbar, 1 Dec. 1945, Still-Arvey Papers.

76. Still to Langston Hughes, 11 Aug. 1948, Still-Arvey Papers.

77. Still, "How Do We Stand in Hollywood," 130.

78. Arvey to Dwight D. Eisenhower, 17 May 1953, Still-Arvey Papers.

79. Carl Van Vechten, introduction to Johnson, *The Autobiography of an Ex-Coloured Man*, ix.

80. Hall Johnson, "Porgy and Bess—a Folk Opera: A Review," *Opportunity* 14, no. 1 (Jan. 1936): 25.

81. Johnson, "Porgy and Bess," 26.

82. Johnson, "Porgy and Bess," 28.

83. Rudolph Dunbar to Still, 5 Apr. 1942, Still-Arvey Papers.

84. Rudolph Dunbar to Still, 19 May 1942, Still-Arvey Papers.

85. Zora Neale Hurston, "Characteristics of Negro Expression," in *Voices from the Harlem Renaissance*, ed. Nathan Irvin Huggins (New York: Oxford Univ. Press, 1976), 235.

86. Frank Hains, "William Grant Still: An American Composer Who Happens to be Black," *High Fidelity/Musical America* 25 (Mar. 1975): MA-27.

87. Still, "A Symphony of Dark Voices," 140.
88. Arvey to Nora Holt, 24 Dec. 1950, Still-Arvey Papers.
89. James Oppenheim to Johnson, 18 Dec. 1930, Johnson Collection.
90. Roland Hayes to Still, 2 July 1943, Still-Arvey Papers.
91. Still to Roland Hayes, 7 July 1943, Still-Arvey Papers.
92. Hortense Love to Still, 15 Oct. 1946, Still-Arvey Papers.
93. Still to Hortense Love, 15 Nov. 1946, Still-Arvey Papers.
94. Mattiwilda Dobbs to Still, 16 Feb. 1970, Still-Arvey Papers.
95. Arna Bontemps to Still, 28 Nov. [1950s], Still-Arvey Papers.
96. James Baldwin to Locke, 4 Feb. 1949, Locke Papers.
97. Still to Claude A. Barnett, Associated Negro Press, 17 Feb. 1943, Still-Arvey Papers. Also see William Grant Still, "William Grant Still Tells of Screenland's Many Tricks," *Chicago Defender,* 13 Feb. 1943, 18–19.
98. Still, "The Negro and His Music," 106–7.
99. Still, "Spirituals, Blues Important Section of American Music," 101.
100. P. L. Prattis to Still, 24 July 1946, Still-Arvey Papers.
101. Still to Prattis, 10 June 1946, Still-Arvey Papers.
102. Locke, *The Negro and His Music,* 118.
103. Arvey to Delores Calvin, 23 July 1946, Still-Arvey Papers.
104. Jean Toomer to Johnson, 11 July 1930, Johnson Collection.
105. Eddie Burbridge, "Bowl Audience Also Hears Nash Singers, Wm. Gillespie," *California Eagle* (Los Angeles), 29 Aug. 1946, 12.
106. R. Nathaniel Dett, "Negro Music," in *The R. Nathaniel Dett Reader,* ed. Spencer, 128. Originally published in *The International Cyclopedia of Music and Musicians.*
107. "Men Who Do Things: William Grant Still," *Opportunity* 16, no. 9 (Sept. 1938): 273, 284–85; "Music for 50 Million People," *The Crisis* 46, no. 4 (Apr. 1939): 107–8.
108. Robert D. Kohn to Still, 5 Feb. 1938, Still-Arvey Papers.
109. Robert D. Kohn to Still, 18 Feb. 1938, Still-Arvey Papers.
110. See "'The World of Tomorrow' as It Will Be Seen by Visitors to New York's World Fair," *New York Times,* 27 July 1938, 12L.
111. Still to Locke, 6 Aug. 1938, Locke Papers.
112. William Grant Still, "The Music of My Race," *Musica* 1, no. 5 (Aug. 1941), 103.
113. Locke to Still, 9 Aug. 1939, Still-Arvey Papers.
114. Arvey, *In One Lifetime,* 115.
115. Katherine Garrison Chapin to Still, 23 Aug. 1940, Still-Arvey Papers.
116. Chapin to Still, 14 Sept. 1940, Still-Arvey Papers.
117. Locke to Mason, 6 Apr. 1940, Locke Papers.
118. Chapin to Still, 13 May 1940, Still-Arvey Papers.
119. Locke to Mason, 3 June 1940, Locke Papers.
120. Locke to Still, 2 July 1940, Still-Arvey Papers.
121. Alain Locke, "Ballad for Democracy," *Opportunity,* Aug. 1940, 228.

122. Mason to Locke, 3 Sept. 1940, Locke Papers.
123. Verna Arvey, "Stokowski, Negro Musicians Friend, Loses Symphony Job," *Washington Tribune,* 8 July 1944.
124. Chapin to Still, 22 Apr. 1942, Still-Arvey Papers.
125. Leopold Stokowski to Still, 10 Apr. 1942, Still-Arvey Papers.
126. *Los Angeles Tribune,* 20 July 1942.
127. James Weldon Johnson, *Along This Way: The Autobiography of James Weldon Johnson* (New York: Viking, 1933), 203.
128. Locke to Still, 31 Aug. 1941, Still-Arvey Papers.
129. Mason to Locke, 20 Sept. 1941, Locke Papers.
130. Locke to Still, 14 Nov. 1941, Still-Arvey Papers.
131. Mrs. Arthur M. Reis, executive chairman, to Still, 13 July 1943, Still-Arvey Papers.
132. Arvey, *In One Lifetime,* 137.
133. William Grant Still, "Politics in Music," in *The William Grant Still Reader,* ed. Spencer, 148–49. Originally published in *Opera, Concert and Symphony,* Aug. 1947.
134. Cited in Chapin to Still, 14 Jan. 1944, Still-Arvey Papers.
135. William Grant Still diary, 9 and 10 Jan. 1944, Still-Arvey Papers.
136. "White Woman Tells Hope for Racial Tolerance," *Los Angeles Tribune,* 19 Feb. 1945.
137. White to Johnson, 31 Dec. 1934, Johnson Collection.
138. Johnson to White, 12 Jan. 1935, Johnson Collection.
139. Delores Calvin to Arvey, 3 Apr. 1944, Still-Arvey Papers.
140. Cited in Robert D. Kohn to Still, 29 Sept. 1939, Still-Arvey Papers.
141. Edward Johnson, general manager, Metropolitan Opera Association, to Still, 9 Sept. 1935, Still-Arvey Papers.
142. Edward Johnson to Still, 31 May 1939, Still-Arvey Papers.
143. Edward Johnson to Still, 31 May 1939, Still-Arvey Papers.
144. Arna Bontemps to Still, 21 Aug. 1939, Still-Arvey Papers.
145. Still diary, 23 Jan. 1946, Still-Arvey Papers.
146. Arvey, *In One Lifetime,* 141.
147. Dick Campbell, "'Troubled Island' Set for New York," *Pittsburgh Courier,* 26 Mar. 1949.
148. Arvey to Locke, 14 Sept. 1944, Locke Papers.
149. Still diary, 28 Jan. 1949, Still-Arvey Papers.
150. Alain Locke, "The Negro and the American Stage," in *The Critical Temper of Alain Locke,* ed. Stewart, 85–86. Originally published in *Theatre Arts Monthly* 10 (Feb. 1926). See also Alain Locke, "The Drama of Negro Life," in *The Critical Temper of Alain Locke,* ed. Stewart, 91. Originally published in *Theatre Arts Monthly* 10 (Oct. 1926).
151. Still diary, 21 Feb. 1950, Still-Arvey Papers.
152. Paul Creston to Arvey, 19 Oct. 1949, Still-Arvey Papers.
153. John Gutman, assistant manager, to Still, 2 June 1960, Still-Arvey Papers.
154. Rossly Neave, secretary to music consultant George Schick, to Still, 15 Apr. 1964, Still-Arvey Papers.

Chapter 4. A Problem Which Could Be Solved
by the Simple Rules of Justice

1. Baker, *Modernism and the Harlem Renaissance,* 12.
2. Baker, *Modernism and the Harlem Renaissance,* xiii–xiv.
3. Huggins, *Harlem Renaissance,* 303.
4. Alain L. Locke, "Beauty and the Provinces," in *The Critical Temper of Alain Locke,* ed. Stewart, 29. Originally published in *The Stylus,* June 1929.
5. Harold Cruse, *The Crisis of the Negro Intellectual* (1967; rpt. New York: Quill, 1984), 37.
6. Huggins, *Harlem Renaissance,* 190.
7. David Levering Lewis, *When Harlem Was in Vogue* (New York: Knopf, 1984), 305.
8. Frank Hercules, "An Aspect of the Negro Renaissance," *Opportunity* 20, no. 10 (Oct. 1942): 306.
9. Blum, "Black Music," 74, 76.
10. Samuel A. Floyd, Jr., "Music in the Harlem Renaissance: An Overview," in *Black Music in the Harlem Renaissance,* ed. Floyd, 23, 24.
11. Baker, *Modernism and the Harlem Renaissance,* 17, 24, 27, 30.
12. George Pullen Jackson, "Nathaniel Dett's Real Artist," cited in Simpson, *Follow Me,* 101. Originally published in *Nashville Banner,* 27 Feb. 1923.
13. Baker, *Modernism and the Harlem Renaissance,* 56.
14. Baker, *Modernism and the Harlem Renaissance,* 60.
15. Kelly Miller, "Negro Nudity in Art," *New York Amsterdam News,* 11 June 1930, 24.
16. Cited in Mark Tucker, "The Renaissance Education of Duke Ellington," in *Black Music in the Harlem Renaissance,* 122.
17. Benjamin Stolberg, "Classic Music and Virtuous Ladies: A Note on Colored Folks' Prejudices," *The Crisis* 38 (Jan. 1931): 23–24.
18. Albert Morini to Robert Ogden Purves, 18 Mar. 1930, Music Collection, Hampton Univ. Archives, Hampton, Va.
19. George P. Phenix to George F. Ketcham, 21 Apr. 1930, Music Collection.
20. James E. Allen, in "Our Readers Say," *The Crisis* 38 (Feb. 1931): 63–64.
21. Baker, *Modernism and the Harlem Renaissance,* 91–92.
22. Alain Locke, "Freedom through Art: A Review of Negro Art, 1870–1938," in *The Critical Temper of Alain Locke,* ed. Stewart, 268. Originally published in *The Crisis* 45 (July 1938).
23. Johnson, *Along This Way,* 152.
24. Johnson, *Along This Way,* 193.
25. James Weldon Johnson to Heywood Broun, 2 May 1924, Johnson Collection.
26. Carl Van Vechten to Johnson, 23 Mar. 1925, Johnson Collection.
27. Aaron Douglas to Johnson, 6 June 1927, Johnson Collection.
28. Pickens, *The New Negro,* 15.
29. Johnson, *Along This Way,* 203.

30. Reverdy C. Ransom, "The New Negro," *New York Amsterdam News,* 3 Jan. 1923, 12.
31. Marian P. Saul, "Negro Ability Gaining Recognition through Efforts of Harmon Foundation," *Opportunity* 6, no. 2 (Feb. 1928): 46–47.
32. "Six New Yorkers Among Harmon Award Winners," *New York Amsterdam News,* 8 Jan. 1930, 1, 2.
33. Harry V. Richardson, "The New Negro and Religion," *Opportunity* 11, no. 2 (Feb. 1933): 42, 44.
34. Thelma E. Berlack, "New Author Unearthed Right Here in Harlem," *New York Amsterdam News,* 23 May 1928, 16.
35. J. A. Rogers, "'The Green Pastures' and Other Ruminations," *New York Amsterdam News,* 13 Apr. 1935, 8.
36. Alain Locke to Charlotte Mason, 9 Sept. 1932, Locke Papers.
37. Kelly Miller, "Watchtower," *New York Amsterdam News,* 15 Sept. 1934, 8.
38. Zora Neale Hurston, *Dust Tracks on a Road: An Autobiography,* 2nd ed. (1942; rpt. Urbana: Univ. of Illinois Press, 1984), 278.
39. Johnson, *Along This Way,* 30.
40. Cited in Wilber P. Thirkield to Johnson, 10 Nov. 1933, Johnson Collection.
41. Beverly Smith, "Harlem—The Negro City," *New York Herald Tribune,* 11 Feb. 1930.
42. Johnson, *Negro Americans, What Now?* 21.
43. Johnson, *Negro Americans, What Now?* 23.
44. William Lloyd Imes to Locke, 6 Mar. 1924, Locke Papers.
45. "Young People's Fellowship of St. Philip's in Three-Day Session," *New York Amsterdam News,* 2 May 1928, 3.
46. "Many Brave Storm to Hear Lecture of Carter G. Woodson, Historian," *New York Amsterdam News,* 8 Dec. 1926, 9.
47. "Du Bois Asserts Race Problem Will Vex Champions of Justice 100 Years Hence," *New York Amsterdam News,* 8 Jan. 1930, 3.
48. Hurston, *Dust Tracks on a Road,* 278.
49. Langston Hughes, "Hughes Tells Why He Wrote Poem Entitled 'Goodbye Christ'," *New York Amsterdam News,* 9 Jan. 1941.
50. Henry Smith Leiper to Johnson, 4 Feb. 1936; William Lloyd Imes to Johnson, 6 Feb. 1936, Johnson Collection.
51. See Leiper to Johnson, 2 Mar. 1936; Leiper to Imes, 10 Mar. 1936, Johnson Collection.
52. Howard Thurman to Johnson, 23 Sept. 1937; Thurman to Johnson, 3 Dec. 1937, Johnson Collection.
53. Thirkield to Johnson, 10 Nov. 1933.
54. Johnson, *Negro Americans, What Now?* 20.
55. Johnson, *Negro Americans, What Now?* 23, 52.
56. Locke to Mason, 30 July 1934, Locke Papers.
57. Undated typescript, Locke Papers.
58. Locke to Mason, 28 Aug. 1933, Locke Papers.
59. Locke to Floyd J. Calvin, 21 Feb. 1928, Locke Papers.
60. Locke to Mason, 30 July 1934, Locke Papers.

61. Claude McKay to Johnson, 1 Feb. 1929, Johnson Collection.
62. Reverdy C. Ransom to Johnson, 21 May 1927; Adam Clayton Powell to Johnson, 17 June 1927, Johnson Collection.
63. "Out of Debt," *New York Amsterdam News,* 11 Jan. 1928, 14.
64. James Weldon Johnson, "Harlem: The Culture Capital," in *The New Negro,* ed. Locke, 306.
65. George Phenix to George Ketcham, 21 Apr. 1930, Music Collection.
66. George Foster Peabody to R. Nathaniel Dett, 25 Apr. 1930, Music Collection.
67. "Salvation Army Station Feeding 250 as Civil Groups Plan to Fight Want," *New York Amsterdam News,* 29 Oct. 1930, 3.
68. Shirley Graham, "Black Man's Music," *The Crisis* 40, no. 8 (Aug. 1933): 179.
69. Locke to Mason, 10 Nov. 1932, Locke Papers.
70. Locke to Mason, n.d., Dec. 1932, Locke Papers.
71. Alain Locke, "The Saving Grace of Realism: Retrospective Review of the Negro Literature of 1933," in *The Critical Temper of Alain Locke,* ed. Stewart, 225. Originally published in *Opportunity* 13, no. 1 (Jan. 1934).
72. Locke to Mason, 13 Jan. 1935, Locke Papers.
73. See Alain L. Locke, "The Negro's Cultural Contribution to America," manuscript, Bennett College lecture, 12 Jan. 1935, Locke Papers.
74. Alain L. Locke, "The Negro's Cultural Contribution to American Culture," *Journal of Negro Education,* July 1939: 521–29.
75. Alain L. Locke, "Sterling Brown: The New Negro Folk-Poet," in *The Critical Temper of Alain Locke,* ed. Stewart, 53. Originally published in *Four Negro Poets,* ed. Alain L. Locke (New York: Simon and Schuster, 1927).
76. Locke to Mason, 9 Sept. 1932, Locke Papers.
77. Alain Locke, "1928: A Retrospective Review," in *The Critical Temper of Alain Locke,* ed. Stewart, 201. Originally published in *Opportunity* 7, no. 1 (Jan. 1929).
78. Alain Locke, "The Year of Grace: Outstanding Books of the Year in Negro Literature," in *The Critical Temper of Alain Locke,* ed. Stewart, 205–6. Originally published in *Opportunity* 9 (Feb. 1931).
79. Locke, "The Saving Grace of Realism," 221.
80. Van Vechten to Johnson, 25 Feb. 1934, Johnson Collection.
81. Johnson, *Negro Americans, What Now?* 92–93.
82. Van Vechten to Johnson, 26 June 1937, Johnson Collection.
83. Cruse, *The Crisis of the Negro Intellectual,* 52.
84. Alain Locke, "Jingo, Counter-Jingo and Us: Retrospective Review of the Literature of the Negro: 1937," in *The Critical Temper of Alain Locke,* ed. Stewart, 259. Originally published in *Opportunity* 16, nos. 1–2 (Jan. and Feb. 1938).
85. Claude McKay to Charlotte Mason, 13 Feb. 1930, Locke Papers.
86. Hughes, *The Big Sea,* 228.
87. Alain Locke, "The Negro: 'New' or Newer: A Retrospective Review of the

Literature of the Negro for 1938," in *The Critical Temper of Alain Locke,* ed. Stewart, 271–72. Originally published in *Opportunity* 17, nos. 1–2 (Jan. and Feb. 1939).

88. Locke to Mason, 6 Apr. 1940, Locke Papers.

89. "'Second Negro Renaissance in Arts'—Langston Hughes," *Now,* second-half Jan. 1946.

90. "The Courier's 40th Anniversary in '50," *Pittsburgh Courier,* 7 Jan. 1950, sec. 2.

91. W. E. B. Du Bois, "20th Century: The Century of the Color Line" ["The American Negro from 1901–1950"], *Pittsburgh Courier,* 14 Jan. 1950, 6.

92. Du Bois, "20th Century," 7.

93. Du Bois, "20th Century," 7.

94. James W. Ivy, "Fifty Years of Progress in Literature," *Pittsburgh Courier,* 11 Feb. 1950, 6.

95. Ivy, "Fifty Years of Progress in Literature," 7.

96. James A. Porter, "Progress of the Negro in Art During the Past Fifty Years," *Pittsburgh Courier,* 29 July 1950, 6–7.

97. Ira De A. Reid, "Fifty Years of Progress in the Professions," *Pittsburgh Courier,* 1 July 1950, 7.

98. William Grant Still, "Fifty Years of Progress in Music," *Pittsburgh Courier,* 11 Nov. 1950, 15.

99. Benjamin E. Mays, "Fifty Years of Progress in the Negro Church," *Pittsburgh Courier,* 8 Apr. 1950, 6–7.

100. Walter White, "Civil Rights: Fifty years of Fighting," *Pittsburgh Courier,* 28 Jan. 1950, 6.

101. White, "Civil Rights," 7.

102. Edwin R. Embree, "Fifty Years of Progress in Human Relations," *Pittsburgh Courier,* 11 Mar. 1950, 6.

103. Embree, "Fifty Years of Progress in Human Relations," 7.

104. Alain Locke, "The American Negro as Artist," in *The Critical Temper of Alain Locke,* ed. Stewart, 174. Originally published in *The American Magazine of Art* 23 (Sept. 1931).

105. Jean Toomer to Johnson, 11 July 1930, Johnson Collection.

106. Baker, *Modernism and the Harlem Renaissance,* 91–92.

107. William Grant Still, "A Composer's Viewpoint," in *The William Grant Still Reader,* ed. Spencer, 228. Originally published in *William Grant Still and the Fusion of Cultures in American Music,* ed. Haas.

108. Still, "The Negro and His Music," in *The William Grant Still Reader,* ed. Spencer, 108. Originally published in *War Worker,* Oct. 1943.

109. Alain Locke, "A Critical Retrospect of the Literature of the Negro for 1947," in *The Critical Temper of Alain Locke,* ed. Stewart, 329. Originally published in *Phylon* 9 (first quarter 1948).

Select Bibliography

Books and Periodicals

Abdul, Raoul. *Blacks in Classical Music*. New York: Dodd, Mead, 1977.

Albus, Harry J. *The Deep River Girl: The Life of Marian Anderson in Story Form*. Grand Rapids, Mich.: William B. Eerdmans, 1949.

Anderson, Jervis. *This Was Harlem: A Cultural Portrait, 1900–1950*. New York: Farrar Straus Giroux, 1982.

Anderson, Marian. *My Lord, What a Morning*. New York: Viking, 1956.

Arvey, Verna. *In One Lifetime*. Fayetteville: Univ. of Arkansas Press, 1984.

Baker, Houston A., Jr. *Afro-American Poetics: Revisions of Harlem and the Black Aesthetic*. Madison: Univ. of Wisconsin Press, 1988.

———. *Modernism and the Harlem Renaissance*. Chicago: Univ. of Chicago Press, 1987.

———. *Singers of Daybreak: Studies in Black American Literature*. Washington: Howard Univ. Press, 1983.

Bennett, Gwendolyn B. "Edmund T. Jenkins: Musician." *Opportunity* 3 (Nov. 1925): 338–39.

Blum, Martin. "Black Music: Pathmaker of the Harlem Renaissance." *Missouri Journal of Research in Music Education* 3, no. 3 (1974): 72–79.

Bontemps, Arna, ed. *The Harlem Renaissance Remembered*. New York: Dodd, Mead, 1972.

Brawley, Benjamin. *The Negro Genius: A New Appraisal of the Achievement of the American Negro in Literature and the Fine Arts*. New York: Dodd, Mead, 1937.

Brown, Sterling. "Roland Hayes." *Opportunity* 3 (June 1925): 173–74.

Butcher, Harold. "The Dawson Folk Symphony." *The Crisis* 42, no. 2 (Feb. 1935): 47, 52.

Butcher, Margaret Just. *The Negro in American Culture*. New York: Mentor, 1957.

Campbell, Mary Schmidt, David Driskell, David Levering Lewis, and Deborah Willis Ryan. *Harlem Renaissance: Art of Black America*. New York: Harry N. Abrams, 1987.

Cruse, Harold. *The Crisis of the Negro Intellectual*. 1967. Rpt. New York: Quill, 1984.

Cuney-Hare, Maud. *Negro Musicians and Their Music*. Washington, D.C.: Associated Publishers, 1936. New York: Da Capo, 1974.

Curtis, Natalie, ed. *The Indians' Book: An Offering by the American Indians of Indian Lore, Musical and Narrative, to Form a Record of the Songs and Legends of Their Race*. New York: Harper and Brothers, 1907.

De Lerma, Dominique Rene, ed. *Black Music in Our Culture*. Kent, Ohio: Kent State Univ. Press, 1970.

———, ed. *Reflections on Afro-American Music*. Kent, Ohio: Kent Univ. Press, 1973.

Dett, R. Nathaniel. *The R. Nathaniel Dett Reader: Essays on Black Sacred Music*. Edited by Jon Michael Spencer. A special issue of *Black Sacred Music: A Journal of Theomusicology* 5, no. 2 (Fall 1991).

Duberman, Martin Bauml. *Paul Robeson*. New York: Alfred Knopf, 1988.

Du Bois, W. E. B. "Criteria of Negro Art." *The Crisis* 32, no. 6 (Oct. 1926): 290–97.

———. *The Gift of Black Folk*. Boston: Stratford Company, 1924.

Du Bois, W. E. B., and Alain L. Locke. "The Younger Literary Movement." *The Crisis* 27, no. 4 (Feb. 1924): 161–63.

Floyd, Samuel A. Jr., ed. *Black Music in the Harlem Renaissance*. 1990. Knoxville: Univ. of Tennessee Press, 1993.

Graham, Shirley. "Black Man's Music." *The Crisis* 40, no. 8 (Aug. 1933): 178–79.

———. "Spirituals to Symphonies." *Etude* 54 (1936): 691–92, 723, 736.

Haas, Robert Bartlett, ed. *William Grant Still and the Fusion of Cultures in American Music*. Los Angeles: Black Sparrow, 1975.

Helm, MacKinley. *Angel Mo' and Her Son Roland Hayes*. Boston: Little, Brown, 1942.

Hercules, Frank. "An Aspect of the Negro Renaissance." *Opportunity* 20, no. 10 (Oct. 1942): 305–6, 317–19.

Howard, John Tasker. *Our American Music: Three Hundred Years of It*. New York: Thomas Y. Crowell, 1931.

Huggins, Nathan Irvin. *Harlem Renaissance*. New York: Oxford Univ. Press, 1971.

———, ed. *Voices from the Harlem Renaissance*. New York: Oxford Univ. Press, 1976.

Hughes, Langston. *The Big Sea*. New York: Alfred A. Knopf, 1940.

Johnson, Charles S. "Public Opinion and the Negro." *Opportunity* 1, no. 7 (July 1923): 201–6.

Johnson, Hall. "Porgy and Bess—a Folk Opera: A Review." *Opportunity* 14, no. 1 (Jan. 1936): 24–28.

Johnson, James Weldon. *Along This Way: The Autobiography of James Weldon Johnson*. New York: Viking, 1933.

_____. *The Autobiography of an Ex-Colored Man*. Boston: Sherman, French and Company, 1912.

———. *The Autobiography of an Ex-Coloured Man*. New York: Alfred A. Knopf, 1927.

———. *The Autobiography of an Ex-Coloured Man*. New York: Alfred A. Knopf, 1937.

———. *The Autobiography of an Ex-Coloured Man*. New York: Pelican Mentor, 1948.

———. *The Autobiography of an Ex-Coloured Man*. New York: Hill and Wang, 1960.

———. *The Autobiography of an Ex-Colored Man*. In *Three Negro Classics*. New York: Avon, 1965.

———. *Black Manhattan*. New York: Knopf, 1930.

———, ed. *The Book of American Negro Poetry*. 1922. Rpt. Rev. ed. New York: Harcourt, Brace and World, 1959.

———, ed. *The Book of American Negro Spirituals*. New York: Viking, 1925.

———. *God's Trombones: Seven Negro Sermons in Verse*. New York: Viking, 1927.

———. "The Larger Success." *The Southern Workman* 52, no. 9 (Sept. 1923): 427–36.

———. *Negro Americans, What Now?* New York: Viking, 1934.

———. "Negro Authors and White Publishers." *The Crisis* 36, no. 7 (July 1929): 228–29.

———, ed. *The Second Book of Negro Spirituals*. New York: Viking, 1926.

Kramer, Victor A. *The Harlem Renaissance Re-examined*. New York: AMS Press, 1987.

Levy, Eugene. *James Weldon Johnson: Black Leader Black Voice*. Chicago: Univ. of Chicago Press, 1973.

Lewis, David Levering. *When Harlem Was in Vogue*. New York: Alfred A. Knopf, 1984.

Locke, Alain L. *The Critical Temper of Alain Locke: A Selection of His Essays on Art and Culture*. Edited by Jeffrey C. Stewart. New York: Garland, 1983.

———. *The Negro in America*. Chicago: American Library Association, 1933.

———. *Negro Art: Past and Present*. Washington, D.C.: Associates in Negro Folk Education, 1936.

———. *The Negro and His Music*. Washington, D.C.: Associates in Negro Folk Education, 1936.

———, ed. *The New Negro*. 1925. Rpt. New York: Atheneum, 1980.

———. *Race Contacts and Interracial Relations: Lectures on the Theory and Practice of Race*. Edited by Jeffrey C. Stewart. Washington, D.C.: Howard Univ. Press, 1992.

Locke, Alain L., and Montgomery Gregory, eds. *Plays of Negro Life: A Source-Book of Native American Drama*. New York: Harper and Brothers, 1927.

Logan, Rayford W., Eugene C. Holmes, and G. Franklin Edwards, eds. *The New Negro Thirty Years Afterward*. Washington, D.C.: Howard Univ. Press, 1955.

Lovell, John. *Black Song: The Forge and the Flame*. New York: Macmillan, 1972.

Martin, Tony. *Literary Garveyism: Garvey, Black Arts and the Harlem Renaissance*. Dover, Mass.: Majority Press, 1983.

McBrier, Vivian Flagg. *R. Nathaniel Dett: His Life and Works (1882–1943)*. Washington, D.C.: The Associated Publishers, 1977.

McKay, Claude. *Harlem: Negro Metropolis*. New York: Dutton, 1940.

Ogren, Kathy J. *The Jazz Revolution: Twenties America and the Meaning of Jazz*. New York: Oxford Univ. Press, 1989.

Pickens, William. *The New Negro: His Political, Civil and Mental Status and Related Essays*. New York: Neale Publishing Company, 1916.

Preece, Harold. "The Negro Folk Cult." *The Crisis* 43, no. 12 (Dec. 1936): 364, 374.

Rampersad, Arnold. *The Life of Langston Hughes*. 2 vols. New York: Oxford Univ. Press, 1986, 1988.

Rauschenbusch, Walter. *For God and the People: Prayers of the Social Awakening*. Boston: Pilgrim Press, 1909.

Richardson, Harry V. "The New Negro and Religion." *Opportunity* 11, no. 2 (Feb. 1933): 41–44.

Richardson, Willis. "The Hope of a Negro Drama." *The Crisis* 19, no. 1 (Nov. 1919): 338–39.

Robeson, Paul. *Here I Stand*. New York: Othello Associates, 1958.

Rogers, William F., Jr. *Dorothy Maynor and the Harlem School of the Arts: The Diva and the Dream*. Lewiston, N.Y.: Edwin Mellen, 1993.

Saul, Marian P. "Negro Ability Gaining Recognition through Efforts of Harmon Foundation." *Opportunity* 6, no. 2 (Feb. 1928): 46–47.

Simpson, Anne Key. *Follow Me: The Life and Music of R. Nathaniel Dett*. Metuchen, N.J.: Scarecrow, 1993.

———. *Hard Trials: The Life and Music of Harry T. Burleigh*. Metuchen, N.J.: Scarecrow, 1990.

Southern, Eileen. *The Music of Black Americans: A History*. 2nd ed. New York: Norton, 1983.

Still, William Grant. *The William Grant Still Reader: Essays on American Music*. Edited by Jon Michael Spencer. A special issue of *Black Sacred Music: A Journal of Theomusicology* 6, no. 2 (Fall 1992).

White, Clarence Cameron. "The Musical Genius of the American Negro." *Southern Workman* 62 (Mar. 1933): 108–18.

Wintz, Cary. *Black Culture and the Harlem Renaissance*. Houston: Rice Univ. Press, 1988.

Woll, Allen. *Black Musical Theatre: From Coontown to Dreamgirls*. Baton Rouge: Louisiana State Univ. Press, 1989.

Newspapers

Boston Herald, Nov. 1939.

Boston Evening Transcript, 11 Mar. 1929.

California Eagle (Los Angeles), 29 Aug. 1946–30 Nov. 1950.

Chicago Defender, 14 Mar. 1931–13 Feb. 1943.

Christian Advocate, 20 Jan. 1927.

Christian Science Monthly, 10 May 1930.

Colonist (Victoria, British Columbia), 14 June 1930.

Norfolk Journal and Guide, 25 Nov. 1939–18 Jan. 1947.

Los Angeles Tribune, 8 Nov. 1943–19 Feb. 1945.

New York Amsterdam News, 3 Jan. 1923–9 Jan. 1941.

New York Herald Tribune, 11 Feb. 1930–17 Jan. 1932.

New York Post, 22 Nov. 1939.

New York Times, 29 Nov. 1926–27 Oct. 1940.

Pittsburgh Courier, 26 Mar. 1949–11 Nov. 1950.

San Diego Tribune, 2 Aug. 1939.

Washington Tribune, 8 July 1944.

Collections

Black Sacred Music Collection. Hampton Univ. Archives, Hampton, Va.

Dett, R. Nathaniel. Collection. Hampton Univ. Archives, Hampton, Va.

Hampton Institute European Tour Collection. Hampton Univ. Archives, Hampton, Va.

Howe, Arthur. Papers. Hampton Univ. Archives, Hampton, Va.

Johnson, James Weldon. Collection. Beinecke Rare Book and Manuscript Library, Yale Univ., New Haven, Conn.

Locke, Alain. Papers. Manuscripts Division. Moorland-Spingarn Research Center, Howard Univ., Washington, D.C.

Music Collection. Hampton Univ. Archives, Hampton, Va.

Peabody, George Foster. Papers. Hampton Univ. Archives, Hampton, Va.

Phillips, Solomon. Collection. Hampton Univ. Archives, Hampton, Va.

Still, William Grant and Verna Arvey. Papers. Special Collections. Univ. of Arkansas, Fayetteville.

Trenholm, H. Councill. Papers. Moorland-Spingarn Research Center, Howard Univ., Washington, D.C.

Index

Thirkield, Wilber P., 22, 24, 121
Three Rhythmic Spirituals, 99
Three Visions, 86
Thurman, Howard, 121
To You America, 86
Toomer, Jean, 6, 30, 96, 135
Trotter, James, xvi
Troubled Island, xviii, 76, 86, 88, 93,
    104–5
Truman, Harry S., 70
Tucker, Sophie, 75
Twain, Mark, 69
Twelve Negro Spirituals, 99

Uncle Remus, 82
Uncle Tom's Cabin, 101
United Negro Improvement Associa-
    tion, 2
Universal Christian Council, 121
University of Arkansas, 80
University of Pennsylvania, 44
University of Southern California, 80

Van Vechten, Carl, xiii, 4, 5, 12, 17, 39,
    77, 89, 92, 104, 116, 129
Varèse, Edgard, 75, 80
Villiard, Oswald, 39
vindication, racial, xv, xvii, xviii, xxi, 2–5,
    9, 12, 13, 19, 22, 30, 33, 35, 45, 46–

64, 66–67, 71, 74, 77, 78, 81, 97,
    100, 102–6, 110, 134
Voorhees, Don, 75, 80–81

Waghalter, Ignatz, 76–77
Warner Brothers Films, 75
Washington, Booker T., xiv, 6, 7, 8, 9,
    11–12, 14, 16, 30, 40, 109, 113,
    114, 116–17
Ways of White Folks, The, 129
Weary Blues, The, 13
"Were You There," 67, 68
Westminster Abbey, 54–55
Westminster Choir School, 65–66
When Harlem was in Vogue, xix, 108
White, Clarence Cameron, 64, 65, 66,
    73, 85, 103, 124, 132
White, Portia, 7, 104
White, Walter, 77, 133
Whiteman, Paul, 75
Wilberforce University, 74, 79
Williams, George Washington, 114
Woodson, Carter G., 120, 121
Work, John, 63–64, 124
Works Progress Administration, 77
Wright, Richard, 99, 137

Yerby, Frank, 12